ALL
OVER
BUT THE
SHOUTIN'

ALL
OVER
BUT THE
SHOUTIN'

Rick Bragg

PANTHEON BOOKS · NEW YORK

Library of Congresss Cataloging-in-Publication Data

Bragg, Rick.
All over but the shoutin' / Rick Bragg.
p.   cm.
ISBN 0-679-44258-8
1. Bragg, Rick.   2. Bragg, Rick—Childhood and youth.   3. Journalists—
United States—Biography.   4. Working class whites—Alabama—
Biography.   5. Alabama—Biography.   6. Alabama—Rural
conditions.   I. Title.
PN4874.B6625A3   1997
070'.92—dc21
[B]   97-9918
                                                                                            CIP

Random House Web Address: http://www.randomhouse.com

BOOK DESIGN BY DEBORAH KERNER

Printed in the United States of America
First Edition
2   4   6   8   9   7   5   3   1

Grateful acknowledgment is made to the following for permission to reprint
previously published material: *EMI Music Publishing:* Excerpt from "I Been
to Georgia on a Fast Train" by Billy Joe Shaver. Copyright © 1972 by
Sony/ATV Songs LLC. Administered by EMI Blackwood Music Inc. (BMI).
All rights reserved. International copyright secured. Reprinted by
permission of EMI Music Publishing. • *Warner Bros. Publications U.S. Inc.:*
Excerpt from "I'm So Lonesome I Could Cry" by Hank Williams. Copyright
© 1949 (renewed) by Acuff-Rose Music, Inc. and Hiriam Music for the
U.S.A. World outside of U.S.A. controlled by Acuff-Rose Music, Inc.
• Excerpt from "Pancho and Lefty" by Townes Van Zandt. Copyright ©
1972 by Columbine Music & EMI U Catalog Inc. All rights reserved.
Reprinted by permission of Warner Bros. Publications U.S. Inc.,
Miami, FL 33014

To my momma
and my brothers

Contents

2   LIES TO MY MOTHER

3   GETTING EVEN WITH LIFE

Living on the road my friend
Was gonna keep you free and clean
Now you wear your skin like iron
And your breath is hard as kerosene
You weren't your momma's only boy
But her favorite one, it seems
She began to cry when you said goodbye
Saddled to your dreams

—T. VAN ZANDT

Prologue

Redbirds

I used to stand amazed and watch the redbirds fight. They would flash and flutter like scraps of burning rags through a sky unbelievably blue, swirling, soaring, plummeting. On the ground they were a blur of feathers, stabbing for each other's eyes. I have seen grown men stop what they were doing, stop pulling corn or lift their head out from under the hood of a broken-down car, to watch it. Once, when I was little, I watched one of the birds attack its own reflection in the side mirror of a truck. It hurled its body again and again against that unyielding image, until it pecked a crack in the glass, until the whole mirror was smeared with blood. It was as if the bird hated what it saw there, and discovered too late that all it was seeing was itself. I asked an old man who worked for my uncle Ed, a snuff-dipping man named Charlie Bivens, why he reckoned that bird did that. He told me it was just its nature.

This is not an important book. It is only the story of a strong woman, a tortured man and three sons who lived hemmed in by thin cotton and ragged history in northeastern Alabama, in a time when blacks and whites found reason to hate each other and a whole lot of people could not stand themselves. Anyone could tell it, anyone with a daddy who let his finer nature slip away from him during an icebound war in Korea, who allowed the devil inside him to come grinnin' out every time a sip of whiskey trickled in, who finally just abandoned his young wife and sons to the pity of their kin and to the well-meaning neighbors who came bearing boxes of throwaway clothes.

Anyone could tell it, anyone who had a momma who went eighteen years without a new dress so that her sons could have school clothes, who picked cotton in other people's fields and ironed other people's clothes and cleaned the mess in other people's houses, so that her children didn't have to live on welfare alone, so that one of them could climb up her backbone and escape the poverty and hopelessness that ringed them, free and clean.

Anyone could tell it, and that's the shame of it. A lot of women stood with babies on their hips in line for commodity cheese and peanut butter. A lot of men were damaged deep inside by the killing and dying of wars, then tried to heal themselves with a snake oil elixir of sour mash and self-loathing. A lot of families just came to pieces in that time and place and condition, like paper lace in a summer rain. You can walk the main street in any small town, in any big one, and you will hear this story being told behind cigarette-scarred bars, before altars, over fresh-dug ground in a thousand cemeteries. You hear it from the sixty-five-year-old woman with the blank eyes who wipes the tables at the Waffle House, and by the used-up men with Winstons dangling from their lips who absently, rhythmically swing their swingblades at the tall weeds out behind the city jail.

This story is important only to me and a few people who lived it, people with my last name. I tell it because there should be a record of my momma's sacrifice even if it means unleashing ghosts, because it is one of the few ways I can think of—beyond financing her new false teeth and making sure the rest of her life is without the deprivations of her past—to repay her for all the suffering and indignity she absorbed for us, for me. And I tell it because I can, because it is how I earn my paycheck, now at the *New York Times*, before at so many other places, telling stories. It is easy to tell a stranger's story; I didn't know if I had the guts to tell my own.

This is no sob story. While you will read words laced with bitterness and killing anger and vicious envy, words of violence and sadness and, hopefully, dark humor, you will not read much whining. Not on her part, certainly, because she does not know how.

I have been putting this off for ten years, because it was personal, because dreaming backwards can carry a man through some dark rooms where the walls seem lined with razor blades. I put it off and put it off until finally something happened to scare me, to hurry me, to make me grit my teeth and remember.

It was death that made me hurry, but not my father's. He died twenty years ago, tubercular, his insides pickled by whiskey and beer. Being of long memory, my momma, my brothers and I did not go to the cemetery to sing hymns or see him remanded to the red clay. We placed no flowers on his grave. Our momma went alone to the funeral home one night, when it was just him and her.

No, the death that made me finally sit down to write was that of my grandmother, my mother's mother, Ava, whom we all called by her pet name, Abigail. Miss Ab, who after enduring eighty-six years of this life and a second childhood that I truly believed would last forever, died of pneumonia two days before Thanksgiving, 1994. The night her grown children gathered around her bed in the small community hospital in Calhoun County, Alabama, I was in New Orleans, writing about the deaths of strangers.

I was sitting in a cramped living room in a crumbling housing project, listening to a hollow-eyed and pitiful young woman tell how her little boy had been killed one morning by a stray bullet as he stood in the doorway, his book satchel in his hand, like a little man going to work. She told me how the Dr. Seuss and Winnie the Pooh just fell out on the stoop, how the boy looked up at her after the bullet hit, wide-eyed, wondering. And as she talked, her two surviving children rode tight circles around the couch on their bicycles, because she was afraid to let them play outside in the killing ground of the project courtyard. As I left, shaking her limp hand, she thanked me. I usually just nod my head politely and move on, struck anew every time by the graciousness of people in such a soul-killing time. But this time, I had to ask why. Why thank me for scribbling down her hopeless story for the benefit of people who live so far and safely away from this place where the gunfire twinkles like lightning bugs after dark? She answered by pulling out a scrapbook of her baby's death, cut from the local newspaper. "People remembers it," she said. "People forgets if it ain't wrote down."

I reckon so.

The next morning, one of those hotel mornings when it takes you a few uneasy seconds to remember where you are and what you are doing there, the phone shook me awake. You always look at it a second before you reach for it, because it is often the slingshot that sends you hurtling toward a place like Oklahoma City, where you walk quietly and respectfully among the rubble and blood and baby shoes scattered by a monster's bomb, or to some obscure dateline like Union, South Carolina, and into the mind of a young mother who drowned her two sons in a dark lake. And the monstrous thing is that you secretly hope that it is something like that, not something dull.

But this time the summons, the death I was called to, was personal. My grandmother, who fried me whole boneyards of chicken, who got mildly drunk on her prescriptions, played "Boilin' Cabbage Down" on the banjo and stomped so hard on the planks it sounded like Jehovah pounding at the door, was gone. All her songs and sayings, all the beautiful things that filled her, warmed her, were quiet.

I had known she was sick. But my kin, hopeful she would recover, told me not to come home yet, told me she would be there when I came home Thanksgiving. But I came home to a coldly modern funeral home, to the people of our community sitting quietly in their pews, white socks peeking out from under black dress pants. There were not a lot of people, but the ones who came would have been important to her. There were third-cousins who had not seen her in years but gave up half a day's pay at the mill to be there; an old drunk who sobered up for her out of respect and sat pale and quietly shaking in the back pew; an ancient, hawk-nosed, hard-eyed man who had not seen her since he was young, but remembered she had once poured him a glass of buttermilk, or was it coffee? and old women who used to sit beside her on the porch, cutting

okra, holding grandbabies, telling lies. These were people who remembered the weight of the cotton sack, people with grease under their fingernails that no amount of Octagon soap would ever scrub away, people
who built redwood decks on their mobile homes and have no idea that
smart-aleck Yankees think that is somehow funny. People of the pines.
My people.

I came home to a pale and elegant body in an open coffin, her thin
hands crossed on her breast. As I said, I have made my living in grave-
yards of spirit, in the blasted-out, crack-infested streets of Miami's Liberty City, in the insane hallways of Manhattan's welfare hotels, in the
projects in Birmingham and the reeking oceanfront slums of Port-
au-Prince and on death rows in three states. I have seen so many horrible things in so many horrible places that I have suspicions about
God and doubts about heaven, but in that funeral home, I found myself
wishing for it, envisioning it. I bet even God, unless He is an Epis-
copalian, likes a little fais-do-do every now and then, and I like to think of
her Up There, blowing a hurricane on her harmonica and singing a little
too loud.

A million sights and sounds rang through my head as I stared down
at her. I thought about the times when I was still a little boy, no more
than five, when she would let me sleep at the foot of her bed so we could
listen to her Philco, how I drifted off to sleep with the tinny voices of
Faron Young, Little Jimmy Dickens, Bill Monroe and Mother Maybelle
Carter in chorus inside my head. It was one of the benefits of being old,
she told me: "You can play your radio all damn night long if you want to,
and no one can do a damn thing about it." Like everyone in that part of
the world, she had been enraptured by a young, thin man from Mount
Olive, Alabama, who sang with a twisted spine and a tortured spirit, and
she would whirl the dial, over and over, searching for his words.

> *I've never seen a night so long*
> *When time goes crawling by*
> *The moon just went behind the clouds*
> *To hide his face and cry.*

She told me she saw Hank Williams once, back before he died. But she was flying pretty high on her medicine that night and might have told a lie, since she felt that another benefit of old age was that it gave you license to lie like a Republican. But it was then, as that dead man's poetry ran through my mind, as I stared down at that old woman I had seen for just a few hours a year on Thanksgiving and Christmas because I wrongly believed I was doing more important things, that I knew I should not wait any longer to write some of this down, whether anyone ever read it or not.

It is not something I can go look up in a book. Poor people in the South do not make many historical registers unless we knock some rich man off his horse. It is not something I can research standing over the silence of graves. My mother is only sixty, but I cannot take the chance of squandering the knowledge and the stories that she and my people hold inside them, even if—as in the case of my father—some of it is sad and dark as the darkest night.

I miss my grandma most when I drive the back roads of the Deep South, the radio tuned to fiddle music on the Cotton States Network down around Troy, or to some wall-rattling black choir on the AM dial outside Hattiesburg. It is when I have long hours to look, think, remember. I know that any time I want to hear the rest of that haunted song, all I have to do is put on the record. But I want her to sing it to me. After all the dying I have seen, I finally understand what death is: simple wanting. My grandma would have added some happiness to this book, and although her mind had clouded considerably in the past few years—she would ask me how my wife was, and I haven't been married for ten years—she would have remembered for me, set me straight on some things. Maybe, if I tell it right, she will live again in these pages, that all the things she could have shared about who we are, who I am, will not be so badly missed. I like to believe that.

I already know a good bit about my history, stories that were seldom written down, only passed from one to another of us over cones of strawberry ice cream in the gravel parking lot of the tiny store owned by a one-legged man named Tillison. I heard them over the ring of guitar strings on the front porch, over the endless, beautiful, hateful rows of cotton that I still dream about even today, even though the fields lie in trash and weeds.

I know I was born during one of those periods when my father had abandoned my mother or driven her away, that—I still do not know whether to laugh or cry about this—he did not bother to come and see me until I was almost two years old. I know he brought a stuffed panda bear as big as God, and I dragged it around by one leg until he was one-eared and his cotton stuffing leaked out and his eyes fell off. And I remember running with it, too heavy, when I was a few years older, running down a road in the night, from him.

I know I grew up in the time when a young man in a baggy suit and slicked-down hair stood spraddle-legged in the crossroads of history and talked hot and mean about the colored, giving my poor and desperate people a reason to feel superior to somebody, to anybody. I know that even as the words of George Wallace rang through my Alabama, the black family who lived down the dirt road from our house sent fresh-picked corn and other food to the poor white lady and her three sons, because they knew their daddy had run off, because hungry does not have a color.

I know that a few weeks later he whirled through our house in a drunken rage, and as always our momma just absorbed it, placing herself like a wall between her husband and sons. I know that later my brother Sam and I lay in the dark safety of our bedroom and tried to figure out a way to kill a grown man, before he hurt her any more.

I know that I had a third brother, an infant who died because we were left alone and with no money for her to see a doctor, that he did not live long enough to have a name. I know his gravestone just reads Baby Bragg and my momma never mentioned him to us, for thirty years, but carried his memory around deep inside her, like a piece of broken glass.

I know that my grandfather on my momma's side, Abigail's husband, was a strong and good man, who tried the last years of his life to protect her from him, and the fact I never knew my grandfather, never saw his face, is one of the great regrets of my life. I know he was a hardworking roofer who made a little whiskey now and then in a still that sent a perfume into the pines that could knock sparrows from the sky. I know he once was forced to shoot a big woman through both buzzoms with a .410 deer slug because she and her brothers came at him with butcher knives, and that when I inquired as to whether the woman died, my aunt Gracie Juanita only said: "Lord no, hon. Went clean through."

I know that I was surrounded in the later part of my childhood by the love of aunts and uncles, that my aunt Gracie Juanita used to feed me tea cakes and tell me that the chicken cooking in her kitchen was buzzard, and then we would sit and eat and talk about how, *mmmm-mmmm*, that buzzard sure was tasty; that every Friday my aunt Mary Jo would haul us to PeeWee Johnson's Dixie Dip for a foot-long hot dog that is still the best thing I have ever had, better'n anything in New York, crème brûlée or no crème brûlée. I know my aunt Edna fried crappie for us and picked the bones out so we would not choke. I know my aunt Sue rocked and walked me to sleep, but lost her grip on me once and I fell headfirst on the fireplace stones, which could explain a lot of things.

I know that my mother's brother, Uncle Jimbo, once won a twenty-dollar bet by eating a bologna sandwich while sitting on a dead mule. I know he drove a Nash Rambler with a naked lady hood ornament, that my aunt Gracie Juanita was so mortified that she painted a bathing suit over the chromed body. I know that you never ever traded cars with my uncle Bill unless you wanted to walk home.

I know that my mother was not afraid of much—I watched her do in a four-foot rattlesnake with a broken-handled rake and a Red Ryder BB gun—and that she could have handled life with my father, if it had just been him and her, without the ghosts. They came for him in the winter, mostly. I could see them only in my father's almost pathological fear of cold, in his hatred of ice. I saw them on a winter day in 1965, when my little brother stepped through the ice on a tiny, shallow pond, when my daddy snatched him up and ran all the way to the house, his face white as frost.

I know that my father had not always been the tortured man of my childhood, that when he started courting my momma, a tall, serenely beautiful woman who looked like a 1940s movie star, he had worn black penny loafers with dimes in them and pants with creases sharp enough to slice bologna. I know he had once been just a slight, dark, part Cherokee man who had a reputation for being a little too quick to pull his knife, who could not hold his liquor, but who consumed life in great gulps. I know he liked to hear his brother-in-law pick the guitar, that he liked to see dogs and chickens fight, and a pretty woman dance.

And I know that something happened to him in those years when he was a marine in Korea, something involving a bitter cold night in a place he could not spell or even pronounce. And I know that after that he was too often mean and cold, and kept a secret that he only talked about when he was either knee-walkin' drunk or scared of dying, like he was at the end, when he called me to his side and told it.

I know a good bit. But one of the best men I have ever known told me once that to tell a story right you have to lean the words against each other so that they don't all fall down, and I needed more words, more facts. I spent a year just talking to the people close to me, filling in the holes in my memory.

I would not have written it at all if my momma had said no. I asked if I should, and I warned her that for every smile it evoked it would bring an equal number of tears. She was quiet a minute, staring out the window of the car. "Write it," she said. "I sat quiet, for fifty years."

The biggest reason for writing this story is to set one thing straight from now on. My momma believes that she failed, that her three sons, being all she has ever had, did not get enough of the fine things in life because she was our mother. My older brother, Sam, has worked like a dog his whole life, in the coal yard and clay pits when he was eleven, with a pick and shovel and yard rake when was a young man, and now in the cotton mill. If he has ever had a full day of rest in his life, I cannot remember when. She blames herself for that.

My younger brother, Mark, has known the inside of jails. He is a hard drinker and fighter who bears the long scars of knife wounds on his body and still carries a bullet in one arm, who seems to have somehow absorbed the spirit of the father he cannot even remember. She blames herself for that.

Then there is me, the newspaperman who, through the leg-up that she gave him and a series of happy accidents, wound up at the temple of this profession, working under legends. I am no better, no worse than my brothers; in fact they are both smarter than me. But the truth is that I am proud of who and what I am, just as proud of being the son of a woman who picked cotton and took in ironing as I am of working for a place like the *New York Times.* I have always believed that one could not have been without the other. My job has carried me to see things seldom seen by a country boy, without a white-trash, first-pick draft notice, to the other side of the world and into the same columned mansions where my momma used to clean bathrooms. When I was a man of thirty-three they even let me into Harvard, and I was not holding a mop. When I was thirty-six, I won the highest honor our profession bestows.

I hope she blames herself for that, too.

I hope she sees some of her backbone in me, because without it I would have been more accepting of the words of others, of the editor who once looked me dead in the eye and told me I was not sophisticated enough to cover the Anniston, Alabama, city council, of one or two Yankee reporters who allowed that I was mildly talented in a quaint Southern way, of a high school teacher who said a boy like me ought to think about a good trade school. It was my momma who said, "Don't never take nothin' off nobody." And while it was my daddy who taught me to fight dirty, she was the one who taught me not to give a damn when it hurt.

I hope she sees some of her gentleness and sensitivity in my words, because if there is any of that in me still, it came from her. In an important way, her sadness is in every story I write. I have written mostly about people whose lives came and went on tides of whim, apathy and cruelty. Some reporters know Washington. I know this. I have, heaven help me, a talent for it. I have never felt so at home as I did in Haiti, where little girls with dead eyes hold your hands and whisper about fathers who were shot in the back of the head by grinning soldiers. I walked through neighborhoods in my own country where the killing is done with laughter, acting like I was ten feet tall and bulletproof even as my legs trembled, because I believe that if we are going to write about life and death, we should not do it from the cheap seats.

I believe I was drawn to those stories because of her; because of all the lessons my mother tried to teach me, the most important was that every life deserves a certain amount of dignity, no matter how poor or damaged the shell that carries it. The only time I ever made her truly ashamed of me was the day I made fun of a boy from a family that was even poorer than us. His daddy had shaved his head to cheat the lice, and I laughed at him, made fun of him, until I saw the look in my momma's eyes.

So, this story is for her, as have been, in smaller ways, all the stories I have ever told and the method in which I told them. I would like to be able to say, with trite and silly melodrama, that I am sorry that my father did not live to see his son's name on a book. But that would be a bigger lie than I can tell, sober. I will not track the muck of cheap sentimentality into this story by saying that it will be in any way an instrument for healing. I understand him better now, understand the pounding his character endured in that defining time overseas. But somewhere between understanding and forgiveness there is another wall, too wide to get around.

The errors in this book that I know of are omissions, not fabrications, intended to spare people who have enough pain in their lives, a little more.

After my grandmother's funeral I strolled over to his tiny headstone in a corner of the cemetery in Jacksonville. I still wonder sometimes to whom the Marines handed the triangle of American flag that had draped his coffin. I do not want it. I only wonder. I noticed that someone had cared enough to come by and pluck the weeds and wild onions from the grave, to put a pink silk flower in a vase, and I wondered about that, too. But if there was any real regret in me, I could not find it. There was no pain to speak of, I think because the dead place inside me where my father resides is shiny and slick and perfectly symmetrical, polished by a lifetime. It is not pain so much as a sculpture of it. It is hard to the touch, but smooth.

No, this is not an important book. The people who know about books call it a memoir, but that is much too fancy a word for me, for her, for him. It is only a story of a handful of lives, in which one tall, blond woman, her back forever bent by the pull of that sack, comes off looking good and noble, and a dead man gets to answer for himself from deep in the ground. In these pages I will make the dead dance again with the living, not to get at any great truth, just a few little ones. It is still a damn hard thing to do, when you think about it.

God help me, Momma, if I am clumsy.

1
THE
WIDOW'S MITE

1

A man who buys books
because they're pretty

My mother and father were born in the most beautiful place on earth, in the foothills of the Appalachians along the Alabama-Georgia line. It was a place where gray mists hid the tops of low, deep-green mountains, where redbone and bluetick hounds flashed through the pines as they chased possums into the sacks of old men in frayed overalls, where old women in bonnets dipped Bruton snuff and hummed "Faded Love and Winter Roses" as they shelled purple hulls, canned peaches and made biscuits too good for this world. It was a place where playing the church piano loud was near as important as playing it right, where fearless young men steered long, black Buicks loaded with yellow whiskey down roads the color of dried blood, where the first frost meant hog killin' time and the mouthwatering smell of cracklin's would drift for acres from giant, bubbling pots. It was a place where the screams of panthers, like a woman's anguished cry, still haunted the most remote ridges and hollows in the dead of night, where children believed they could choke off the cries of night birds by circling one wrist with a thumb and forefinger and squeezing tight, and where the cotton blew off the wagons and hung like scraps of cloud in the branches of trees.

It was about 120 miles west of Atlanta, about 100 miles east of

Birmingham, close to nothin' but that dull red ground. Life here between the meandering dirt roads and skinny blacktop was full, rich, original and real, but harsh, hard, mean as a damn snake. My parents grew up in the 1940s and 1950s in the poor, upland South, a million miles from the Mississippi Delta and the Black Belt and the jasmine-scented verandas of what most people came to know as the Old South. My ancestors never saw a mint julep, but they sipped five-day-old likker out of ceramic jugs and Bell jars until they could not remember their Christian names.

Men paid for their plain-plank houses and a few acres of land by sawing and hand-lifting pulpwood onto ragged trucks for pennies a ton. They worked in the blast furnace heat of the pipe shops, loaded boxcars at the clay pits and tended the nerve gas stockpiles at the army base, carrying caged birds to test for leaks. They coaxed crops to grow in the up-country clay that no amount of fertilizer would ever turn into rich bottomland, tried in vain to keep their fingers, hands and arms out of the hungry machinery of the cotton mills, so that the first thing you thought when you saw an empty sleeve was not war, but the threshing racks. The summers withered the cotton and corn and the tornado season lasted ten months, making splinters out of their barns, twisting the tin off their roofs, yanking their tombstones out of the ground. Their women worked themselves to death, their mules succumbed to worms and their children were crippled by rickets and perished from fever, but every Sunday morning The Word leaked out of little white-wood sanctuaries where preachers thrust ragged Bibles at the rafters and promised them that while sickness and poverty and Lucifer might take their families, the soul of man never dies.

White people had it hard and black people had it harder than that, because what are the table scraps of nothing? This was not the genteel and parochial South, where monied whites felt they owed some generations-old debt to their black neighbors because their great-great-grandfather owned their great-great-grandfather. No one I knew ever had a mammy. This was two separate states, both wanting and desperate, kept separate by hard men who hid their faces under hoods and their deeds under some twisted interpretation of the Bible, and kicked the living shit out of anyone who thought it should be different. Even into my own youth, the orange fires of shacks and crosses lit up the evening sky. It seems a cliché now, to see it on movie screens. At the time, it burned my eyes.

It was as if God made them pay for the loveliness of their scenery by demanding everything else. Yet the grimness of it faded for a while, at dinner on the ground at the Protestant churches, where people sat on the springtime grass and ate potato salad and sipped sweet tea from an aluminum tub with a huge block of ice floating in it. The pain eased at family reunions where the men barbecued twenty-four hours straight and the women took turns holding babies and balancing plates on their knees, trying to keep the grease from soaking through on the one good dress they had. The hardness of it softened in the all-night gospel singings that ushered in the dawn with the promise that "I'll have a new body, praise the Lord, I'll have a new life," as babies crawled up into the ample laps of grandmothers to sleep across jiggling knees. If all else failed, you could just wash it away for a while, at the stills deep in the woods or in the highly illegal beer joints and so-called social clubs, where the guitar pickers played with their eyes closed, lost in the booze and the words of lost love and betrayal. They sang about women who walked the hills in long black veils, of whispering pines, and trains.

It was the backdrop and the sound track of our lives. I was born into it in the summer of 1959, just in time to taste it, absorb it, love it and hate it and know its secrets. When I was a teenager, I watched it shudder and gasp and finally begin to die, the pines clear-cut into huge patches of muddy wasteland and the character of the little towns murdered by generic subdivisions and generic fast-food restaurants. The South I was born in was eulogized by pay-as-you-pray TV preachers, enclosed in a coffin of light blue aluminum siding and laid to rest in a polyester suit, from Wal-Mart.

I watched the races fall into an uneasy and imperfect peace and the grip of the poverty ease. There was reason to rejoice in that, because while I was never ashamed to be a Southerner there was always a feeling, a need, to explain myself. But as change came in good ways, I saw

Southernness become a fashion, watched men wear their camouflage deer-hunting clothes to the mall because they thought it looked cool, watched Hank Williams and his elegant western suits give way to pretty boys in ridiculous Rodeo Drive leather chaps. And I thought of my granddaddy Bobby Bragg, gentler than his son in some ways, who sat down to dinner in clean overalls, a spotless white shirt buttoned to the neck and black wingtip shoes.

Only the religion held. It held even though the piano players went to music school and actually learned to read notes, even though new churches became glass and steel monstrosities that looked like they had just touched down from Venus. It held even though the more prosperous preachers started to tack the pretentious title of "Doctor" in front of their name and started to spend more time at seminars than visiting the sick. It held even though the Baptists started to beat drums and allow electric guitar, even though—Jesus help us—the Church of Christ conceded in the late 1970s that it was probably not a mortal sin if boys went swimming with girls. It held. God hung in there like a rusty fish hook.

Even my father found Him at the end, or at least he went looking for Him.

It was 1974, when he was still a young man and I was a boy in my first year of high school. Several years after he abandoned us or chased us away for the last of too many times, the phone would ring in the little red house where we lived with my grandmother, through the good graces and charity of my aunt Nita and uncle Ed. It would be him, asking for my momma between bone-rattling coughs, the kind that telegraphed death, promised it. She would stop what she was doing, dust the flour from her hands or turn off the iron or put down her fork at supper, and sit for what seemed hours, silent, just listening, twisting the phone cord around and around her hands until it was so tight her fingers turned white as bone. Funny, the things that rivet themselves in your mind. Finally she would promise to pray for him, and ease the phone back onto its cradle. Then she would pick up what she was doing again, dry-eyed, but would not talk to us for a very long time.

He had been a fearsome man, the kind of slim and lethal Southern man who would react with murderous fury when insulted, attacking with a knife or a pine knot or his bare hands. When I was six I watched him kick the mortal hell out of a man in a parking lot. I cannot remember why he did it. I just remember how the man covered up his head and tried to crawl under a car to get away, but he was too fat and wedged himself half in and half out, while my daddy kicked his ass and spit on his back and called him a son of a bitch. I remember how the man's yellow sport shirt had blood on it, how his pocket change spilled out into the gravel, and how the man's children—I remember a little girl screaming—stood and watched, in terror. I distinctly remember that I was not afraid, because no matter how much red hatred clouded his eyes, how much Jim Beam or beer or homemade whiskey assaulted his brain, he never touched me. In some sick way I admired him. This was, remember, a world of pulpwooders and millworkers and farmers, of men who ripped all the skin off their knuckles working on junk cars and ignored the blood that ran down their arms. In that world, strength and toughness were everything, sometimes the only things. It was common, acceptable, not to be able to read, but a man who wouldn't fight, couldn't fight, was a pathetic thing. To be afraid was shameful. I am not saying I agree with it. It's just the way it was.

But in the end he was very afraid. The years of drinking more whiskey than water had wrecked him, and somewhere along the way, he had picked up TB. People were not supposed to still be dying of it then, in 1974, and he might have lived if he could have quit drinking and cleaned up his life. But it was the drinking that killed him, really, just as sure as if he slipped and fell and cut his throat on the broken bottle.

He was only forty, when the sickness took him down. But by the time he was scared enough of dying to try to live, to truly want to live, he was out of every option except The Cross.

He said he began to see a dark angel perched like a crow on the footboard of his bed, just waiting, expectant. He knew enough of the Gospel to be fearful of fallen angels, and he was afraid that it might have been dispatched from hell, special, to ferry him home. He said he threw shoes at it to get it to flutter away, but it returned, it always returned. I never,

ever liked to listen to him when he talked drunk and crazy that way, and the phone seemed to grow hot in my hand.

He had never been inside a church in his life, back when he was young, indestructible. But as the sickness squeezed his lungs he began to hope that Jesus was more than just a fifty-cent mail-order picture enshrined in a dime-store frame on the hallway wall, that salvation was the trick card he could play right at the end and stay in the money. I know it because I asked my momma what they talked about all those times. "He talked about y'all, a little. But mostly he just wanted to talk about the Lord."

I guess it is what you do if you grow up with warnings of damnation ringing from every church door and radio station and family reunion, in a place where total strangers will walk up to you at the Piggly Wiggly and ask if you are Saved. Even if you deny that faith, rebuke it, you still carry it around with you like some half-forgotten Indian head penny you keep in your pocket for luck. I wonder sometimes if I will be the same, if when I see my life coming to an end I will drop to my knees and search my soul for old sins and my memory for forgotten prayers. I reckon so.

He would ask to see her in some of those calls, but anything my momma had for my daddy had been beaten and starved out of her a long time ago. At least, that is the conviction I had at the time. He would ask to see us, too, his sons, but too much time had gone by since he had been anything close to a father and the overpowering memories were bad, of curses and shouts and my momma motioning us away, out of the room. I had not seen him for more than a few minutes in years, since I was six and we went back to live in my grandmother's house on Roy Webb Road.

We had heard he was sick, but that information registered somewhere far below my second-hand motorcycle and my first real kiss in relevance and importance. My older brother, Sam, who was nine the last time he left us, who went outside to dig crumbs of shattered coal from the frozen mud so that we would have something to burn to stay warm, was scarred more than me by the memories, cared even less than me. My younger brother, Mark, did not have a single cognizant memory of him. I wonder sometimes if that is not a blessing, but then I think that while my older brother and I grew up with a cracked image of a father, with some vague memories of fleeting good times, he had nothing, has nothing now, as if he was hatched into this world.

Then one day my momma told me he had asked for me, only me. She said he was bad sick and it might be the last time. He said he bought me a present, and wanted to give it to me himself.

Even now, over twenty years later, I wonder if the reason I saw my father that one last time, that I heard the closest thing to a confession he would ever make, is because I responded to a dying man's cry for attention or just wanted the present, the bribe. I guess it does not really matter anymore. I went to the little house where he lived and knocked on the door, determined to stare him down, man to man, to let him know exactly what I thought of him for what he did to us, to my momma. I was going on sixteen, six feet two and 185 pounds, and had fought bloody battles over girls in the parking lot of the local Hardee's, and now and then my brothers and I mixed it up just for sport.

I was not afraid of him anymore. I was not helpless now, not some child hiding under the bed.

I know why he wanted to see me. If my daddy had a favorite, I guess I was it. I guess he thought I was smart, because he liked the fact that I would sit quiet with a book about Dick and Jane and read it so many times that I memorized it, then show off in class by reciting my page, not reading it. He liked the fact that if I got into a fight on the playground and someone had a grip on my throat, I would stick my thumb in his eye, just like he taught me when I was still just a very little boy. He was proud of the fact that, if a batter got a hit off me in baseball, I would throw the next pitch at his head. Like he taught me.

I guess he thought I was a lot like him. Even now people say that. They tell me I remind them of him in little ways. As the years slip past, it is easier to hear, but at the time I hated to hear it, think it.

He was living in a little house in Jacksonville, Alabama, a college and mill town that was the closest urban center—with its stoplights and a high school and two supermarkets—to the country roads we roamed in our raggedy cars. He lived in the mill village, in one of those houses the mills subsidized for their workers, back when companies still did things like that. It was not much of a place, but better than anything we had ever lived in as a family. I knocked and a voice like an old woman's, punctuated with a cough that sounded like it came from deep in the guts, told me to come on in, it ain't locked.

It was dark inside, but light enough to see what looked like a bundle of quilts on the corner of a sofa. Deep inside them was a ghost of a man, his hair and beard long and going dirty gray, his face pale and cut with deep grooves. I knew I was in the right house because my daddy's only real possessions, a velvet-covered board pinned with medals, sat inside a glass cabinet on a table. But this couldn't be him.

He coughed again, spit into a can and struggled to his feet, but stopped somewhere short of standing straight up, as if a stoop was all he could manage. "Hey, Cotton Top," he said, and then I knew. My daddy, who was supposed to be a still-young man, looked like the walking dead, not just old but damaged, poisoned, used up, crumpled up and thrown in a corner to die. I thought that the man I would see would be the trim, swaggering, high-toned little rooster of a man who stared back at me from the pages of my mother's photo album, the young soldier clowning around in Korea, the arrow-straight, good-looking boy who posed beside my mother back before the fields and mop handle and the rest of it took her looks. The man I remembered had always dressed nice even when there was no cornmeal left, whose black hair always shone with oil, whose chin, even when it wobbled from the beer, was always angled up, high.

I thought he would greet me with that strong voice that sounded so fine when he laughed and so evil when, slurred by a quart of corn likker, he whirled through the house and cried and shrieked, tormented by things we could not see or even imagine. I thought he would be the man and monster of my childhood. But that man was as dead as a man could be, and this was what remained, like when a snake sheds its skin and leaves a dry and brittle husk of itself hanging in the Johnson grass.

"It's all over but the shoutin' now, ain't it, boy," he said, and when he let the quilt slide from his shoulders I saw how he had wasted away, how the bones seemed to poke out of his clothes, and I could see how it killed his pride to look this way, unclean, and he looked away from me for a moment, ashamed.

He made a halfhearted try to shake my hand but had a coughing fit again that lasted a minute, coughing up his life, his lungs, and after that I did not want to touch him. I stared at the tops of my sneakers, ashamed to look at his face. He had a dark streak in his beard below his lip, and I wondered why, because he had never liked snuff. Now I know it was blood.

I remember much of what he had to say that day. When you don't see someone for eight, nine years, when you see that person's life red on their lips and know that you will never see them beyond this day, you listen close, even if what you want most of all is to run away.

"Your momma, she alright?" he said.

I said I reckon so.

"The other boys? They alright?"

I said I reckon so.

Then he was quiet for a minute, as if trying to find the words to a question to which he did not really want an answer.

"They ain't never come to see me. How come?"

I remember thinking, fool, why do you think? But I just choked down my words, and in doing so I gave up the only real chance I would ever have to accuse him, to attack him with the facts of his own sorry nature and the price it had cost us all. The opportunity hung perfectly still in the air in front of my face and fists, and I held my temper and let it float on by. I could have no more challenged him, berated him, hurt him than I could have kicked some three-legged dog. Life had kicked his ass pretty good.

"How come?"

I just shrugged.

For the next few hours—unless I was mistaken, having never had one before—he tried to be my father. Between coughing and long pauses when he fought for air to generate his words, he asked me if I liked school, if I had ever gotten any better at math, the one thing that just flat evaded me. He asked me if I ever got even with the boy who blacked my eye ten years ago, and nodded his head, approvingly, as I described how I followed him into the boys' bathroom and knocked his dick string up to his watch pocket, and would have dunked his head in the urinal if the aging principal, Mr. Hand, had not had to pee and caught me dragging him across the concrete floor.

He asked me about basketball and baseball, said he had heard I had a good game against Cedar Springs, and I said pretty good, but it was two years ago, anyway. He asked if I had a girlfriend and I said, "One," and he said, "Just one?" For the slimmest of seconds he almost grinned and the young, swaggering man peeked through, but disappeared again in the disease that cloaked him. He talked and talked and never said a word, at least not the words I wanted.

He never said he was sorry.

He never said he wished things had turned out different.

He never acted like he did anything wrong.

Part of it, I know, was culture. Men did not talk about their feelings in his hard world. I did not expect, even for a second, that he would bare his soul. All I wanted was a simple acknowledgment that he was wrong, or least too drunk to notice that he left his pretty wife and sons alone again and again, with no food, no money, no way to get any, short of begging, because when she tried to find work he yelled, screamed, refused. No, I didn't expect much.

After a while he motioned for me to follow him into a back room where he had my present, and I planned to take it and run. He handed me a long, thin box, and inside was a brand-new, well-oiled Remington .22 rifle. He said he had bought it some time back, just kept forgetting to give it to me. It was a fine gun, and for a moment we were just like anybody else in the culture of that place, where a father's gift of a gun to his son is a rite. He said, with absolute seriousness, not to shoot my brothers.

I thanked him and made to leave, but he stopped me with a hand on my arm and said wait, that ain't all, that he had some other things for me. He motioned to three big cardboard egg cartons stacked against one wall.

Inside was the only treasure I truly have ever known.

I had grown up in a house in which there were only two books, the King James Bible and the spring seed catalog. But here, in these boxes, were dozens of hardback copies of everything from Mark Twain to Sir Arthur Conan Doyle. There was a water-damaged Faulkner, and the nearly complete set of Edgar Rice Burroughs's *Tarzan*. There was poetry and trash, Zane Grey's *Riders of the Purple Sage*, and a paperback with two naked women on the cover. There was a tiny, old copy of *Arabian Nights*, threadbare Hardy Boys, and one Hemingway. He had bought most of them at a yard sale, by the box or pound, and some at a flea market. He did not even know what he was giving me, did not recognize most of the writers. "Your momma said you still liked to read," he said.

There was Shakespeare. My father did not know who he was, exactly, but he had heard the name. He wanted them because they were pretty, because they were wrapped in fake leather, because they looked like rich folks' books. I do not love Shakespeare, but I still have those books. I would not trade them for a gold monkey.

"They's maybe some dirty books in there, by mistake, but I know you ain't interested in them, so just throw 'em away," he said. "Or at least, throw 'em away before your momma sees 'em." And then I swear to God he winked.

I guess my heart should have broken then, and maybe it did, a little. I guess I should have done something, anything, besides mumble "Thank you, Daddy." I guess that would have been fine, would not have betrayed in some way my mother, my brothers, myself. But I just stood there, trapped somewhere between my long-standing, comfortable hatred, and what might have been forgiveness. I am trapped there still.

He could not buy my friendship, not with a library, but with the books he bought my company for as long as he wanted it that day. We went back in the living room and he unscrewed the cap on a thin pint of what I believe was George Dickel or some other brown likker. He drank it in little sips, and talked about how pretty my momma was when they were married, about a time when we all went to Texas for a summer so he could work a body and fender job, about the bulldogs he used to fight in the pits over in Rome, Georgia, about the mean woman he used to court over that way who kept a razor tucked down the neck of her blouse. He talked of a hound dog he had that could climb a tree, of the time a rattlesnake bit Boots, his momma's fat Chihuahua, and how she swelled up like a beach ball. I had heard them all before, or thought I had, when I was a child, but I cannot say it was a bad thing to hear them again.

I asked him once or twice to tell me about Korea, because I was a boy and boys are thrilled with war. But he just said nawwwwww, he didn't like to dwell on it, that I should thank the Lord I never had to go.

Finally the bottle was down to a swallow or two and he was huddled back in a corner of the couch, quiet, as satisfyingly, numbingly drunk as a man in his condition could be. The whiskey was like tonic to him, I guess. It warmed instead of burned. I just sat in a chair all the way across the room, waiting. I had experience with drunks, with him as a child, and later with kinfolks who staggered into our house for a place to sleep. I knew it was just a matter of time until he slipped into that deep, deep sleep that no amount of shaking or even a house fire would wake him from. I would take my gun, my books, and leave him forever.

Then, without any explanation of why he changed his mind and without any pretense that by talking about this war he could somehow excuse the way he lived, he told me one last story. He used his aged, ruined voice like an old man's palsied hands to pick the lock on his past, and tugged me inside.

2

A killing, and a man who tried to walk on water

The dead waved from the ditches in Korea. The arms of the soldiers reached out from bodies half in, half out of the frozen mud, as if begging for help even after their hearts had cooled and the ice had glazed their eyes. They had been shot to rags by machine guns and frozen by a subzero wind, leaving olive-drab statues in the killing, numbing cold in the mountains in the north. The young Marine from Alabama trudged past them as he fought the North Koreans and Red Chinese at places with great strategic military importance for a second or two in time. Of all the tales he told that day, more than twenty years ago, the image of dead men reaching to him from the roadside still won't lie still in my head.

The dead have the decency to lie flat in Calhoun County. In my father's time they still laid them out in the parlors and in their own bedrooms, with pennies on their eyes. The women and the very old would take turns sitting up with the dead, because to leave them alone would be disrespectful, and because the very oldest ones still believed that the soul lingered until the final benediction, until the first handful of dirt, and Satan might fly in through a window and snatch it away if someone didn't watch close. Even the littlest children would be led in to stare, to hide their face in the skirts of their momma or the pants leg of their

15

daddy, while the young men stood sentry most of the night on the front porch, smoking, sipping black coffee. It was all about respect, about ceremony, as if by making the dying of a woman or man an event, a happening, it somehow made up for the fact that there was so goddamn little nicety in living. That, for my daddy, was what was wrong with Korea. He just glanced at the dead, and left them where they lay.

Like most other Southern boys who grew up far from the Big House, the ones who fought and died and fought and lived in every armed conflict since Cemetery Ridge, his world had been narrow, and the only way to see the rest of it was to enlist. His father worked for dusty, stifling decades in the cotton mill. He wasn't sure what he wanted to do with his life, but anything that would keep him out of the mills was fine with him. He happened to come of age in one of those eras when America was in the market for rough-as-a-cob country boys who could shoot bumblebees off dandelions with a BB gun. They could knock gray squirrels out of the tops of trees with a .22 rifle, and could bring down quail and even doves on the fly with no. 9 birdshot. It would be like hitting a bear in the ass with a bucket of sand, to shoot a man.

Boot camp had been like a party for him, or at least what he figured a party was like. The Marines, balanced against the harsh world of home, dripped with life, with experiences. He got plenty to eat and unlimited milk to drink. He got weekends off to chase women. He would drink beer with his newfound friends until they were tighter than Dick's hatband and even the fat girls started to look good. They would fight anyone who looked at them funny until the MPs came, then they'd fight them. He got a pure silver cigarette lighter, a gold-plated ink pen and a five-dollar camera, so that he could take all his experiences back to Alabama after they vanquished the communist horde and defended democracy, or whatever it was they were supposed to do.

He rode in a plane, the first in his family to ever do that, and he rode on a boat on the ocean, far, far out on that ocean, the first to ever do that. He had no problem with the notion of killing. He had never seen an Asian man, not in his whole life. I got the impression that because the Chinese and North Koreans were so different, so alien to him, they were somehow less human and therefore easier to kill. I asked him, because I was a boy and dying was a remote thing to me then, how many he killed. He said a few, maybe. All but one, he killed from a distance.

I knew we were getting to the good part now. I had pictured my father in war, a merciless, indestructible warrior, not in olive drab but in faded gray or butternut brown. I pictured him striding through wildflowers and dead Yankees with a saber in one hand, a six-shot revolver in the other and a bayonet wound in his side, his horse shot out from under him. I pictured him that way much as I had sometimes pictured him as taking me places, doing things with me. One daydream was just as silly, as far from truth, as the other. I definitely did not picture him hollow-eyed and shivering, huddled around a portable stove, in this war and country I could not even adequately imagine.

For my father in Korea, there were no grand charges, no standup fights over open ground. The fighting was mostly mean, drawn-out, duck-and-shoot battles fought around bends in the roads and over frozen streams and up the sides of a hundred hills, which the officers ordered them to "take" in the teeth of machine guns and snipers, as if they were going to plant a flag and grow turnips on it or some such, instead of just walking back down it again, fewer than before.

But the violence of it was almost welcome, because for a while he forgot about being cold. He had never been cold. Oh, once or twice a year back home it got cold enough to freeze the ducks on the pond or to dust the ground with snow. This was something else, something as alien as the words the enemy screamed at him as they hurled themselves again and again at the dug-in Americans. This was cold that burned like red-hot needles.

Men were sent home blown to pieces by mines and pocked with bullet holes, but more often with frozen feet, fingers, ears, noses. The ones who were shot were shot through five layers of clothes, so that sometimes the hurt and blood didn't show. It looked like whole platoons of men had just gotten weary, and lain down to sleep.

They did much of their moving through trenches, where every step cracked through the ice underfoot, so that his feet were not just half-frozen but wet, so that the ice collected between his toes.

He reasoned he was there when it came spring and summer, too, but for the life of him it seemed like it was winter all the time. He wandered through a nightmare maze of mine-laden trenches, trails and roads, afraid that every step would rip his legs out from under him and send him home to Alabama a cripple. He even had a dream that it did happen and he had to sit in a wheelchair outside the courthouse. For some reason that only makes sense in dreams, he had to shake the hand of every single person who went in to get married or pay their taxes or get their license renewed, so that they could all see him sitting there like that. He said he dreamed about it more than once, even after he came home whole, or mostly so. It was what he feared, more than dying: losing part of himself.

He was quiet for a little while after that, I remember, maybe because he was remembering, and it made me nervous, sitting quiet with him like that, as if we had reached a point in the story that I wasn't allowed to see. "I hated them mines," he finally said, and I believe he tried to take another swig from that now dead bottle.

Sometimes it seemed like the country itself was just playing with them. Sometimes the ground was so hard that men walked over the mines and did not trip the trigger, and later in the day, when it had warmed a few degrees and the ground turned to mud again, one soldier would walk down a path that a thousand men had already tramped and have his feet ripped out from under him. So you never walked safe, you never walked free. Mortars would come whistling down from the sky and he was sure he was dead, but although men around him died he seemed to dance between the snowflakes of shrapnel, waiting for the next one, and the next. On warmer days the shells would just sink into the mud.

He said he was bound up in so many clothes that he could not effectively run or efficiently fight, that his mind was always thick, sluggish, because he was always tired. He did not talk about the politics of it, or at least if he did it did not register with me then. He did not rail against officers or badmouth MacArthur's insane push into the north that brought the Chinese swarming onto them. He did not talk about things like honor, because while honor is a big thing to the gentility, it is not a word you hear much on the lips of poor whites. It is not that we do not know what it is, or have it, it is just one of those fifty-dollar words you don't hear much. To my daddy, the war was an adventure gone bad, not a family heirloom.

I remember that I asked him then why he had never talked about this war with my momma, and he said he had, but just one time. It was when he was fresh back from it, when the memories were still hot in his mind, and he tried to unburden himself to a new bride. He told her just one story, the worst of it, but if she ever shared the story with her sons I could not remember it. He said she probably thought we were just too little, that we would be scared. Maybe, he said, she was afraid it would give us bad dreams.

I told him I was old enough to hear it now.

He remembered there was a moon that night, one of those winter nights when the sky was clear and mean and bright. He remembered it, because it was easy to get shot dead if you showed your silhouette on a night like that. They had heated rations and ate them mechanically, with spoons out of mess kits, like overgrown children. It was nice to think of home, on nights like that. At home in Alabama, his family would be sitting around the long table, the men pulling a little every now and then on a jug of whiskey as they waited for the cornbread to brown. He would have crawled home on his knees to smell that smell, even though he had been a picky eater and disdained such "country food." He liked a good sandwich, what we called café food. But not having it made it taste good in his mind.

The cold was worse on the clear nights. They camped on a flat place beside a river, almost within sight of the enemy on the other side. As wretched as the days were because of the cold and the fear and the sickness, the night was terror. The rivers froze, and at night the Chinese or North Koreans would inch their way across it, one or two at a time, and do their killing with knives. It was legend, those killings, designed to terrify.

That night, or maybe it was morning, an assassin crept into his group, as he slept, and killed a man just inches away. My daddy reached out to shake him, maybe to shake him awake, and felt the blood that had leaked from his neck.

He scrambled out of the shelter and into the biting cold, and saw him, the killer, on the ice.

The man lay flat on his belly, to keep the ice from breaking, and slithered and squirmed like some kind of slow-moving reptile, just a few feet from the bank. My daddy ran down to the river's edge and, unthinkingly, straight out onto the ice, slipping down hard on his hands and knees, hearing the ice crack. But he lunged forward and grabbed the man. They fought, frantic, crazy. My daddy must have lost his rifle because he never mentioned using it, and if he pulled his knife he never said. He knew the other man had a knife, had to have one, but my daddy did not see it. Maybe, in his rage, his terror, he did see it and didn't care.

Finally he fought to his knees and pushed himself on top of the man, and the ice popped and cracked again. The other man clawed at my daddy's face, screaming, and finally fought free. He tried to do the impossible, to walk on that thin ice, and plunged straight through it.

The man rose up, his hands clutching the edge, and although he didn't know it, he was already dead. The cold, that unbearable cold, would take him even if he could get out of the water. My daddy could have left him that way, could have let the ice have him. Instead, he reached down into the water and put both hands on top of the man's head, and pushed him down, again and again, till there was no need anymore.

When the thing was done, my daddy, freezing, crawled back to where he guessed dry ground was, to the shelter, peeled off his wet, freezing gloves and shoved both hands between his legs to warm the numbness away.

If there was satisfaction in what he had done, he didn't say.

"I remember he had big eyes," my daddy said of the man he killed. "A little feller, but big ol' eyes."

He was done talking then. I left him with his empty bottle and never saw him again, alive or dead.

I don't know anything about wars. I don't think even the most erudite scholars do. I think you have to fight one, to know it.

But I have little doubt that, in that narrow space of time, his life shifted, tumbled off balance. I do not know, not for dead certain, that I can blame his meanness and cruelties, his abandonment of us, my momma, on something as distant as the war. It might be that he was just a flawed man, a man without conscience, who let his wife and children suffer and just didn't care. It might even be that, as he sat dying, he would have told me anything if it would have made me think better of him. Even a legacy of a lie is better than hate.

I choose not to believe that. I believe instead that there, in that wretched place where the ground blows up under your feet and dead men motion to you from the sidelines of war, a boy with thin blood was rearranged. I believe it. I want to. I have to.

I asked Momma, not long ago, to tell me stories about my daddy's war.

"He did some killin', but he only told me about one time," my momma said. "He didn't even talk about it with men, just me, that one time. That one man. That's all I know," and I could tell it was something she would rather not remember. It is a mean thing to do, for a son to ask his momma to remember things like that. Still, I had to know.

I asked her how my daddy killed him. "He killed him a little bit at a time," she said. Then, to show me how, my gentle mother put her hands together with her palms turned toward the floor, and made a pushing motion, again and again and again . . .

He came home from the war to marry my momma. I guess, in the end, he did what we all do when we suffer. He came home, to try and heal.

But in a way, he was dying, failing, even before I was born. My momma's life with him, my life, Sam's and Mark's lives, may have given him some joy, some peace. It might be that we distracted him from his devils. It is the only reason I can come up with, for why he wanted us at all.

He called once, maybe twice more before he died. In the final few weeks he said he could still see the angel on his footboard, just waiting. I could not tell if he was drunk or not, but that is the way drunk people talk. I told him it was just a dream.

3

Fake gold, other people's houses, and the finest man I never knew

Τhe first memory I have is of a tall blond woman who drags a canvas cotton sack along an undulating row of rust-colored ground, through a field that seems to reach into the back forty of forever. I remember the sound it makes as it slides between the chest-high stalks that are so deeply, darkly green they look almost black, and the smell of kicked-up dust, and sweat. The tall woman is wearing a man's britches and a man's old straw hat, and now and then she looks back over her shoulder to smile at the three-year-old boy whose hair is almost as purely white as the bolls she picks, who rides the back of the six-foot-long sack like a magic carpet.

It is my first memory, and the best. It is sweeter than the recollection I have of the time she sat me down in the middle of a wild strawberry patch and let me eat my way out again, richer than all the times she took me swimming in jade-colored streams and threw a big rock in the water to run off the water moccasins. It is even stronger than the time she scraped together money for my high school class ring, even though her toes poked out of her old sneakers and she was wearing clothes from the Salvation Army bin in the parking lot of the A&P. It was not real gold, that ring, just some kind of fake, shiny metal crowned with a lump of red

23

glass, but I was proud of it. I was the first member of my family to have one, and if the sunlight caught it just right, it looked almost real.

But it is the memory of that woman, that boy and that vast field that continues to ride and ride in my mind, not only because it is a warm, safe and proud thing I carry with me like a talisman into cold, dangerous and spirit-numbing places, but because it so perfectly sums up the way she carried us, with such dignity. We would have survived on the fifty-dollar welfare check the government decided our lives were worth. The family could have lived on the charity of our kin and the kindness of strangers. Pride pushed her out into the cotton field, in the same way that old terror, old pain squeezed my daddy into a prison of empty whiskey bottles.

I asked her, many years later, if the strap of the sack cut deeper into her back and shoulders because I was there. "You wasn't heavy," she said. Having a baby with her made the long rows shorter, somehow, because when she felt like quitting, when she felt like her legs were going to buckle or her back would break in two, all she had to do was look behind her. It gave her a reason to keep pulling.

Like I said, it is a perfect memory, but too perfect. It would have been easy for me to just accept the façade of blind sacrifice that has always cloaked her, to believe my momma never minded the backbreaking work and the physical pain as she dragged me up and down a thousand miles of clay. I wish I could just accept the myth that she never went to see me or my brothers play basketball or baseball because she was too tired, and not because she was ashamed of her clothes. I would like to believe she didn't even notice how her own life was running through her hands like water. But the truth is she did know, and she did think about it in the nighttime when her children were put to bed and there was no one left to keep her company except her blind faith in God and her own regret.

There is a notion, a badly mistaken one among comfortable people, that you do not miss what you never had. I have written that line myself, which is shameful to me now. I, of all people, should know better, should know that being poor does not make you blind to the riches around you; that living in other folks' houses for a lifetime does not mean a person does not dream of a house of his or her own, even if it is just a little one.

My mother ached for a house, for a patch of ground, for something. When I was a young man and we would take drives through town, she stared at the homes of others with a longing so strong you could feel it. She stared and she hoped and she dreamed until she finally just got got tired of wanting.

The only thing poverty does is grind down your nerve endings to a point that you can work harder and stoop lower than most people are willing to. It chips away a person's dreams to the point that the hopelessness shows through, and the dreamer accepts that hard work and borrowed houses are all this life will ever be. While my mother will stare you dead in the eye and say she never thought of herself as poor, do not believe for one second that she did not see the rest of the world, the better world, spinning around her, out of reach.

In fact, poor was all she had ever witnessed, tasted, been. She was not some steel magnolia thrust into an alien poverty by a sorry man, but a woman who grew up with it, whose own mother would just forget to eat supper if there wasn't enough to go around. Her sisters wed men who worked hard, who bought land, homes and cars that did not reek of spilt beer. Through their vows, and some luck, they made good lives and had good things that had never been worn or used before. Momma, bless her heart, picked badly, and the years of doing without spun a single, unbroken thread through her childhood, her youth, her middle age, until the gray had crept into her hair.

We have to go back a ways to find the start of it, to a little rented house so deep in the pine barrens that night fell like a black cloth. It is lit by lanterns and ringing with a young woman's cries as a new baby appears, kicking and screaming, like she knew what life had in store.

She was born the daughter of Charlie and Ava on April 23, 1937, just over the state line in Floyd County, Georgia. An elderly doctor named Gray drove out from Rome in an Model A Ford to help with the birth, but no one seems to remember if he left with a live chicken or a ham or a ceramic jug of fine, homemade whiskey in payment. More than likely, if the doctor had any sense and was not a Baptist, or perhaps if he was, it was likker. Charlie Bundrum did not distill whiskey for just any trash, but sold it only to the doctor, the lawyer, the man who owned the drug-store and the man who ran the school board. It was known in the dry counties of northwestern Georgia and northeastern Alabama that a jar of Mr. Bundrum's pale gold, almost clear likker was safe as buttermilk. It would not make you go blind or howl at the moon or shoot your wife. A cup or two—or a few long pulls on the jug—only put a nice little fuzz around the edges of the world, like a soft lens on a camera. It helped you sleep, and some people said it even improved your dreams. A gallon of it, in its purity, was seen as fair payment for a few hours of doctoring, even the bringing forth of new life.

The baby girl had the blond hair and blue eyes of all the Bundrums, who were said to have come from Germany, but later learned that they were maybe Scotch, or maybe Irish. I guess that doesn't matter. It's not like we're searching for a family crest. They named her Margaret Marie, not after anybody in particular, but because it sounded pretty. And be-cause it was a warm April in the north Georgia mountains and because it was tradition—some say superstition—my grandfather bundled the baby up and carried her once around the house. It was said that babies would absorb all the good qualities of the person who walked them that first time around the house in which they were born, that the tiny, weak things would borrow from their strength, their character. We do not know where the tradition came from, only that it has been a ceremony of birth for generations (for me, it had been my great-aunt Plumer, a woman of virtue, abstinence and deep religious conviction. I reckon, sometimes, it don't take good).

There were worse spirits for my momma to absorb than the one of her father. He was a towering, sun-cured man with ears too big for his head, with bright blue eyes and perfect white teeth and light brown hair. His children worshipped him, because, while he whupped them too hard when they were bad, mostly he was kind, warm, laughing, solid. He drank, but instead of unveiling a hard and cruel inner man, as it so often does, the likker only revealed someone much like the sober version of himself, only one who bumped his head on the door facing.

I never saw him with my own eyes. I know him only from faded black-and-white photographs taken during the Depression, and through the rich, vivid, Technicolor memories of his children, mostly from my mother and aunts.

He never had much except laughter to give. He did not want to make his living selling whiskey on a large scale, even though some of his customers said he could have been a Rockefeller or, perhaps more fittingly, a Kennedy. The men who made it by the trunkload were much more inclined to prison, and that would have left his family alone in the teeth of the Depression. So he made a few gallons, enough to bring out the dogs and the deputies now and again, but never the federal men. It would be romantic to picture him as a big-time whiskey man, but it would be a lie. His daughters say he did it because he had to, when he couldn't get work, and because he liked to sip it himself.

It was a big family, as families went back then. He and Miss Abigail had eight children—James, Bill, Edna, Emma Mae, Gracie Juanita, Margaret, Jo, Sue—and he made his honest living in the most honorable way any man could, with a hammer. He was a carpenter, mostly a roofer, and he spent his days up high, tacking down sheets of shingle, and spent some nights and Sunday at his still, measuring the meal, the sugar, the yeast, always wary of the law, always ready to cut and run like hell through the weeds.

The stills where he cooked his whiskey are lost in rust and pine needles now, scattered through the hills. But my brother Sam still has his old carpenter's tools. He hung them, like a shrine, on the inside of his shed. He said he just likes to look at them sometimes, and doesn't have much more to say on it than that. Sam believes in taking life in his two hands and squeezing and pounding it until it gives you something, even if it's just a little bit. But the important thing is to keep squeezing, keep pounding, keep working. I believe that to him those rusted, pitted hammers, rasps and crowbars not only remind him of the first grown man who ever treated him with any kindness and love, but also represent a simple, basic principle of a man's worth, one a man can live a whole life by. He would never say that, because he doesn't talk that way, but I believe it to be so.

My grandfather could not live in town, could not breathe in a place where there were too many people. So, chasing work, he moved his growing family from tiny house to tiny house on both sides of the Alabama-

Georgia line. The whole of his life, he never went to sleep under a roof he owned outright. His children had one pair of shoes, and his wife cooked squirrel and rabbit he hunted and jack salmon he pulled out of the deep blue of Lake Guntersville. If there was not enough, like I said, she would just forget to eat, or say she wasn't hungry, or just walk outside. I have seen my own mother do it.

My mother never had a doll. When she was six, her daddy got her her first real toy, a wooden turtle with wheels that you pulled with a string. She dragged it around the dusty yard till it came to pieces. "Then I saved the pieces," she said. "I pulled 'em out, and just looked at 'em. I saved 'em till I was almost grown."

It would have been a hellish life if her momma and daddy had been the hard, religious fanatics who peopled that part of the world back then, a humorless bunch who prayed and plowed and didn't do much else, if you don't count speaking in tongues or handling snakes, the Holy Spirit coursing through their bodies like antivenin laced with Epsom salts.

I think Charlie Bundrum was unique for his time. He did not beat Jesus into his children, but believed in God. He drank but was prone to work hard and regular. He was fond of living, whereas most hard-drinking men hate life and only want to dull it. He got drunk, and sang.

He had wit like a razor, and while he had never cracked a book he was a wizard with language, with stories. Like a lot of Southern men, he could tell a story and have you sitting dead quiet, waiting for the next word, said the people who knew him well. My momma inherited his love of stories but not his timing, so that when she talks about him the words come out in a jumbled rush, like puppies spilling out of a cardboard box, jumping all over each other. She speaks in the up-country twang of the poor South, not the refined drawl of the Delta, an affectation borrowed by the rich people of our own region. The rich folks, like those of the lower South, do not pronounce their *r* sounds, so that "mother" becomes "mu-thah" and "never" becomes "nevah." You have to try, to talk that way.

My grandfather didn't talk that way. In contrast, he stuck the *r* in even where it don't need to be, and I see the ghost of his language, my language, with every trip home I make. For instance, my aunt Gracie Juanita is "Niter," and Aunt Edna is "Edner." You can pick us out of a crowd that way, as easy as finding a Cockney in the House of Lords. Anyway, I have always liked to hear my mother talk about her father, because when she does she is as close to happy as I think I have ever seen her. Listen to her:

"As each baby was born he give 'em a nickname, and that's all he ever called us. Juaniter was Snag, Edner was Rusty, William was June Bug, James was Shaker. He called Phene, James's wife, Polecat, but she stayed so mad at him that he changed it to Tadpole. I reckon because she was short. I don't really know. He called me Pooh Boy and I don't why, 'cause I was a girl and all.

"I was his pet. He only whupped me twice in my whole life, when I was five and when I was thirteen, because I kicked Jo one night in the bed and she screamed and hollered like I'd kilt her, and then acted like she went into a comer. And Daddy whupped me and whupped me and I thought Lord God he's gonna kill me, and I didn't talk to him for three months until one day his ol' car was broke down and he had to walk to the store and he asked me if I wanted to walk with him. And I went but I wouldn't walk beside him. I walked a long way off behind him. But then I got to lookin' at his old clothes, how he walked kind of stooped over, sad, and then with every step I'd just run up a little bit, closer and closer, till finally I was walkin' beside him."

Even though his pockets were empty as a banker's soul, even though his family was as poor as poor got outside the shantytowns of the Depression, he wore pride like a suit of mail. Like my father, and yet so very unlike him, the big-eared man in the raggedy overalls would fight a man at even the vaguest insult. His hands were so strong from decades of manhandling mules across rock-strewn fields, of gripping that hammer, he could squeeze an apology out of a man just by taking his arms and pressing a little bit at a time. If a man pulled a knife on him, he went and got his hammer, which in his hands was about as lethal as a thunderbolt. Again, I understand how people who grew up in other places, in gentler cultures, might not understand why men had to fight each other. I think it is much more civilized to knock someone of your own gender on their ass than it is to stand on a street corner cussing yourself into an embolism, like they do in New York.

We know of only one time when one of these arguments resulted in a shooting, when my mother was four or five, and a man accused him of stealing. He might as well have spit in my grandaddy's face, shot his mule, talked down his dog and called his momma a bad name, 'cause you don't tell a good man that he stole, and expect to walk away.

What happened next remains one of those pages of family history that no one really wants to tell, but just can't help themselves. My momma can tell it better than me, but not quite as good as Aunt Gracie Juanita, who is the only person who can do so without giggling. Listen to them.

"It was them Reardens. I don't know what they said Daddy stole but Daddy didn't steal, so Daddy just loaded his shotgun and walked to meet 'em when they come to the house," said my momma. "I was little. I laid in the bed and covered my head up, but I heard the shot."

Aunt Gracie Juanita was an eyewitness.

"This big woman come at Daddy with a long ol' knife, and he shot 'er," said my aunt Gracie Juanita, who has always been willing, ready and able to plug someone her ownself if they got her mad. "It went clean through 'er buzzoms. Both of 'em. Clean through, hon."

I surmised that the woman had been standing sideways.

"Mmm-hmmm," said my aunt Gracie Juanita.

I asked her, not sure if I wanted the answer, if the woman was killed.

"Lord no, hon, they was this big," and she made a circle with her hands about the size of a truck tire.

The wounding of their matriarch seemed to take the fight out of the Reardens, who retreated, carrying the big woman. I think that Granddaddy helped haul her to the car. I do not know if the Reardens ever apologized for accusing my grandfather of stealing, but I guess once you've shot one of their women in the buzzoms with a deer slug, any apology would be a long time coming.

Like my mother, my granddaddy had no luck at all. "He used to go fishing up in Guntersville for jack salmon, and he'd always holler when he caught one, and you know I do that, too, I holler like a wild woman when I catch one," said my momma, thinking back. "Then he'd just put them jack salmon in his coat pockets, and we'd laugh when he'd tell us that when Momma washed his coat we'd see minners in the tub, and when I was little I used to stand over it, waitin'. And one time when he was up there on the lake his ol' car broke down and he had to catch the bus and ride it home, and the police arrested him in Anniston when he got off the bus and sent him to Birmingham because he walked off behind these men and they thought he was with them, that he was a, what do you call it, a vagrant, and we couldn't find him and he had no way of tellin' us, and it was days and days and days and we didn't know what had happened to our daddy, until finally we called all the jails and found him. They had spelled his name so bad wrong that they couldn't find him the first time, and then he come home and we was all afraid to even talk because he was so mad, so mad somebody could do that to him. And while he was in jail for nothin' the floodwaters come up at Lake Guntersville and washed over his ol' car, and rurnt it. No, he never did have no luck."

If nothing else validates the decency of that man, then the story of Jessie Klines will. Everyone called him Hootie, back before rock bands thought that name was cool, and he was a harmless, simpleminded man who lived with my mother's people their whole life. When I asked where he came from, my momma just said: "Daddy got 'im off the river." He had lived like an animal in a shack on the Tallapoosa until my grandfather rescued him, took him into his own home, and fed him and clothed him like he was a member of the family. Sometimes he toted the shingles my granddaddy hammered in place, and sometimes he didn't, but there was always a place for him at their table. I asked my momma why, in a time when they had so little, my granddaddy adopted this man. My momma just told me he felt sorry for him.

Hootie had only one real job, and that was to ride in the back of the pickup with the children and keep them from falling out. He rode miles and miles with his legs stretched out across the open back of the pickup, taking his job seriously, because Mr. Charlie had told him it was important to arrive at a place with roughly the same number of kids they left with. He was an old man in ragged overalls, and the children loved him because he would play with them, and was tall enough to fix things like tire swings and tree houses. He loved my grandfather and his children, but Miss Ab scared him a little bit.

Abigail was a Hamilton, a Presley on her momma's side, and yes, the same ones as Elvis, although I don't think her branch of the family ever got anywheres close to Tupelo. The Hamiltons were quick-tempered and sometimes hard-hearted people, but the Presleys were gifted, could play anything and sing like angels. All my grandma's people picked banjo, guitar, mandolin, blew the harmonica—which we called the French harp—and played the piano, fiercely. Miss Ab never had a music lesson in her life, but could play anything. I have no doubt that if she had ever heard it she could have played Beethoven. She knew all the words to all the songs on the radio and in the hymnal, and made her children laugh with verses like:

> *Where the steak it is cooked rare*
> *and the biscuits have gray hair*
> *at that hungry hotel where I dine*

Miss Ab picked cotton for Walter Rollins, a good-humored fat man who pretended not to notice that her children and grandchildren were stealing his watermelons by the wheelbarrow load. In the hot summer she wore a bonnet and in the cold she wore a man's knit cap, which we called, for reasons I will never understand, a "bogan." Indoors she wrapped her long gray hair up in a bun and covered it with a rag or scarf twisted tight around her head, like the black people of that time. I reckon it was to keep the gray hair out of the biscuits.

Like a lot of women in that time, she walked in the shadow of her man even as she kept him upright. But like a lot of creative people, she was prone to periods of brief . . . well, she could go a little peculiar. When she got mad she could cuss paint off the wall, cuss crows from the trees, cuss the lame straight and the wicked pure. She could cuss Hootie and he would drop what he was doing and run for the woods. When she got really wound up she could talk loud for ten, twelve hours straight. My granddaddy would just bow his head and let it rain over him like hail, or flee.

It was this world, of rich poverty, that shaped my mother. Her older sisters helped raise her and her older brothers tormented her, especially William. Instead of throwing a rock in the creek to scare off the snakes, "he just throwed one of us," my momma said. When little Emma Mae died of fever when my momma was just four or five, he told her that she was still alive and one day they would go dig her up. "I dragged a hoe around with me everywhere I went, for weeks, because I believed we was goin' to get Emma Mae."

Her two brothers escaped jail, though no one is really sure how. They stole chickens, and worse, because they got hungry. When they got thirsty, they crawled under the plank floor of their Uncle Newt's house to the spot where they guessed he stored his whiskey barrels. They took a brace and bit, and drilled a hole through the floor and the barrels and drained it into jugs.

My uncle Bill used to wait until my grandma would leave the house and then cut my momma's hair. He would cut one side of her head short and leave one side long, and even though Grandma would whup him he would laugh and laugh and laugh. "I was sixteen years old before I knowed people wasn't supposed to have hair like that," my momma said.

The girls were better behaved, but they were not delicate flowers. They learned how to use a hammer and saw and level, and even now, as most of my granddaddy's girls near or have passed sixty, you still see them toting two-by-fours around the yards of their houses. My aunt Gracie Juanita could build Tara if you gave her a year and a key to the Home Depot. They dropped out of school, all of them, to go to work, to help the family live. Some of them even climbed the roofs of houses and worked beside my grandfather, others picked cotton beside my grandmother.

Sit long enough with the people in my family and the talk always turns to the fields, because all of them did their time there. They were the center of the family's life, even though they never owned land, never made more than a few dollars a day. When carpentry and whiskey making failed to put food on the table, there was always cotton. The big sacks could hold more than a hundred pounds. The best pickers picked out the trash and sticks, the worst would shove a big rock in the bottom of the sack and hope no one saw it when it was upended into the cotton wagon. Whites and blacks picked together, but did not make the same money. It wasn't right but it was the way it was.

"Even when Momma was old, she was still pickin'," said my momma. "She could pick purty good. She could outpick Niter, but then anybody outpick poor ol' Niter. She could pick a hundred pounds, too, but it took her five years."

The only work the family did not share was the still. Like most cultures where hard likker and religion flowed together, Granddaddy did his whiskey making and drinking away from the children. It was fine for a man to drink, as long as he didn't expose his children to it, and it was fine to get blind drunk as long as a man could keep his dignity and his hands off his wife and children when he was angry or had the blind staggers. It is an odd thing now, thinking back, that even though I grew up surrounded by drunks, not one time can I remember any man besides my father openly drinking. I would see an uncle or two sneak a nip from a bottle hidden under the seat, but they did it furtively, almost ashamedly. It is why my grandfather never respected my father. He couldn't hold his likker or his temper, but we will get to that later.

Now and then, the law would come to visit. The sheriff would make a perfunctory trip out, but instead of searching through the pines for the still he would sit on the porch until suppertime, and have some beans and cornbread. Other sheriffs were more vigorous, but my granddaddy fooled them again and again. He would walk the hills until he found a nice bluff, hollow out a place to put the still, and cover the opening with brush. He would walk a different way to the still every time, to avoid wearing down the grass and weeds and leaving a trail. He probably could have ridden a rhinoceros through the ragweed for all the danger he was in of being found out, since the typical Southern sheriff was not exactly Daniel Boone when it came to following a trail. My uncle Jimbo likes to tell the story of the time a sheriff came out and stood on top of the hill, sniffing the air, smelling the whiskey cooking almost under his feet, but just stomped around and cussed. Then my grandma invited him to supper.

The lifetime of drinking killed Charlie Bundrum in the end just as surely as it did my own father. The doctor called it cirrhosis of the liver. He did not die a little at a time, like most people do. He kept walking, kept working, kept laughing, until one day he just didn't get out of bed, and died that same day.

He lived long enough to see most of his family married off, to sit knee-deep in a pool of squirming grandchildren. He saw my mother fall in love with the good-looking, dark-haired, part Cherokee boy, and did not stop them when they drove up to Tennessee to get married by a justice of the peace. She was almost eighteen, and if she was not the most beautiful woman in the county, I do not know who was. The photographs from that time show a tall, slim, blond woman with high cheekbones and a peace about her that comes through even in faded black-and-white. She looks serene. I don't know. Maybe that is how she stood it.

My grandfather lived long enough to hold her first child, David Samuel, named from the Bible. He took one look at the long body and nicknamed him Bone. Sambone. And while he loved his grandchildren he seemed to love him most of all, and would hold him in his big hands for hours, or just watch him play in the dirt between his big boots. It was as if he knew his own death was coming, and he wanted to be close to this precious life as much as he could.

He lived long enough to see the true nature of his son-in-law's character emerge, saw the cruelty, and his first inclination was to hunt him down and kill him. The second time my momma had to flee my father, my grandfather told her, matter-of-factly, that she could go back to her sorry husband if she felt she had to, but she could not take the boy, Sam.

When my daddy came to get her my granddaddy met him at the door, and ordered him away like a beggar. My daddy slid his hand in his pocket for his knife but he never pulled it. It probably saved his life, because that tough old man would have come down on him like the strong right hand of God.

Charlie Bundrum died later that year, in April of 1958. He was fifty-one. "He still had his hair, he still had all his teeth, he didn't have a gray hair in his head," said my momma, of when they laid him out. "He was purty."

After the funeral, my daddy came for her.

Her life might have been much different if she had refused to go. She might have found a new man, a decent man, while she still had her youth and her looks. But she had a baby, and the man she loved so much, for a lifetime, was dead and in the ground. There was hope, not much hope, but some, that her husband would change. She dreamed he would stop drinking up his paycheck, stop disappearing for days, for weeks, for months. She dreamed he would stop running around and shaming her, dreamed she would not have to beg him for money for milk for the baby, Sam. She dreamed that this time it might be bearable, it might last.

She didn't want much, really, just something decent.

All she got was me.

4

Dreaming that a crooked man will straighten up and fly right

I t was there, sitting in the glow of that gigantic screen, that I saw Alan Ladd call Jack Palance a no-good Yankee liar, send him to his Maker in a haze of gunsmoke and then ride off into the sunset, bleeding, with a little boy frantically chasing him, crying, "Shane! Shane! Come back, Shane!"

There, I saw Robert Duvall call John Wayne a one-eyed fat man, saw Big John yell out, "Fill yer hand, you sonofabitch!" and charge down across a wide, beautiful valley, reins in his teeth, shooting a Winchester from one hand and a Peacemaker from the other.

There, I lusted after the unattainable Elizabeth Taylor's Cleopatra, and, years later, lusted after others, oh so attainable. There, I tasted my first orange slush, my first beer, my first kiss, whispered "I will love you forever" to people whose faces and names I can hardly recall. I am sure they cannot remember mine.

The Midway Drive-In Theater is long gone now, as if, by providence, someone saw fit to remove the scene of so many lovely lies. The Midway, so named because it stood like a beacon midway between Jacksonville and Anniston, is now a lot where they sell mobile homes and prefabricated buildings. The screen is blank, the romance is dead. Sometimes on

Friday and Saturday nights I drive past and I forget, and I glance over at the marquee to see what's playing or glance up into the night sky to catch a fleeting glimpse of some B-movie heroine's eight-feet-tall lips, and all there is, is dark. It is a shame, really. I have a kinship with the place that goes far beyond simple nostalgia.

I was almost born there, during the stirring closing moments of *The Ten Commandments*.

I am told it was a hot, damp night in late July 1959, one of those nights when the setting of the sun brings no relief. It might have been the heat, or something she ate—an orange slush and a Giant Dill Pickle—but about the time Charlton Heston laid eyes on that golden calf and disowned the Children of Israel as idol worshippers and heathen sons of lewd women, I elected to emerge.

Some births are marked by a notation in the family Bible, others are acknowledged with the hoisting of glasses. For me, it all began with wandering Hebrews, flying gravel and a dangling speaker.

The front seat of a 1951 Chevrolet, roomy as it is, is a damned inconvenient place for the miracle of birth, and as the car sped north on Highway 21, my momma gritted her teeth and prayed. It would have been closer to take her to Anniston, but it was cheaper to take her to Piedmont, where most of the country people in our part of the county went to have their babies and kidney stones delivered.

As it turned out it was hours before her ordeal was over, and during her pains she talked on and on in the emergency room about the parting of the Red Sea and staffs that turned into snakes, so that the doctor began to question his decision to give her painkillers.

"The main nurse told everybody, 'Y'all come listen to this woman, she's gone plumb crazy,'" said my momma, laughing.

Finally, about dawn on Sunday morning, she held her second son in her arms. He was kind of puny looking, actually, with pale blue eyes and hair the same color as her own, and because she had hoped for and believed strongly it would be a girl, she had to dress him in pink, including a pink hat with pink lace on it. She named him Ricky, after Ricky Ricardo. I guess I should be grateful she didn't name me Lucy.

All this is the honest to God truth, every word. But for much of my lifetime, I had some of the important details all wrong. I asked her once, a long time ago, if my daddy had paced the waiting room, smoking Camels, worrying about her, about me. That was a father's duty back then, to worry from a safe distance, protected from the actual birth by a thick sheet of glass and concrete. Men would have no more entered the delivery room to watch the birth than they would have insisted on going to a slaughterhouse to watch their sausage made—the result was what was important, not the process—but it was expected of them to wait outside with the nervous kinfolks. But my momma told me no, he had not been there at the hospital, so I just naturally assumed he had gone off somewhere to get drunk and await word, another acceptable tradition. But that was not true, either.

I had believed it was Momma and Daddy at the Drive-In that night, believed it was him who calmly steered that sedan along the dark highway to the hospital. But in fact it was my momma, my grandma, my aunt Gracie Juanita, my aunt Jo, my aunt Sue, my brother Sam, and probably a cousin or two they smuggled in inside the trunk. My daddy was nowhere around, had not been seen for months, and had nothing to do with my momma and me making it to the hospital in time. The hero was my aunt Gracie Juanita, and the route to the hospital was anything but a beeline. Because the kinfolks all started hollering at once, giving directions and advice and threatening to ruin her concentration—Aunt Gracie Juanita cannot navigate if she cannot concentrate—she had to make a ten-minute detour past her house to let 'em all out before heading for Piedmont Hospital. She has never been what you call a fast driver, but I understand that, feeling the urgency of the situation, she might have blistered down that highway at forty miles per hour. Looking back, it is a wonder I was not born in transit.

The first six years of my life followed a ragged pattern. There were brief periods when my mother and father were together, longer ones of separation, her family growing ever larger even as he became less and less a father.

I was born in one of those many periods in which my father had either abandoned my momma or driven her away, and she was living in my grandmother's little house, picking cotton, taking in ironing. It was weeks, maybe months before word finally reached him that he had a son, and if he gave a damn he never showed it. My first birthday passed without word from him. On the second birthday, he came bearing gifts. I was walking. I was talking. My brother, Sam, was five, and he had forgotten what his daddy looked like.

I have little firsthand information about that time, since I was still not trusted with anything more dangerous than a sharp spoon, but I know he eventually talked my momma into coming back home with him, and kept her, this time, just long enough to leave her with another child, my baby brother, Mark. Then he disappeared again, leaving her with a six-year-old, a three-year-old, and the infant, but with no money, no car, not one damn thing. So she just swallowed her pride and went home again, to the fields and the manual labor that slowly turned her from a beautiful young woman into one old before her time, until the next time he snatched us up and moved us to places in and around Piedmont, Possum Trot, Spring Garden, Jacksonville. Once, we followed him to Dallas, but that didn't last, either.

I guess it is hard for some people to understand why this was, why she kept going back to him when he treated her so badly. I guess trying to explain it is futile, since it would be like trying to explain starving to someone who thinks hungry is being late for dinner. Her life had slipped into a dull routine of sacrifice and loneliness, and these times with him offered at least a sliver of hope, a promise of what other people had. She kept going back, even after she realized he might never change, not because she loved him in that pitiful way some women love bad men, but because there were whole months at a time when he did pay the electric bill, when he did give her money for groceries. There were long months when he held his children with something very close to love, when he was sober, mostly, and kind. There were nights at the table when he sat with a baby on his lap and spoon-fed him, and laughed when one of us daubed food in his face. It never lasted. It was a dream sandwiched by pain.

There would always come a night when she put our clothes in paper sacks and buttoned our coats, begging us not to cry, to shush, baby, we're goin' to see Grandma. He never bought her presents, never bought her anything, so there was nothing for her to pack of her own, nothing precious. Sometimes we left in the still dark hours of morning, when he was passed out, and walked fast down the dark roads for miles, just getting away. We walked until she could find a phone and call for help, and we would wait for the headlights of an uncle or aunt's car to appear, and then we knew we were safe.

She did what she could to support us with her own work, her own sweat, but sometimes it was just too hard. I know it killed her deep inside to go begging, but it would have destroyed her to watch her three sons do without. She stood in line at the welfare office, stood in line for government cheese. She fawned over the church people, year after year, who showed up at Christmas with a turkey or a ham. I saw her follow them back to their big cars, thanking them, a hundred times, and walk back to the house pale and tight-lipped.

I did not know then, like I know now, that my momma never ate until we were done, or maybe I did know but was too young to understand why. I did not know then that she picked all the meat out of the soup and stew and put it on our plates. I did not hear her scraping pots, pans and skillets to make her own plate, after her three little pigs ate most of what we had. But I can still see her sliding the bones off plates and gnawing them clean, after we were done, saying how she liked that meat close to the bone, that we just didn't know what we were missing. It is not that we were starving, just that the quality of life for her children inched up a little, if she did without.

She stood in line at the checkout counter at the Goodwill, ten-cent dresses draped across her sunburned arms. I can remember walking the aisles of that store, remember trying on other people's clothes. Mostly, as I grew from a toddler into a boy of five or six, I wore Sam's hand-me-downs, which was fine except I am longer from my shoulders to my belly button than he is, and so spent the first five or six years of my life with my navel showing. His legs are longer than mine, so my momma had to hem my pants, or tried to. She may be a saint but she has no depth perception, and always left one leg shorter than the other. I am easy to find in our old black-and-white photos taken by my aunts and uncles. Just look for the little boy with the shining navel, who, even when he is standing on flat ground, looks like he is walking around the side of a hill.

I remember we scavenged the city dump at Jacksonville, and I was too little to be ashamed. We picked through the latest leavings, burrowed into mountains of trash, not for food, because it never got that bad, but for treasure. We came home with moldy, flat footballs, melted army men, radios that never made a sound. My momma looked for anything she could sell, copper wires, aluminum, Coke and Orange Crush and RC bottles, worth a penny. And I remember, with a clarity that I wish would fade, the smell of that stuff, that treasure. It is a sickly sweet smell laced with rot and smoke, because they burned trash back then, and often we had to race the flames to claim it. I have no doubt that this is what hell smells like.

It would be years before I was old enough to realize that the way we lived was somehow less than the way of other people, years before I began to chafe under it, until finally I was ashamed to bring friends into our house. It would be years before I had to duck my head when we went to the dump to burrow, and years before I knew that I was supposed to be ashamed that when a teacher called roll for lunch money, my name was never called. It was stamped "FREE." Welfare lunches.

You lose a lot in your memory, over so many years. But I distinctly remember, before I was old enough to cover myself in what my mother called false pride, that there was also some happiness there. While I was often frightened and troubled by the drastic changes in our life, because of our father, I was too damn little and too damn stupid to be miserable.

The little wood-frame house seemed huge then, a place to run and jump and hide and climb, but now I can stand in the middle of the living room and touch one wall with my right hand and the other with my left. I had an Ashley wood heater, and the sink in the kitchen was the only indoor plumbing it had. There was no hot water unless you heated it in a pan, and the light came from naked bulbs that dangled from the ceiling. There was no basement, no attic, just a little wooden box that sat solid on four legs of concrete block, so that the dogs and children could find sanctuary underneath in the cool dirt. I played for hours under it, digging holes with an old spoon, until the wasps or the snakes or my momma ran me out. I buried treasures, balls of aluminum foil, a button, anything that had a shine, and went back the next day, the next month, the next year, to dig it up again.

The bathroom was fifty yards away, a plywood outhouse. I know it is a cliché, but it really did have a Sears, Roebuck catalog on the floor, and a sawn-off broom handle, to do in the five-inch centipedes and black widow spiders and the odd snake. A lot of people did have indoor plumbing on our road, of course. For many men it was the first thing they did, when they got a steady paycheck. They put in a bathroom for their family. My momma had to iron forty pounds of clothes to make four dollars, so we were probably the last family on Roy Webb Road to experience the joy of twentieth-century ablution.

I cannot say I am nostalgic for the outhouse, because anyone who has ever had to visit one at 2 A.M. in January with a flashlight and a rolled-up back issue of the *Anniston Star* will tell you that the first contact with that cold pine board is damned exhilarating. When I was five, as I was then, I had to get a running start from the willow tree to leap high enough to reach the seat, and then was left with the uncomfortable truth that there was no way to shut the door. Sometimes Momma would see me and, understanding, close the door for me, and she would not grin about it. Sam would not only leave the door open but would sneak around the corner of the house and throw rocks at me, once my britches were down, and once he locked a mean tomcat in there with me and just leaned against the door, laughing. It sounds, now, like a cartoon. I damn near died.

Once, I badly miscalculated my jump to the throne, and instead of landing to the side of the diamond-shaped hole, on solid plank, I jumped clean into the heart of darkness. I skinned my legs and scared myself, and thanked God that the hole was not quite big enough to swallow me. No one would have believed I didn't do it on purpose, since I was in some ways a peculiar child.

I caught crawfish in the bright, clear waters of Germania Springs, and dammed streams with my brother until the water was neck deep and freezing cold. We built homemade boats and sailed them a good six or seven feet before they sank like stone and half-drowned us. I was a water baby, and when it rained I would run laughing through the big, hard drops, the red mud squishing between my toes. I would fling myself belly down into mud puddles, scattering tadpoles, squishing some. Yet I kicked and screamed when my momma tried to give me a bath, because there was just no sport in it, and was liable to run naked if she ever sat me down and let go the death grip she had on my skinny arms.

I climbed trees and was prone to fall out of them. Sometimes in the summer I would climb into the big willow in the side yard and wedge myself into the limbs, and sleep. You have never slept until you have been rocked to sleep by a willow tree, the whole thing creaking as the wind pushes it back and forth. There was something about being up high, up in the green and the breeze, something safe about it. That is, unless you shifted out of the crook of the limb and came hurtling down like a sack of rocks.

I came close to dying only once, if you don't count the time I was almost swallowed up by the outhouse, or the falling out of trees, or the tomcat, or the time Sam shot me with the bow and arrow. It involved a plastic poinsettia, and I was drawn to it like a gnat to butter pecan ice cream.

It is one of the peculiarities of poor white folks, and poor black folks, too, I reckon, that even though we lived surrounded by trees and flowers and the visual wealth of a very real and beautiful world, we were fascinated by anything fake or phony. With my family it was plastic flowers, and as a child I grew up with at least one vase of phony flowers on the table. I never asked where we got them, but some of them looked a lot like the ones people left at the graveyard. It is one of those things that I guess it is better not to think too hard about. Anyway, some of them, especially the poinsettias, had little plastic berries, and now and then I would pluck one of the berries and chew the plastic. One day, for reasons I cannot readily explain, I accidentally sucked one of the berries up my nose.

I was rushed to the hospital, screaming, until Dr. James R. (I think that stood for Roundtree) Kingery finally prized it out with what felt like a set of posthole diggers. He calmly asked my momma: "Reckon how that happened?" and said he believed I had made medical history. He said he could not remember a time when he had to pluck a plastic poinsettia berry out of any child's nostril, or any orifice, for that matter. My momma just shrugged, muttered something about the boy not being quite normal, and gave him five dollars she could not spare. She held my hand as we walked out to the car, obviously afraid I would have some other form of mental breakdown and try to run in front of cars. Perhaps naked.

For the record, I should say here that one of the reasons I was able to enjoy that time at all is because my momma's kin were kind to us, and helped make it so. In those years, the early 1960s, there was barely enough for their own families, yet they shared their lives with us. We enjoyed only two luxuries: the Midway Drive-In Theater, which charged two dollars a carload; and PeeWee Johnson's Dixie Dip, where a foot-long hot dog cost fifty cents and my mother often cut hers in half, to share with the smallest child. I was ten or older by the time I realized that my aunts and their husbands usually just dumped the money she gave them for our food back into her hands, all of it, as change.

Even though it has been a quarter-century since PeeWee shut down his hot dog and hamburger joint, I can still taste them. During the week we lived on beans and cornbread, or buttermilk and cornbread, or poke salad (Yankees call it pokeweed) and cornbread, but on Saturday night someone would get a sack of footlongs from PeeWee's, and the smell alone would make us start to grin. It was just a weiner of unknown origin, covered in a watery but spicy chili and yellow mustard, topped with a chopped, hot, Spanish onion. We could have gotten fries with it it for a quarter, but that was beyond our means. I guess I was thirty years old before, when a waiter asked me if wanted fries, I stopped saying: "Damn straight I want some fries."

The one great meal of the day was breakfast, because breakfast is cheap. Every morning of my childhood I woke up to the smell of biscuits, and to the overpowering aroma and popping sound of frying fatback, which we called white meat. Momma fried eggs laid by our own chickens, and made gravy and grits. Sometimes there was nothing but biscuits and gravy made from yesterday's bacon grease, which I would take right now in place of just about anything I usually eat. We always had a hog—not hogs, A hog—and at hog killin' time we ate like kings until he had been reduced to snout and toenails. If I was late for the school bus she would shove a piece of fatback or bacon into a biscuit and I would eat it on the run. To this day I dream not of beautiful women and wealth and power as often as I dream of sausage gravy over biscuits with a sliced tomato on the side, and a small lake of real grits—not that bland, pale, watery restaurant stuff I would not serve on death row, but grits cooked with butter and plenty of salt and black pepper.

Momma kept a garden, which sounds romantic to people who have never held a hoe. She grew corn and tomatoes and okra and squash, and spent hours a day on her knees, pulling ragweed and the Johnson grass that was sharp as razors. I remember once seeing the fat, four-foot body of a massive copperhead, one of the meanest, most aggressive snakes in the South, sunning himself between the rows. She killed him with a hoe, white-faced, because once you piss off a copperhead it is him or you. The Yankee biologists who say they won't bother you if you don't bother them have obviously never had to remove one from the pole beans with a stick with a dull blade on the end of it.

Sometimes, even though I know it is my own foolish romanticism, I think about having a garden again, to see if I retain any of the skills of my people, or if I have just become too citified to do anything real. I loved the way it smelled when it was fresh-tilled, loved the way the red tomatoes and the yellow squash looked against the green leaves, like candy. Sometimes my momma would quit working and pluck three big tomatoes, one for her, one for Sam, one for me, and salt them with a shaker she had brought from the kitchen, thinking ahead. And we would sit in the dirt and eat them there in the field, and I would get seeds all over me, and Sam would laugh at me and call me a baby until I bounced a dirt clod off his pumpkin head. She would sit the baby, Mark, down amongst us, and try to keep him from eating dirt.

Sometimes she would take the yellow squash and carve them into boats and submarines. We would take them to the creek and play and play until one of us figured out that, if you hold a squash just right, it looks a lot like a club. And someone almost always sneaked up behind someone else and clobbered them with it—usually Sam, because I was never violent until provoked—and we would hammer each other with them until they flew apart in yellow chunks and seeds.

She would pick May Pops for us, and show us how the tiny stem inside looked just like a woman dancing if you twirled it between your fingers. She taught us that the hooting of owls and the cries of night birds are bad luck, and showed us how to find the best worms for fishing by looking under rotten planks. She showed us how to bait a hook so that the worm did not go flying free but mortally wounded across the water when you flicked your wrist. She showed us how to make a stringer for fish out of a tree branch, showed us how to spit on the hook, for luck. If we passed a store, she bought us Golden Flake barbecue potato chips and Grapicolas while she pretended that "No, child, I ain't hongry, I'll just ask them if I can have some water."

She tried to teach us how to throw a baseball and shoot a basketball and kick a football, but the fact is she was no damn good at it and spent most of her time running to get the balls she missed, till we finally said, that's okay, Ma, we can take it from here. She built kites out of newspaper and twigs which never flew, but somehow that did not seem to matter. At Halloween we never had a costume, but our cousins would paint a black eye or some freckles on us with Maybelline and let us go with them, anyway. "What do we tell people when they ask what we are," we asked her. She said: "Tell 'em you're hongry." (One year they put a pillowcase over my head with two eyeholes cut in it, and I was supposed to be a ghost but someone drew a cross on it with red lipstick so I looked like a midget Klansman.)

And all this mothering she did with a baby on her hip, my little brother, Mark, who had red-brown hair that she left long, because she had hoped for a girl that time, too. What she wound up with was three sorry boys, who ran her ragged, fought like cats in a sack and thought it was just plain damn hilarious to put snapping turtles in the outhouse when a grownup was inside, engrossed in the garden implements section.

To say we were rotten little children would be like saying John Brown was a little on the impetuous side, but I cannot remember her striking me, shaking me, screaming at me. Sam was older and needed constant beating, but he found a way out of it. It was brilliant, really, thinking back on it. When he did something heinous, like chunking a rock through the back window because he barely missed my ducking, weaving head, he would run like a Tennessee racehorse. But Momma, long and lean, could run, too, and as she bore down on him he would drop to his knees and raise his arms to heaven, asking God to deliver him from the sure-for-certain killing he was about to receive. Sometimes, if he had drawn blood and figured his whipping would be intense, he would prostrate himself flat on the ground and pray, and I think once he even tried to speak in tongues. I suppose it is hard to beat a child as he is getting right with God, and she would just turn around and walk off, muttering to herself, shaking her head. Sam would wait until she was safely away, then give God a wink and go about his business.

Grandma Ab, who was still spry in body and mind, watched it all from the front porch, grinning, her dentures wide and bright as the grill on a 1957 Cadillac.

People have often asked me, when I talked of how I grew up, how awful it was that I did not have a solid male influence in my life, but the fact is that we had two, my uncles John and Ed, who were married to my aunts Jo and Nita. Every Friday night, without fail, my uncle John and aunt Jo came to visit. He rough-housed with us for hours, and while I didn't know it then he was standing in for our daddy. They had no children, and it was John Couch, who worked hard for his money in the blast furnace heat of the pipe shop, who gave us an allowance of twenty-five and later fifty cents a week, and once, when I was older, a silver dollar. People say sometimes that it must have been hard, growing up without a father figure. But if I have ever met men who were more decent than my uncles, I cannot recall.

The small house we lived in with my grandma sat on land owned by my uncle Ed and aunt Gracie Juanita, and for most of my life they just let us live there, never asking anything in return. Ed Fair had been crippled as a boy when a car struck his legs, but he was the hardest-working man, except for my brother Sam, I ever knew. In the winter when the water pipes froze, it was Ed Fair who took the pick and hacked at the frozen clay until he found the leak, and patched it so we would have water to drink. It was him who brought us the coal, when he had some extra, so we could keep warm. It was him who paid the doctor bill when I slid into home and peeled all the skin off my legs.

No, by the time I was six years old, I had already witnessed what a man should be, how a man should act. I saw it in my own momma, who put on a man's britches and worked in the field all day, then ironed mountains of clothes at night, for pocket change. Our father's face, his voice, his character had faded to this wispy thing that needed only a soft wind to sweep him away forever, for good.

As hard as life was for my momma, I had come to expect certain things in my own. I expected to have homemade ice cream once every three months with my uncles and aunts, sometimes with a can of peaches added for flavoring. I expected to sit with my grandma Ab, singing "Uncloudy Day" at the limit of my lungs. I expected to wake up to the warmth of a woodstove, and drift off to sleep under piles of soft, frayed quilts stitched by hand generations ago.

I came to see the little house we lived in, surrounded on two sides by the cotton field, on one side by a vast green pasture and on the other by creek and swamp, as the place we belonged. I knew that if I ran outside at precisely 6:30 A.M., I could see the big yellow bus come and take my brother to Roy Webb Elementary School. I knew that most of the time he would throw a rock at me before he got on that bus but sometimes he would wave, and I thought that was the best thing in all the world.

I knew that the man who ran the Crow Drugstore would give me presents when my momma went in for cough syrup for the baby, and one year he even gave me an Easter basket. He had run out of the blue ones for boys, but he had a pink one left, and my momma told him, "He won't know the difference," and I didn't. I expected to follow my momma to the cotton field, expected to climb on board that sack, expected to ride.

I knew that sooner or later my daddy would show up and we would live someplace else for a while, but never long enough to be thought of as home, as this little house was.

He came for us in the spring of 1965, for the last time.

I will never forget the sight of him that day. He had on dress pants and loafers and a pretty shirt unbuttoned at the neck, to show his tattoo, but I cannot remember if he was sober or just well groomed. He had always been a clean drunk, a well-dressed drunk, what people in that time called a pretty man. He might be cross-eyed drunk but his shoes were always shined, always the best-dressed man in jail. His children and wife might go without, but his shirts were always pressed. Some people had backbone to lean on. Daddy had starch.

He said he had a steady job working body and fender for Mr. Merrill, who ran a big auto body shop in rural Spring Garden in Cherokee County. He promised her that this time he would straighten up and fly right. That's what he always said: straighten up and fly right. Three decades have whipped by since that day, but I remember, as the car pulled away, how the beer bottles clinked in the floorboards and my brother Sam sat still as stone, his hair slicked down with Rose Hair Oil, because my momma had wanted us to look nice. I remember I stood in the backseat and stared out the rear window, and saw my grandma Ab run up the walk from the house in that curious, jerking way that old people run. She had sat quiet in the kitchen as we packed our clothes, not talking, not even looking at us. But as the car pulled away she stood in the middle of the driveway, her dew rag on her head and her apron wadded in her hands, not waving, just staring and staring until we slipped over a rise in the blacktop, out of sight.

5

When God blinks

We were raised, my brothers and me, to believe God is watching over us. The day we left our grandma standing in the driveway for that massive, hateful house on a hill, I guess He had something in His eye. Maybe it was Vietnam. Maybe it was Selma. Either way, as my daddy's Buick rumbled between the low mountain ridges and crossed into Cherokee County from Calhoun, we were on our own. I was six years old.

I will forever remember my first look at that house. It stood like a monument on the hill, smack-dab in the middle of a little farming community called, idyllically, Spring Garden. It was high and white, a two-story farmhouse with big, square columns in front, too big to reach around. There was a massive gray barn, and a smokehouse, and off in the distance, a string of shacks. The house stood sentry over fields of cotton and corn, and was ringed with live oak trees, trees that had outlived generations of men. There was an apple orchard and a pasture and acres and acres of empty, lonely pines.

He had told Momma he had a good job, but to rent this house, we thought, he would have to be a county commissioner, at least. For all our lives we had lived in tiny mill houses or in relatives' homes, places so small that people sit with their knees touching and their arms tucked in tight at their sides, the way prisoners sit when they are fresh out of jail. This, we thought, as the car rolled toward it on the blacktop, was a mansion.

But as the car pulled closer and turned up the long driveway, I saw that it was no mansion, only the corpse of one. I saw peeling paint and missing boards, and looking back on it now I know that my father must have rented it for a song, because it was a house no one else would have. We would have said it was straight out of Faulkner, if we had known who Faulkner was. The bathroom, like the one we had back at our grandma's little house, was out back, down a dirt trail, bordered by ragweed.

Inside, where the wallpaper hung like dead skin, a great mahogany staircase stretched up to a sinister, deserted second floor, a floor that we never used, one that remained covered in a fine gray powder of dust, like old graveyard dirt, the whole time we lived there. Even now, I can close my eyes and see the footprints in it, left by someone a week before, a month, years.

The house was almost empty. There was a bed in one room where Sam and I slept with our little brother, Mark, who was still just a baby, and a bed in another room for them. I remember a couch and a chair in the living room and a kitchen table, and nothing else, just space. It had a fireplace and a wood heater, which is fine when you have something to burn, and electric lights that only worked in a few rooms. The floor had so many cracks that the wind reached up to tickle your ankles, like cold, invisible fingers reaching out of the ground. I jumped the first time I felt it, and my daddy laughed.

I believe now that if I would have listened very carefully, I could have heard my mother's heart break and tinkle down in pieces on the warped floor. She did not say anything, of course. She never said anything. It was just one more broken promise, one more sharp slap to her pride. But if that was all she had to endure, she could.

I was afraid of that house. Sam was afraid. I think even she was afraid. For the first month I slept with my head covered up, but there was no hiding from the monster in that old house. It was quiet at first, but it was only resting. It was with us just as sure as if it had been locked into one of those closets in the abandoned second floor.

For a little while, I believe, we were something very like a family. My momma cleaned up the ground floor of the old house, stuck our baby pictures on the wall with Scotch tape and put a few plastic flowers on the empty shelves. For weeks, our daddy woke up early and went off to work at Merrill's body shop, carrying a lunch box full of bologna sandwiches and a Little Debbie snack cake. He came back home smelling of dust and paint, not whiskey, and on Fridays he cashed his check and put money in my momma's hand for groceries before going to get drunk. We had not one bottle of milk in the refrigerator but two. One pure white— what we call "sweet" milk—and one chocolate. We could drink as much milk as we wanted. The milkman came back for the half-gallon bottles, and left more. I thought it was free.

Our daddy came home almost every evening and we sat around a table and ate supper. I can remember him holding three-year-old Mark on his lap, trying to get him to eat off his plate, remember how the food got in his hair and his son's hair, how my momma would run over, wiping, fussing, and my daddy laughing and laughing and laughing. It was nice, like I said, to hear that deep voice laugh.

I remember him sitting in the living room with a cigarette in his thin fingers, talking about living, about life. He talked of life beyond cotton fields and Goodwill stores and commodity cheese.

I guess he was trying, to be a daddy, a husband. But even at six years old I knew not to count on him, believe in him. I walked around him like he was a sleeping dog, afraid every minute that he would wake up and bite me. But the weeks turned into months, and still the demons in him were quiet, till the summer vanished into fall and the giant oaks around that giant house began to burn with orange, yellow and red.

Sam and I grew less and less afraid of the house. We climbed the stairs and slid down the bannister until Momma hollered at us to quit or she would whup us, which was an empty threat if ever there was one. We even dragged her up there, herself, one day, when Daddy was gone. She laughed like a schoolgirl.

But I never got completely over my fear of that second floor, so empty, like a family of ghosts lived over our heads. I would imagine they were chasing me as I flung myself on the bannister and slid down to safety, down to my momma and my brothers and the smell of baking cornbread and boiling beans and the sound of the Gospel Hour drifting from the plastic radio.

It was about that time I had my first taste of education in the Alabama public school system. We went to school at Spring Garden, where, in the first grade, I fell in love with a little girl named Janice. Janice Something. But the first grade was divided into a rigid caste system by the ancient teacher, and I was placed clear across the room from her. They named the sections of the divided classroom after birds. She was a Cardinal, one of the children of the well-to-do who studied from nice books with bright pictures, and I was a Jaybird, one of the poor or just plain dumb children who got what was left after the good books were passed out. Our lessons were simplistic, and I could always read. I memorized the simple reader, and the teacher was so impressed she let me read with the Cardinals one day. I did not miss a word, but the next day I was back with the Jaybirds. The teacher—and I will always, always remember this—told me I would be much more comfortable with my own kind. I was six, but even at six you understand what it means to be told you are not good enough to sit with the well-scrubbed.

Her name is lost in my head. She was an aristocrat, a white-haired woman with skin like a wadded-up paper bag that she had smeared red lipstick on and dusted with white powder. I did not know it then, but I was getting my first taste of the gentry, the old-money white Southerners who ran things, who treated the rest of the South like beggars with muddy feet who were about to track up their white shag carpeting. She drove a big car with fender skirts, probably a Cadillac, and wore glasses shaped like cat's eyes.

❖   ❖   ❖

On Sunday evenings, we visited my daddy's people, strangers to me then, strangers to me now. But for one slender ripple in time I had a second family, a people unlike my momma's people. These were people, the menfolk anyway, without any governors on their lives, not even the law. They drove the dirt roads drunk, the trunks of their cars loaded down with bootleg liquor and unstamped Old Milwaukee beer, the springs squealing, the bumpers striking sparks on the rocks, the men driving with one hand and alternately lighting cigarettes and fiddling with the AM radio with the other, searching for anything by Johnny Horton.

They fought each other like cats in a sack, existing—hell no, living—somewhere between the Snopeses of Faulkner's imagination and the Forresters of *The Yearling*. It is a point of fact that the whole male contingent of the family got into a brawl in town—"they wasn't fightin' nobody else, just each other," my momma said—and, as a family, went to jail. One cousin by marriage—and I am not making this up—refused to wear shoes, even in winter. They were constantly bailing each other out of jail, not for anything bad, merely for refusing to march in step with the twentieth century. If they had been machines instead of men, they would have had just one speed, wide-open, and they would have run at it until they blew themselves apart. I guess, in a way, they did. They are all dead now, not from age, but misuse.

Against my will, I grew fond of them. I would have liked to have known them better.

What I know I learned from those Sunday evenings, when we visited my granddaddy Bobby and granny Velma Bragg's house to eat a meal that took hours to cook and a solid thirty minutes just to put on the table. I remember fine fried chicken, and mashed potatoes piled high with a small lake of butter in the middle, and cracklin' cornbread, and butter beans with a white chunk of fat pork floating like a raft in the middle, and sweet tea poured from gallon pickle jars. They lived in a big, rambling farmhouse, paid for with money from Bobby's steady job at the cotton mill, and they had a short, fat dog named Boots who was about 150 in dog years and moved stiffly around the yard, blind as a concrete block.

Bobby Bragg, a white-haired little man, was what we would now call an eccentric. He still had a horse and wagon, and it was not too uncommon then to see Bobby riding around the mill village in his long underwear, drunk as a lord, alternately singing and cussing and—it must be said—shouting out bawdy limericks to mill workers and church ladies.

The town's police officers seldom bothered the ornery old man, mainly because arresting him would would have left them not only with an unmanned horse and wagon but Bobby himself, and everyone with even a lick of sense knew Bobby would cut you as soon as look at you.

I was amazed by him. His hip bone was prone to come out of joint and when it happened he would not go to a doctor or do anything else that was remotely sensible, but he would limp and cuss and drink and limp and cuss and drink until all he could do was lie on the bed and cuss and drink. Until, one day, my granny Bragg had enough. She reached down and got his bad leg by the foot, and commenced to jerking and twisting and jerking and twisting until his hip bone popped back into place with a sound like, well, a pop, and he was cured.

When sober, he often dressed for dinner, not in a suit but in a fresh pair of overalls, and a white button-down shirt that was stiff as a board with starch. "Clean as a pin," Momma said. Of the bad things that can be said about my granddaddy, no one could ever say he did not have a certain style. (It is widely believed in my family that a good many of my peculiarities, I most certainly got from him.)

My granny Velma Bragg was a sad-eyed little woman who looked very much like the part Cherokee she was, a sweet-natured woman with great patience who hovered over the men when they drank whiskey at a beautiful dining room table, trying to wipe up what they split before it ate away the varnish. I remember she was always kind, always gentle, especially to my momma. I guess, in a way, she had an idea what was in store for her. Momma and Granny Bragg still talk, every week. Survivors, both of them.

After supper the men went one way and the women went another. The old man, Bobby, would hold court on the porch, surrounded by his sons. The men drank—Lord, how they could drink—from endless cans of beer or from a jug when they had one. They even talked about drinking as they drank, and smoked Camels down to the barest nub before flipping them out in the dirt of the yard. When I close my eyes I can still see the trail of orange sparks it made. My momma often would holler for me to come inside, but I was enthralled. These men were what my momma's kinfolk called sinners, and it seemed to me like sinning was a lot of fun.

Listening to them, I learned much of of what a boy should know, of cars, pistols, heavy machinery, shotguns and love, all of which, these men apparently believed, can be operated stone drunk. I learned that fighting drunk is better than sober because a clear-headed man hurts more when hit. I learned that it is okay to pull a knife while fighting drunk as long as you are cautious not to cut off your own head.

I learned that whiskey will cure anything from a toothache to double pneumonia, if you drink enough. (Once when I was bad sick with flu, they even gave it to me. They heated it in a pan, being careful not to let it get anywhere close to an open flame, and poured it over honey in a coffee cup. Then someone, my granny probably, squeezed a lemon into it. I drank it down in four gulps, took two steps, a hop, a skip and a staggering leap and passed dead out on the floor. From what I heard later, everyone except my momma thought it was pretty amusing. I cannot say it cleared up any congestion, but it made my head hurt so bad that I did not notice it so much.)

They talked about the mill. They talked about dogs. They talked about fistfights and bootleggers and, a little, about war, but not my daddy's war. They talked about the new war, Vietnam, but my daddy never joined in, that I remember. He drank, smoked his cigarettes. Once, I recall, he came off the porch and walked off into the night for a long time. I remember it because Momma came outside, some time later, ready to go, and we had to search for him. We found him in the car, just sitting, smoking.

Now and then, the men talked of what they called "the nigger trouble," but I could not attach any significance to that. We had no contact with black people beyond a wave, now and then, from a car or from the side of a road. I was not of a world where there were maids, cooks or servants. When they picked in the cotton field beside white pickers, like my momma, they kept to themselves. There were no black people in my school, and at that time no black person had ever been in my house or in my yard. So how, I wondered, could there be trouble between us? They lived in their world, and we lived in our world. It became gradually clear, as I sat there listening, watching the orange comets of their cigarettes arch across the dark, what the trouble was about.

They were sick and tired of living in their world. They wanted to live in our world, too.

6

The free show

Everybody seems to be here, everybody white. The city auditorium
is packed with sweating, jostling bodies, and two little blond-
haired boys try hard not to get stepped on as their momma, holding tight
to their hands, steers them through the cheering crowd. A band is playing "Dixie" as the people clap their hands in time, and someone is waving a Confederate battle flag back and forth, back and forth. There are
pipe shop workers still in their soot-covered, dark-blue work clothes, and
big-haired ladies who work behind the counters of the Calhoun County
Courthouse, and old, sun-scorched men in Liberty overalls and brown
fedoras who drove all the way from Rabbit Town and Talladega and
Knighten's Crossroad, just to see the free show. Up on the big stage a
beautiful woman in a lime green minidress, knee-high go-go boots and a
Styrofoam boater hat with WALLACE on it prances out and starts to sing
loud about the day "my momma socked it to the Harper Valley PTA,"
and though it did not register at the time, I am certain a few of the
church ladies swallowed their snuff.

Then, some time later, I see him.

He walks out onto the stage to a roar of welcome that seems to swell
and swell until I finally put my hands over my ears. I catch only glimpses

of him as the forest of grownups sway and shift in front of me, but I can make out the well-oiled, slicked-down, coal-black hair, and the pugnacious face, the wrinkled and baggy suit, the kind the men at the courthouse have on when you go beg the judge to let your daddy out of jail. I see him raise his balled fists above his head and bring one down hard, hammering at the air as if he is smashing the heads of those pointy-headed intellectuals and outside agitators, and the people roar again. He strokes their anger, their resentment, like a mean cat.

The look on those faces, on all those upturned, adoring faces, reminds me of the faces of people in church, the people who have been touched deep down by the preacher's words, who raise their hands into the air, reaching out to Jesus, saved. They are in The Rapture. They are packed tight into this smoky auditorium in the pipe shop town of Anniston, Alabama, but that little man in the rumpled suit is taking them someplace higher.

Sam and I stand together, understanding only a little of what is being said. The governor talks about a lot of things but mostly he seems to be telling us we are better than the nigras.

We had not known we were better than anybody.

I grew up in a house where the word *nigger* was as much a part of the vocabulary as "hey," or "pass the peas." If I was rewriting my life, if I was using this story as a way to make my life slickly perfect, this is the part I would change. But it would be a lie. It is part of me, of who I was, and I guess who I am.

It does no good to try and qualify it, certainly not to the people whom that word slashes like a razor. It does no good to say we didn't know any better or that it was part of our culture or that Yankees just don't understand that, when a Southerner uses it now, he doesn't "mean anything" by it.

But if you sit and talk to old black people, the people who recall the time of my childhood, that time in history, they will tell you that there are degrees of meanness in this world, degrees of hatred, degrees of ignorance, and calculating those degrees, over decades, was a means of survival. They will tell you that the depth of that meanness and hatred and ignorance varies from soul to soul, that white Southerners are not the same and symmetrical, like the boards in a white picket fence. They will tell you that the depth of that meanness often depends on what life has done to a person, on the impressions left by brushes with people different from you, on those rare times when the parallel universes came close enough to touch.

To find our own, to find what ultimately shaped and softened my own family, I have to reach back into the darkest and ugliest time of my childhood. To find the good in it we have to peel back layers of bad, the last few months we lived with our daddy, the year we went to sleep every night afraid.

It unfolded against a backdrop of a broader meanness, a racial one. It was a year of burning buses and Klan picnics, and looking down on it from up high was the man they called the "Fighting Judge." Wallace had lost his first run for governor because he claimed he was "out-niggered," and vowed never to lose another race because he seemed soft on segregation. The people and the governor fed off each other, until both grew full on their own doomed ideal. They thought it would last forever.

But in the midst of it, in the middle of the hating and fear, was a simple kindness from the most unexpected place, from people who had no reason, beyond their own common decency, to reach across that fence of hate that so many people worked so hard to build.

The closet door banged open in the fall of 1965, and the old monster was loose among us, again.

Someone had sold my daddy several bottles of aged moonshine of high quality, or so he believed. It was not in ceramic jugs or Mason or Bell jars, but in thin, dark brown bottles of about a half pint. One night, he drank one straight down, standing up in the kitchen, and another. I cannot remember exactly what happened next, but it ended with Momma slamming the door to our bedroom, to protect us.

The next day I came home from the first grade at Spring Garden Elementary to find her standing over the sink, slowly pouring bottle after
bottle of it down the drain.

I was six years old. I was still trying to figure out what nine plus nine
was, still trying to color between the lines. But as I watched her, I distinctly remember thinking: "He's gonna kill you, Momma. He's gonna
kill you for that."

That night, when he came home, Sam and I, pitiful in our inability to
help her, to protect her, stood in the door of the kitchen and watched as
he opened the cupboard and reached for his home brew. "Not all of it?"
he asked, and she nodded. My momma did not run, did not hide. She
stood there like a statue. Then, slowly she took off her glasses.

"Don't hurt my teeth," she said.

I guess the angels were with her. He looked at her, hard, and she
nodded her head, slowly. Then he just went over to the Formica table
and sat down.

"Margaret," he said, "you couldn't have hurt me no worse if you shot
me dead." He got up, after a while, and walked out the door, to find a
bottle somewhere else. I didn't know then, like I do now, of the devils
that rode his back, flogging him, didn't know that he was free of them
sometimes, for weeks, for months, and he lived upright, then, mostly
sober. But that when they descended shrieking on him the only place to
hide was in the bottom of a bottle. But instead of freeing him, it only fed
them.

She never moved until the door banged, and then she just walked
kind of stiff-like into her bedroom, and shut the door.

He quit work. He stayed drunk most of the time, instead of weekends, and he yelled at her and told her how sorry he was that he ever
married her, what a mistake it was when she brought a passel of brats
into his life, cluttering it up. Once, drunk, he tried to cut my hair. My
momma stopped him, and he hit her.

And there was nothing, nothing we could do. I would stand beside
Sam, a little behind him, because like her he always seemed to be between him and me. Once, I guess because I couldn't stand it anymore, I

screamed at him to leave our momma alone, and he got up out of his chair and reached for me, but what might have happened I will never know. Sam launched himself at our daddy like a wildcat, and in my mind's eye I can see him swinging his little balled-up fists into that grown man, again and again. My daddy grabbed his hands, and then Sam commenced to kicking his shins, or trying to, as my daddy swung him wildly around the room.

I remember that my own fear seemed to break then, and I ran in and grabbed one of his legs above the thigh, and bit him hard, behind the leg in the bend of his knee, and heard him howl. I do not remember him hitting us, only that my momma, one more time, somehow got between us, saving us. Mostly I remember how helpless and weak and useless I was.

It was a cold winter that year, and it seemed that with each passing day of December the temperatures dropped a little more. Once it got so cold that the small pond near our house froze, which is no big deal to Yankees but was amazing to us. We skidded rocks over it, and gingerly stepped out on it, never more than a few inches. But my little brother, Mark, was fearless at age three.

He was wearing two coats and two pairs of pants, so trussed-up his arms stuck almost straight out at his sides. As my daddy stood with his hands in his pockets, smoking, lost in thought, Mark decided to go skating in his baby shoes.

He walked straight out to the edge of the pond and was fine, laughing, too light to even break the ice, but then one of us, Sam or me, made the ice crack with a rock or a footfall, and the next thing I saw was my daddy running, wild-eyed, crazy-looking, snatching up my little brother and running with him to the house. That night, for no reason at all beyond the fact he was drunk, he went mean again. Momma, as always, tried to fend him off even as she herded us out of harm's way, back into the bedroom. We hid not in the bed but under it, and whispered to each other of how you reckon you can kill a grown man.

A few days later he left us, with no money, no car, nothing. I remember my momma sitting at the table, crying. At the time I thought it was because she missed him, but now I know that had nothing to do with it.

I remember how the meals got smaller and smaller, plainer and plainer. The welfare checks, the government cheese and peanut butter and grits and meal had quit when she went back to our daddy, so there was not even that. Once a week she would bundle us up in our coats and we would walk the mile or so to the old, gray, unpainted store, where an elderly man sold us groceries on credit, and then we would pull them home again in Sam's wagon. She carried Mark, to keep him from running out into the road, and Sam I took turns pulling the wagon. People rode by us and stared, because no one—no one—walks in the Deep South. You ride, and if you don't have something to ride in, you must be trash. I remember how the driver of a pulpwood truck made a regular run up and down the road, and when he would see us he would throw sticks of chewing gum out the window, sometimes a whole pack.

Eventually the credit ran out. The milkman came by one day to get his empties and left nothing for us. Weeks went by and we ate what was in the house, until finally I remember nothing but hoecakes. Usually, her sisters would have come to our rescue, but her decision to go back to my father had caused hurt, and bad feelings. Out of pride, she wanted to wait as long as she could.

Then she got sick. She lay for days in her bed, dragging herself out just long enough to fix us something to eat, then she would struggle down the path to the outside bathroom, hunched over, and stay out there too long, in the cold. Finally she would struggle back into her bed, and sleep like the dead. We did not know it then, but she was going to have another baby.

We were at rock bottom.

Then one day there was a knock at the door. It was a little boy, the color of bourbon, one of the children who lived down the road. He said his momma had some corn left over and please, ma'am, would we like it.

They must have seen us, walking that road. They must have heard how our daddy ran off. They knew. They were poor, very poor, living in unpainted houses that leaned like a drunk on a Saturday night, but for a window in time they had more than us.

It may seem like a little bitty thing, by 1990s reasoning. But this was a time when beatings were common, when it was routine, out of pure meanness, to take a young black man for a ride and leave him cut, broken or worse on the side of some pulpwood road. For sport. For fun. This was a time when townspeople in nearby Anniston clubbed riders and burned the buses of the Freedom Riders. This was a time of horrors, in Birmingham, in the backwoods of Mississippi. This was a time when the whole damn world seemed on fire.

That is why it mattered so.

We had seen our neighbors only from a distance. They drove junk cars and lived in the sharecroppers' shacks, little houses of ancient pine boards, less than a mile from our own. Their children existed beside us in a parallel universe, climbing the same trees, stealing the same apples, swimming in the same creek, but, somehow, always upstream or downstream.

In the few contacts we had with them, as children, we had thrown rocks at them. I knew only one of them by name. He had some kind of brain condition that caused tremendous swelling in his head. The others called him Water Head, and he ran slower than the rest and I bounced a rock off his back. I heard him cry out.

I would like to say that we came together, after the little boy brought us that food, that we learned about and from each other, but that would be a lie. It was rural Alabama in 1965, two separate, distinct states. But at least, we didn't throw no more rocks.

We stayed in that big house for a little while longer, until the trees were naked and black and the cold numbed our feet as we waited for the yellow school bus. Daddy would return from God knows where every now and then, but only to terrorize us, to drink and rage and, finally, sleep like he was dead. He would strike out at whoever was near, but again it always seemed that she was between him and us, absorbing his cruelty, accepting it. Then he would leave, without giving her a dime, without asking if we had food, without giving a damn.

She continued to be sick a lot of the time. For months, she had nothing healthy to eat or drink for her or the unborn child, unless you count cornbread. There was no money for a doctor and no way to get there.

Finally there was nothing. We packed our clothes for the last time on a February afternoon in 1966, as my daddy lay drunk. We moved silently through the house, packing, my momma shushing us when we would try to ask what we were doing. We loaded Sam's wagon—he refused to leave without his wagon—and we walked down the railroad tracks to the store, to use the phone.

It must have been a pitiful sight. A tall, pale, blond woman carrying a brown suitcase, a three-year-old child stumbling along beside her, holding on to her hand, and two other little boys, one tugging a wagon, the other, me, holding tight a squirming, half-starved stray puppy that had just showed up there a few days before. I wish I could remember its name. I'm sure it had one.

Momma called a taxi from Piedmont. She had hidden seven dollars, just for this, but seven dollars was not nearly enough to carry us the twenty miles to our grandma Bundrum's house. "I reckon the taxi man felt sorry for us," my momma said. He took us there anyway.

A few months later my momma had her baby, another boy. He died in the hospital. Later, back in my grandma's house, my brothers and I stood around the bed and wondered, for weeks, why she just lay there.

Thirty years later, I drove out to the big house myself one day, to look, to see what time had done to the place. The old store, built from brick during the Depression, was still standing, but the windows were broken out and the door had a rusty chain across it. I peeked in the windows and through the gloom I could see the counter, the empty shelves that should have been lined with tins of mackerel and sacks of beans and giant jars of pickled pigs' feet. Someday, I believe, some Yankee photographer will drive past, see it as quaint, and put a picture of it in a coffee-table book. That is where a big part of the Old South is, on coffee tables in Greenwich Village.

The fields and apple orchards, where we stole green apples and ate them until we thought we would burst, are abandoned. The fields are waist high with weeds. It has not been profitable to grow cotton, corn and other big field crops for a long time, so the ground is worthless, at least until some developers decide the time is ripe for another pod of identical, vinyl-sided tract houses at $63,000 a shot.

The railroad tracks we walked as a shortcut to the store are overgrown with weeds, more a scar on the ground than a remnant of rails. When I was six I had lain awake at night and listened to the freight trains hurtle by in the dark, and it was a lullaby. There, I used to think, is my way out of here. If all else goes to hell, I can always sneak away in the middle of the night and flag down that train, and leave this place. I was six. I didn't know any better. I thought it would stop for me.

Finally, I worked my courage up and drove to where the hateful old house used to sit. I expected to find it in sticks, falling down, abandoned. I believed it was in its death throes when we were there, so long ago. But as my own car crept closer and closer I could not believe my eyes. I do not believe in ghosts, I do not believe—now that I'm grown—in haunted houses. I have not been afraid to open the closet door for a long, long time. But this looked like magic.

The big house had been reborn. It was like new, covered in a new skin of gleaming white aluminum siding. Instead of finding any flaws and decay as the car crawled near, I noticed that it became more perfect, more precious. It was like a postcard for the gentility, framed by a canopy of massive trees and surrounded by manicured grass. I noticed a swing hanging from one of the huge oaks, and toys, in bright plastic, scattered around the yard.

I wanted to scream.

7

No papers on him

All of my life, when I thought of my mother's sons, I thought of only three. The fourth brother, the one without a name, faded from my mind's eye, like an old newspaper left in the back window of a car. I was still six years old when they buried him beside my grandfather, my mother's father, and the sliver of life he had was too narrow, too fleeting, to register very much in my memory. I never saw my momma rock him, feed him or sing to him, like she sang to our baby brother, Mark. But it was the fact he never got a name, more than anything, that made it so easy to forget him. At least, it made it easier to think about him when we did remember.

The gravestone in our town cemetery just reads "Baby Bragg." It has a kneeling lamb on top of a plain granite slab. When I was little my momma would take me with her to the grave and let me touch it. I thought it was pretty, then. I still do.

Our father did not come to the hospital, did not come to the cemetery. Our kinfolks, on the Bundrum side, helped her through it as they have helped us through so many other things. They cooked us food and they told us stories while our momma lay in my grandmother's bed, the most comfortable one, and as the weeks passed I began to wonder if she would ever get up again. It was the first and only time we had ever seen her whipped by anything. Not even Daddy had been able to do that.

We shouldn't have worried. One morning she just slid her legs over the side of the bed and went to make biscuits, and except for the fact we couldn't make her laugh quite so easy anymore, she seemed the same.

For thirty years, she never mentioned it, any of it. For a while she went to the cemetery to put flowers on the grave and pluck the wild onions from it, but over time she just stopped going. I figured she had mourned all she could, and moved on. I thought that, maybe, she had squeezed it out of her mind. I was stupid to think that.

I had never asked her about him, over the years. I envisioned my questions about her fourth child, somehow, as throwing open a door she had nailed shut, and dragging out some old, forgotten pain.

Instead, when I finally asked, I found it fresh as yesterday.

It was August of 1996. The little air conditioner in her house, really my late grandma's house, had finally died, and it was damp and hot. The oscillating fan chased the flies around the living room.

"Momma," I said, "do you ever think about the baby?" She nodded her head, and spoke without looking at me.

"He had a birthday, the other day," she said. "He would have been thirty. I was sittin' down in the living room, just yesterday, countin' back. That's how I can tell, by countin' back. Y'all come three years apart. First it was Sam, and three years later it was you, then three years later it was Mark, and then three years later, it was him. Ain't it funny, how that was? When he died, I tried to make Mark the baby again, I babied him too much, I reckon. I tried to keep him a baby as long as I could."

If she felt that way, then surely she had given the child a name, at least a name she called him in her head. I did not want to ask that, either, but I had to know.

"Yes," she said, and for a few minutes she was quiet, and I thought that was all she was going to say. "I wanted to name him Randy John," she finally said. "I thought it sounded real nice. Randy. I always liked that name, Randy. And I thought it would be real nice to name one of y'all af-ter your uncle John, 'cause he was good to us, like we named you Ricky

Ed, for your uncle Ed. If he had lived a little while, I would have named him that. But he didn't."

Apparently, the people at the hospital and courthouse did not bother to record the name of dead babies of women who picked cotton. Officially, he never existed. People where I come from would have just said that he "didn't have no papers on him."

I waited for her to tell me more but there wasn't anything more to say. That night, on the drive back to my home in Atlanta, I thought of the baby for the first time as a human being who was connected to me, by blood, family, and, finally, name. It was not a name that you'd find on the fancy letterhead of some big shot Atlanta lawyer or in the social register of the weekly paper, but it had a ring to it. It was honest and Southern, and fit just fine there in the hills of home.

For a little while, I thought that maybe he should have a new grave-stone, one with his name on it. It would be small like the other, with a lamb on it, too, but there would be a name. There ought to be a name.

Then I thought of the pain that act would draw from my momma, and I knew it was better to let the baby rest as he is. I cannot fix everything that is wrong, flawed or broken in my past, in her past. I cannot recast those years in smooth, cool marble, and believe that my meddling will make things all better again. The name of the child is etched into her head, her heart, her soul. Now, because of my meddling, it is etched in mine.

As the car ate up the miles to Atlanta, dodging the wobbling tourists and drunken pickup trucks and eighteen wheelers that hurtled by in the dark, I started to cry.

When we first went back to my grandma's house to live, I went to bed every night afraid there would be a knock at the door, that he would come for us, mad, drunk, enraged. But he never did. He never would. I did not miss him. I did not even wonder what happened to him. After a while I did not think of him at all. I learned what became of him only from the gossip of kinfolks.

After we left the last time, he began the steady process of drinking himself to death. It took a long, long time. By the time it was accomplished, my childhood was done. My mother's youth was burned away, more by working in the fields than by the time, making her old much too soon.

It would be years before I spoke to him in person again. To be accurate, I did see him from time to time from a distance. It was a small place, our world, and I would see him slide by in his car.

A year or two after we left him, I saw him in the parking lot of a grocery store in Piedmont. He saw me, too, and got out of his car, motioning to me, staggering across the asphalt like it was a deck pitching and rolling beneath his rubbery legs. I ran.

8

In the mouth
of the machine

There were still three of us to raise, in the summer of 1966, back in the peace and safety of my grandmother's tiny house. My momma enrolled us in Roy Webb Elementary School, the closest public school, and begged a ride to the county seat in Anniston to sign us up again for welfare. It killed her pride to do it, but she knew that her chances of making enough money to clothe, feed, care for and educate us—her with no skills, no education to speak of—were damn slim. She signed us up for free lunches. She hated it, but she did it. To not do it, she said, would have been "false pride."

She went back into the fields, picking for a few dollars a day again, but there was always work for her because she was good and fast at it, and because she always picked clean, without a bunch of trash in the sack. She worked at it for two or three more years, until one day a gigantic mechanical monster roared out of some nightmare and into the field, and took the work away.

The mechanical pickers had been used in the bigger fields down South for a long time, but it was the late 1960s before they began to gnaw their way through the fields that ringed our lives. At first there was still work on the smaller fields, and later my momma picked the "trash" cotton, the wisps and dirt-crusted bolls that were left after the big pickers passed through. The first time I ever saw one I stood amazed. It was big as God, and picked rows and rows at a time. I did not know it then but I was seeing a way of life disappear into the maw of the thing. No matter how poor or desperate you were, back then, there had always been the field. It did not matter that most white people considered it "nigger work." It was our work.

When that work was gone she did whatever she could find. She stripped long rows of sugar cane and picked tomatoes and picked up pecans, doing backbreaking stoop labor, sometimes for money and sometimes for "halves." She cleaned the houses of the rich folks and flipped hamburgers at a café and took in washing and ironing. People would drive up to our house in nice, big cars and leave off bundles tied up in sheets. She washed some of the clothes in a sink and some in the old ringer washing machine on the back porch. Once, I remember with brutal clarity, I stuck my fingers between the ringers to see what would happen. It hurt. That was about what I expected would happen.

She ironed in the tiny bedroom I shared with my brothers. I used to go to sleep, countless nights, with the clothes of strangers heaped around my bed, under strict orders not to touch them. I touched them anyway. She only made a few pennies a shirt or blouse, but she worked hours and hours at it, dripping sweat, the hiss of the iron like a live thing. I touched the bottom once, to see what would happen. That, too, was about what I expected. (I did not know it then, but I was in training to be a reporter, or an imbecile.)

It seemed all she did was work. She did not go on dates even though she was still a pretty woman in those early years. She did not go to church because she did not want people to stare at her, because she did not want to have to explain where her husband was. At least, that was part of it.

It would be years before I realized the main reason she exiled herself to the little house, going out only to buy groceries. She avoided crowds, even our school. It was a long time before I realized that she stayed home because she was afraid we might be ashamed of her, ashamed of the woman with rough hands like a man and donated clothes that a well-off lady might recognize as something she threw away. She could live with the fact that she wore old tennis shoes with the toes worn clean through, but she was afraid we would be ashamed of her.

So that we would be proud of her, so that we could say our momma had a high school education, she went to a night school with Aunt Gracie Juanita and began her education again, almost from the beginning. Momma had quit school as a little girl. She resumed her studies as a grown woman, hunched over a fifth grade reader. Momma studied at home mostly, at the kitchen table, and she flew through those math, literature, grammar and science books, passing a grade every few months, sometimes in just weeks. "I liked the literature, because it had poems in it," she told me.

Some twenty years after she quit school, she took a hard test and got her GED, her diploma.

I do not ever remember being ashamed of her, not when I was a little boy. Later, when I was older, when I was discovering girls and making friends, I admit I was content to let her remain hidden there, in her own exile. But I will get to that later. As children, we never knew how tenuous our existence was. She absorbed that unpleasantness, too.

We wore hand-me-downs and charity clothes and slept on sheets that our kinfolks made from the sacks of a brand of hog feed called "Shorts," but every fall we got brand-new underwear—genuine Fruit of the Loom—and a few pairs of pants and shirts and socks that no one had ever worn before. And there were always new shoes. She walked around with her toes sticking out, but we got new shoes. Because we were children, we begged for things we couldn't have, but instead of slapping us or yelling at us, the way so many mommas did, she just said no, she was sorry. There was a look on her face, then, that I now know was the look of someone who is just flat beat down. I saw it other times, when she stood in line at the grocery store with one hand frantically flipping through the one-dollar bills in her change purse, praying that the cash register would stop ringing before long. Still, we kept kept asking, kept wanting.

In the second grade, it was a pair of cowboy boots.

❖   ❖   ❖

They were jet black on the bottom and bright blue on the top, like the television cowboys wore, like Hank Williams wore. I was certain there would not be a finer pair of boots in all of Roy Webb School and certainly not in Imo Goodwin's second grade class. I begged and I begged, for excruciating days. For her, it must have been like fingernails being dragged slowly down a blackboard.

One morning I found them at the foot of my bed.

And I was transformed. I had been little towheaded Ricky Bragg. Now, I was Steve McQueen, "the bounty hunter." I was "Have Gun, Will Travel."

I was so proud of them that I would sit with my feet splayed way out into the aisles so that you couldn't help but see them, and sometimes trip over them. Mrs. Goodwin warned me to put my feet under my desk like a gentleman and quit slouching, but what good are new shoes if no one can see them, so I would slide them back under the desk for a few minutes and then ease them back out into the aisle, an inch at a time. I would actually even work the boot half off my foot, so I could stick it even further into view.

Then, one day, Goodwin caught me by surprise. It was study hall. She snuck up on me from behind and drop-kicked my half-on, half-off boot to the front of the room, then chased it down and kicked it again, clear out the open door and into the hall. The second graders, me included, held our breath. Mrs. Goodwin was seventy if she was a day. We thought she had lost her mind. She actually cackled as she did it, hopping around the room like some skinny old bird dusted with DDT.

I cannot begin to tell you how ashamed I was. She stood over me and dared me to go get it, saying she would paddle me if I did, so I just sat there with one boot on and one off, my face hot. But there was no way she was going to make me cry.

In study hall, she usually let us go, one at a time, to get a drink of water. I saw my opportunity. She did not let me go, but I gave Woodrow Brown a nickel—my milk money—and he brought my boot in for me.

❁   ❁   ❁

Like I said, we were too stupid to realize that, as our lives spun round and round on these trivial things, my momma's life was running through her hands like water.

As the years went by, she went out less and less when she didn't have to, to chase the work. She never went to church. She just prayed at home. She almost never went to the PTA meetings, or Halloween Carnivals, or Christmas parades, or, later, to see us play basketball or baseball. Our aunts Nita and Jo drove us where we needed to go. Years later when I was in junior high school, I won the Calhoun County public speaking championship sponsored by the 4-H Club. My momma didn't go.

A hundred times in my life, people have asked me why didn't she just get another husband. One idiot, one of those trust fund babies that the newspaper business is riddled with, even asked why she didn't just go to college.

You have to understand the time and place. She was a married woman in Alabama in the 1960s. Divorce was shameful at best, and impossible if the man did not agree. She was not weak. She was never weak. But convention bound her, and something else. Despite everything she had been through, all the hopeless times, I believe she felt some loyalty to him. She was a product of the rural, poor, Protestant South. She was in her mid-twenties, alone, and trapped.

I guess that, somewhere, there was still the ghost of some love. She never talked about him, never pined for him in any way we could see. But all her life she kept a small brown suitcase stashed high on a shelf in the hall, containing all the things that were valuable or precious to her. It didn't hold much. It had three birth certificates, and a bundle of letters from him, when they were still young, before Korea.

It burned in a fire in 1993, with just about everything else she owned, and the last tangible link to the boy she had met and fallen in love with was gone.

Two tiny black-and-white photographs, the only ones we have of him now, survived that fire. In one, he is fresh-faced and fearless and probably more than just a little drunk, dressed in his winter uniform in Korea, one arm slung over the shoulders of a buddy who is swigging on a bottle of whiskey. They seem to be someplace warm and safe and dry, and it must have been taken before the killing began, because he looks too brave, too fresh, too dashing.

The other is so unlike my memories of him that I almost can't believe it is him. It is springtime, maybe, because he is in a T-shirt, on what seems to be a military base. The hills in the background look like the hills of pictures I have seen of Korea. He is cuddling a puppy to his cheek.

Like I said, the pictures are very small. It hurts my eyes to look at them for long.

9

On the wings of a great speckled bird

If I live to be a hundred, I will never forget her, eyes closed, lips moving in prayer, both hands pressed to the warm plastic top of the black-and-white television. On the screen was a young Oral Roberts in shades of gray, assuring my momma that God was close, that she could feel Him if her faith was strong enough, coursing through that second-hand Zenith.

The fact that my momma did not go to church did not mean that she did not seek God. The television preachers—beamed to us from Baton Rouge, from Tulsa, from the Birmingham Municipal Auditorium—brought not only His Word, but salvation. All you had to do was reach out and feel the screen, feel that warmth, that electricity, and be Saved. I reached out to touch it myself once or twice, but all I felt was the hot glow of the picture tube.

I am not making fun of this. I mention it at all only because faith is part of my momma's life, and because my own struggle to understand, to believe, to accept, consumed so much of my childhood. That faith, that belief, made the unbearable somehow bearable for her, and the loneliness, less. I am descended from a people who know there is a God with the same certainty that they know walking into a river will get them wet.

The promise of heaven, the assurance of it, was balm, even if you had to turn the antenna to fix the prophet's horizontal roll.

I was only nine years old, but I knew even then that God didn't live in no damn TV. But I never told my momma. She needed to believe that somebody bigger and stronger than her was looking out for all of us, so on Sundays she turned on the television for her preaching, and worshipped. The prophets on Channel 6 did not know or care that she was wearing old blue jeans cut off at the knee and rubber dime store flip-flops, as long as she sent them a list of prayer requests every month wrapped around a one-dollar bill. They praised God and said that, of course, it would be nice if she could send five dollars or maybe ten, but that kind of salvation was too rich for our blood. When I was little, I truly believed that the reason we had it so hard was because we could only afford a dollar's worth of salvation a month.

The TV preachers peddled promises, and offered hope to people who had none. There would have been great good in that, I believe, if they had not followed every sermon with a request for a portion of their flock's old-age pensions. Instead, it was an odd mix of good and evil, and people like my momma understood their avarice but forgave it, because the words the men spoke were comfort to her and their preaching was first-rate. I remember a jolly fat man named Wally Fowler who banged on a piano like he was pounding at Lucifer himself, and a young Jimmy Swaggart before there were any prostitutes in his life that we knew of.

It was a ritual on Sunday mornings. She would get up early and make a special breakfast, maybe biscuits with apple butter, and scrambled eggs mixed with crumbled-up sausage. She would take a diced-up tomato from the garden, a big, red thing, not those fake, pink things that New Yorkers eat because they don't know no better, and drizzle over it a tablespoon of fresh-brewed coffee and a little hot grease from the skillet where she cooked the sausage, and then dust the whole thing with black pepper. She called it red-eye gravy.

We would eat with our plates balanced on our knees in the living room, listening to the gospel music shows that were a warm-up to the evangelists. I remember the Florida Boys—"Here they are folks, up from Pensacola, Florida, with sand in their shoes!"—and the Dixie Echoes, and the Happy Goodman Family, and others. They were quartets, mostly, men in good suits who never, ever moved their legs as they sang. Everyone knew that people who moved too much when they sang were inviting hell and damnation. Look what happened to Elvis.

They sang the same songs that filled the church hymnals, mostly, songs we knew from heart even though we had seldom been anywhere close to a church. My daddy had not believed in them. You could not have forced him into a church pew with a bazooka. But we did not need a hymnal. We did not need an eighty-year-old woman pecking on a church organ. We got out of bed at 6 A.M. on Sunday and heard "Closer Walk with Thee" sung by people who owned a tour bus.

Just like in the real thing, our electronic church had singing first, then the Gospel. The preacher, usually the young-looking Oral Roberts—the one who would later say that God threatened to take his life if he failed to raise a specific dollar amount in his crusade—read from the Scripture and explained it to us. The message I got was that sleeping with your neighbor's wife would sock you into hell just as quick in 1967 as in the age of Pharoah. I listened, and I think I understood. I just never felt anything.

I never felt any fear of The Pit, or felt a joy at the notion of harp music and milk and honey, which sounded pretty dull to a nine-year-old boy raised on fiddle music and biscuits and gravy. Because they had to devote so much time to begging, things like fire and brimstone and eternal bliss got a little less attention than they should have. The pay-for-pray preachers all seemed frantic to build a new cathedral or a Christian amusement park. All my momma was praying for was enough money to last till the first of the month.

Some of those TV preachers did good things with their millions, and some lied, cheated and stole, so it's unfair to lump them all into one pile. But I wish those bad ones could have seen my momma with her hand on her thirty-five-dollar television, believing. Maybe they would have done better. Probably not.

I was lucky, in a way. Other mommas and daddies beat Jesus into their children, or used the Son of God as an anvil to hammer out their behavior. I remember one time when we were stripping cane for a farmer, and a little girl, no more than six or seven, was exhausted. It was a tedious process, even for a grownup. You reached as high up on the stalk as you could reach, wrapped the fingers of your other hand around the top of the stalk, and ripped downward, leaving the naked stalk standing. The little girl didn't have any gloves, and her hands must have hurt.

Her daddy, the farmer we worked for, asked her why she had stopped working. She said she couldn't do it any more.

"Baby," he said, "do you love the Lord?"

The little girl nodded her head.

"Well," the farmer said, "the Lord wants you to strip that cane."

The little girl started to cry, and I worked on by.

That didn't happen in my world. God was a benevolent force. He stared down at us from the wall in The Last Supper, or from the cross, His head bowed in its crown of thorns. But in all those pictures, all dime-store images painted on cardboard, the face of Christ was beatific, as, I believed, would be the face of God. I had no doubt that They existed. I was as sure of Them as I was of other people I had never met but had heard of, like my grandfather Charlie Bundrum, or John Kennedy, or Alan Ladd. I believed. I just didn't feel that feeling, that joy, that religious charge that others did. I thought I had something bad wrong with me.

My momma, a little worried, finally sent me to the source a few years later. She sent me to a real church.

Maybe they thought I needed to hear The Word without any electronic interference. Maybe they believed The Spirit was lost somewhere over Tupelo, snagged by a power line. Either way, one grim Sunday morning, I found myself bathed like I had never been bathed before—she cleaned so deep inside my ears I thought she would gouge all the way through and pull the washrag out the other side of my head—and dusted with so much talcum I was chemically unable to sweat. She had bound my feet up in hand-me-down shoes—handed down from people I had never seen—and slicked down my hair with the slimy residue from that bottomless, dust-covered bottle of Rose Hair Oil that she had used to weigh down a million cowlicks on the untamed head of my brother Sam. In one hand I held a Bible I had never even cracked, and in the other I had a quarter my momma had told me to deliver unto the collection plate, if it came my way.

I noticed I was the only one going. Mark was still too little to waste good religion on, and Sam, at the faintest notion of church, had cut and run. That morning, I had stomped and rolled my eyes and even said "damn" under my breath at the prospect of church, of being forced to "have fellowship" with strangers. I did not understand exactly what "having fellowship" meant, but I knew it couldn't be good. But my grandma Bundrum, who wasn't big on churches her ownself, had whispered to me that if a really competent sinner enters church, the whole thing splits right down the middle. That alone, I reasoned, would be worth seeing.

At worst, it would be a show.

After I was pronounced clean, dusted and oiled, I stood in the white chert of the driveway, waiting for my ride to Hollis Crossroads Baptist Church, waiting for the One Living God to reveal himself to me or at least whisper in my ear. I was nine, and a little afraid.

I went that day with my cousins Linda, Wanda and Charlotte, my aunt Edna's girls, in a 1962 Thunderbird that wouldn't go in reverse. You had to park it with its nose facing the wide-open spaces or you were trapped.

We pulled up to the solid, concrete-block building—but not too close up—and the car doors swung open to the unmistakable smell of grilling meat. It almost made a good Christian out of me, then and there.

It was a special Sunday, I later learned. It was Dinner on the Ground.

In Protestant churches throughout the South, Dinner on the Ground is nothing more than a big picnic held at dinnertime, which to us is the noon meal. But imagine a hundred church ladies, all schooled in the culinary genius of generations, unloading trunkloads of potato salad, homemade pickles, barbecued pork chops, beans (butter, green, pole, lima, pinto, baked, navy and snap), deviled eggs dusted with cayenne pepper, pones of cornbread cooked with cracklin's, fried chicken, squash casserole, a million biscuits, a bathtub-sized vat of banana pudding, pies (lemon, cherry, apple, peach, fig, pecan, chocolate-walnut), cakes (you name it) and enough iced tea and RC Colas to drown a normal man. Off to one side a woman fried up shrimp in an electric skillet, but the children kept running over the extension cord that led to the church and cutting her power off. And over there, a man grilled hamburgers and served them up with a big round slice of Vidalia onion. If this is church, I thought, let me in.

This was religion without pretension. The church was brand-new, a big, square box made from concrete blocks, painted white, the whole gigantic thing resting on a massive concrete slab. The men of the church, who paid the bills for construction with money they couldn't really spare, did not care much for aesthetics, but they knew their Bible, particularly Matthew. Only a fool will build on sand, and since there was no solid rock, they built their own out of cement. I think Matthew was referring to character, not architecture, but the fact remains, that was one damn solid church.

The people were solid, too. You could look down the pews and not see one necktie. The men came to church in what we called "dress shirts"—that was any shirt that didn't have the red, telltale spots of transmission fluid on its arms or tiny pinpoint black holes made from the flying sparks of the foundry. They wore blue jeans, neatly ironed. In every shirt's pocket, there was a pack of Camel cigarettes—no filter tips, only sissies smoked filter tips—and on the ring finger of every left hand, a band of gold. A man who had no family, who had no roots and responsibilities, was no man at all.

The women wore dresses they made themselves on Singer sewing machines or bought on sale at J. C. Penney in Anniston. A few of them worked but mainly they raised babies and gardens. Their mommas taught them how to cook, sew and can, and they had no way of knowing, none of us truly did, that they would be the last of their kind, the last generation to live that way and to use those skills. It is a cliché to call it a simple time, but it was.

The old sat up front. You could snap a rubber band down the first pew and, no matter how lousy your aim was, sting somebody with a bam-

boo cane or a set of support hose. But such an act would have been suicide. The old were of value. The old men could look at a leaf a younger
man brought to church in his shirt pocket and tell him what kind of
worms were gnawing at his tomato plants, and how to kill them. They
could peek under the hood of a car that was running rough and, with a
Case pocketknife, adjust the idling, reset the points and adjust the gap
on the plugs, all before the first strains of "I'll Fly Away" drifted from the
door.

The old women had an almost magical power. They were the
shamans of their world, who could lift a crying baby from its own
momma's arms and, by pressing a wrinkled finger to its lips in just the
right way, make it shush. They were the historians of the community, and
kept a neat record of births and deaths in the blank pages of their Bibles,
or just in their heads. They *knew everything*. They visited the sick, sat up
with the dead and watched over their men, which they had grown accustomed to.

If any of them had had any money, young or old, they would have
gone to one of the big churches over the mountain in Jacksonville or Anniston, where the people who owned the car lots and the banks and the
insurance companies went, where men in suspenders and seersucker
suits and women in heels—not too awfully high, for that would be scan-
dalous—sat in churches with red stained glass, on pews softened by
cushions. There were no cushions at Hollis Crossroads.

There was no choir, at least no robed choir. The entire congregation—every man, woman and child—was its choir, and if you didn't sing,
some old woman would whip her head around and give you a dirty look.

They were Baptists, not Church of Christ, so they strummed guitars
and beat drums and tickled the piano. I remember one young man with
a fine, strong bass voice who hit them low, low notes, like he was singing
from the bottom of a well, and one old woman, her hair piled into an im-
pressive beehive, who sang through her nose and gave out peppermints,
and one old man who sang so loudly, so badly, that people used to gossip
about whether someone should speak to him about it, but no one did. It
was deemed un-Christian.

There was a whole, new, fascinating culture to this big whitewashed building. I went to Sunday school, not so much to study the Bible as to sit, covertly, by pretty girls. The teacher only asked us to memorize one verse every week. I used the same verse every Sunday.

"Jesus wept," I would recite every week, short and sweet.

The teacher would glare.

The weeks rolled by. My momma would ask me, very eagerly, what I had learned, what the preacher said, who I had seen, what they wore. Every time, we begged her to come with us, but she always said no, she reckoned not, she would stay home. Maybe next Sunday.

Meanwhile, I heard a Sunday school teacher haltingly explain the Immaculate Conception. We drew names at Christmas and I got a Batman you catapulted into the air with a slingshot. I tried to learn a few hymns so ancient protectors-of-the-faith would stop looking mean at me. I thought, stupidly, that I belonged here.

But there was more to it than that. As so many Sundays flew by, there among those good people who treated me like a member of the family, the warm, decent people who found a pure joy inside the walls of that church, I learned that you can't just come to have Dinner on the Ground. You can't just come to listen to the guitar picker, or to sit with the girls or pretend to sing when you don't know the words or the meaning behind the words. You can't just see the show. You have to give something in trade.

The minister was a kind-looking older man who, instead of scaring his congregation, spoke of the loveliness, the wonder, the bliss of salvation, not only in heaven, which was its reward, but here on earth. He promised a peace and a happiness and something more, something that lit the darkness around you and frightened off the things that might do you harm. He was not an eloquent man, I remember, but he stood with his old Bible open in one hand, his voice warm and a little weak but clear and coaxing, and ushered those people into the outstretched arms of God.

I was a reporter, even then. I believed what I could see and hear and sometimes what I could feel, but there is no doubt in my mind that something powerful, something fierce, rippled along that bare, gray concrete floor.

It happened at the end of every service, when the singing and the preaching was spent and the minister gave what was known as the call to the altar. The people in the congregation sang, softly, "Just as I Am," as the old man in his sweat-stained polyester sport coat begged them to come forward, to kneel, to be Saved.

This was no confessional—that was for the Catholics—but a simple trade. One soul, for salvation, for peace, for across-the-board absolution. It began with a trembling of the lips, and then the tears would start to flow and before long the Lost would be coming, by ones, by twos, by threes. Some walked quietly to the preacher's side, to kneel before the simple wooden cross on the simple wooden dais. Others came clawing out of their pew, frantic, enraptured, as if the bench had suddenly grown too hot to sit on, and maybe it had. In the congregation, the already Saved raised their hands to the ceiling, and heaven, waving them slowly from side to side as the old minister held the hands of the Now Found, welcoming them to Canaan.

He saved them one by one, the young ones and the old ones and even the ones who had been saved once or twice already, but had felt their faith weaken some, and needed it shorn up with another visit to the altar. He saved children—he said you were never too young—and caressed their necks as they knelt, weeping, not really understanding what they felt or why they felt it, as their mommas and daddies wept for them, from joy. He kept at it Sunday after Sunday, until he had enough of them to hold a decent baptismal. I saw one, only one. I think it was the most beautiful thing I have ever seen.

They did them only in warm weather, in a fishing lake not too far from the church. First someone threw in a rock to chase the cottonmouths away, then the minister and his deacons walked into the dark green water, in their nicest clothes; nothing in this culture, our culture, was more important. The rest of the congregation lined the banks, singing of the River Jordan. I cannot recall the words, but even now I can hum those songs in my head.

Those about to have their sins washed clean waited, some weeping, some laughing. I remember that the women and the girls always wore white, some with flowers in their hair, and went barefoot into the murky water. I can still see the rapture in their faces as the preacher took them in his arms, then ever so gently leaned them back, back, until the waters closed over them and the thing was done. I remember how the mascara ran down their faces, and how completely, utterly alive they looked. I have never seen a look like that, as if something was racing through their very veins, stronger than heroin.

And I remember how odd it seemed, to see grown men, men who fed pipe shop furnaces, who heaved around 200-pound sticks of pulpwood like firewood, lie like children in the preacher's arms, and go so passively under the water as the congregation silently mouthed the words "Praise God" and "Thank you, Jesus."

Then it was back to the church, back to The Word, back to that old man's quiet faith and his unyielding crusade to save us all.

Every Sunday, I waited. I waited for the invasion, the infusion, the joy. I waited for the Holy Ghost to slip inside my heart and my mind and, as He had done to those all around me, lift me out of the pew and up to that altar, Saving me. I waited for it like a boy waiting on a train.

But while I felt wonder and maybe a little fear, I never felt what I had seen, or maybe sensed, in the others. I was not refusing Him, rebuking Him. I wanted it, I wanted the strength of it, the joy of it, but mostly, I wanted the peace of it. The preacher promised it. He promised.

I just sat there. I could have pretended—I think some did pretend—but what good would that have done. I sat, as the Sundays drained away.

I never felt so alone before.

I don't think I ever have, since.

I stopped going, after a while. I never went to church again, but I am not sorry I went then. I saw the power in it. I saw the need. Over the years, in every place I've gone where people lived surrounded by danger or misery or just pure evil, there was always one place of escape. Sometimes there was a cross nailed to the door, sometimes other symbols, but it was still sanctuary.

In every hopeless place I have ever been, there was that hope. And I always think the same thing, of how good it would be to feel what they feel, that peace in the midst of all that suffering. I guess it is envy, and maybe jealousy. How sad, to envy them heaven.

I don't buy all of it or even most of it, what those preachers said. I don't think you have to do anything to get into heaven except do right. If you have ever pushed a wheelchair for somebody and nobody paid you, then you might get in. If you ever peeked inside an old person's screen door and cracked open their loneliness with a simple "hello," you might get in. My momma will. That, I know. Even with her hands pressed to the dusty top of a dully glowing electric box, she was closer to God than most people will ever get. I will take my peace from that.

I remember her, in that time, sitting in the living room, sewing up our ripped blue jeans, singing.

What a beautiful thought I am thinking
Concerning a great speckled bird
Remember that her name is recorded
On the pages of God's Holy Word

10

If you got to kill somebody,
better it ain't family

For three good years, from the time I was ten until I turned thir-teen, I lived in a beautiful oblivion, safe from the past, unaware of what waited for us when our childhoods ran out. In the summer, I would sit for endless hours in the middle of high clover, idly searching for one with four leaves, then pressing it between the pages of *Tom Sawyer* or *The Hardy Boys.* Even today I flip through those old books and search for one, but they have all either turned to dust or just disappeared, as if any luck they had in them was for the boy, not the man.

In winter I would settle into a spot where the pale, weak sunshine reached but the wind couldn't find, and daydream myself away, far, far away. Sam and Mark used to think I was a little odd, and they would ask our momma what was wrong with me. "He's travelin'," she would say. "His daddy done it, too."

As the 1960s gave way to the 1970s, Sam was thirteen, I was ten and Mark was seven, and when we stood side by side, with our matching cowlicks, huge ears and varying degrees of blond hair, we looked like steps in a staircase. Sam was exactly one foot taller than me, and Mark was exactly a foot shorter, with freckles. I know because our uncle John used to measure us every Saturday night with a fold-up ruler, or a tape measure, or by guessing, I disremember. We had the same one-dollar haircut by an absentminded barber who was prone to cut at an angle, so that the hair slanted down over one eye, like a patch. On any given day, we only had three eyes between us that actually saw anything. People used to see us in the grocery store, standing behind Momma, and grin.

"They growin' like weeds, Margaret," some old woman would say at the Piggly Wiggly, and Momma would politely say that, yes'm, and they eat like hogs.

But while we were so obviously similar, our characters, which had long since formed, were as different as people could be who had the same blood in their bodies. Sam was the solid one, the one most like Momma, the one who washed cars for a quarter, toted in wood for the heater and slopped the hog every morning before the school bus came through. Mark would become, even at such an early age, the wildly unpredictable one, the one most like our daddy, the one with mean and gentle streaks that seemed to blur and merge. Both of them were good with their hands, could build anything with a hammer and a saw, or fix anything with a wrench. But while Sam worked steadily at a thing until it was done, Mark was always dissatisfied, restless, as if something was nibbling at him, inside. Even when he was still a little child he had a rage in him.

I was not much like either of them. I couldn't hammer a nail without bending it or severely damaging myself or someone standing near, and if you had depended on me to feed the fire or the hog we would have froze to death, huddled with our emaciated pig. I was a dreamer, and while I loved the woods and the creeks and the natural bounty of our world, I also loved to bury myself in books. After all the lights were shut out, I would cover up my head, click on a flashlight, and read as long as the batteries lasted from *You Were There* books about the Alamo, the Creek Indian Wars, the Battle of New Orleans. I solved mysteries with the Hardy Boys, and drifted down the Mississippi with Mark Twain. By the time I was in the eighth grade, I had read every book—except the ones for the little kids—in the tiny library at Roy Webb Junior High School. I am not bragging. I was just hungry. When I was out of books, I just found a quiet place to dream.

Sam and Mark built tree houses. I sailed them to China.

You wouldn't have known any of this, of course, if you had driven up into our chert driveway when we were all involved in some major disagreement, which sometimes resulted in a trip to the emergency room. All it took was an angry word or some insult, however slight, and the subtle differences in our characters vanished and you would have thought we were children of Beelzebub, unbound. Momma had hoped that the passing of time would make us more passive, more peaceful, but all it did was make us stronger so we could hit harder. Like our inherent weakness for liquor, we had brawling in our DNA.

Like our father, his father, his brothers, we fought with our fists, with rocks, with mud clods, sticks, baseball bats and, once, a hambone. Sam shot me once in the hand with a bow and arrow—I was protecting my eyes—and Mark stabbed me in the forehead with a pine splinter. I bled a quart. We shot each other with slingshots and BB guns (once I shot my cousin Connie by mistake). A snowball fight in those rare hard winters could kill. We packed the snow around chert rocks, to give us heft and distance. We knocked each other out of trees. We held each other under the water until the last, lonely bubble had trickled to the top. We choked each other, to see if you really did turn blue. Once, Mark hit me in the knuckle with a rock he threw from fifty yards. We walked it off, just to see.

We only quit when we made our momma cry. We worried her to death, and made her chase us through the hills and fields with a hickory in her hand and the wrath of God in her eyes. But if she ever broke down and cried, it shamed us, and we behaved for a while, or until she went inside. Once, I recall, she called us into the living room to ask us for help.

She didn't have many sit-down talks with us, so when she did, it was serious. She had one with me, in tears, the day I took the scissors and cut the legs out of a new pair of jeans so they would fit me, jeans she had bought for Sam by ironing clothes. She whipped me a little, halfheartedly and not very effectively, the only time she ever did, and explained that there was no money left to undo what I had done.

This time, she explained that she was doing all she could to feed us and clothe us so that we could live decent, and she actually apologized for not being able to spend as much time with us as she would like. But she said we were worrying her to death, and she extracted three promises from us, before we went out to play.

One: Don't kill yourself.

Two: Don't kill each other.

Three: Try hard not to kill nobody else, but if you have to, better if it ain't fam'ly.

She might as well have been talking to a telephone pole. We built go-carts and minibikes and motorcycles out of junk—well, actually, Sam made them, but I was always the test pilot—and wrecked them all in spectacular fashion. I burned myself so bad in one wreck, from the hot muffler, that I lay under the cold spray of water from the outdoor hydrant (Yankees would call it a faucet) because it was the only thing that stopped me from screaming.

Once, Sam came into possession of an old moped, a boring, half-bicycle, half-motorcycle conveyance that looked better fit for some Parisian sissy or an old woman. But we stripped it down to—near as I could tell—a seat with a motor under it, attached it to two wheels, and then he gave me a push-start. It would run sixty miles an hour on a straightaway. I jumped ditches with it. I should have worn a helmet, but that would have slowed me down. My momma thought I was crazy, and would run, screaming at me, until she disappeared in a cloud of red dust and the *grrrrrroooooowwwwwwwwwwwllllllllll* of that sawed-off, two-inch muffler. On every slope, on every hump, I was airborne, and I thought, as I cheated gravity, that I was Captain Zoom. It had no fenders, either, so it covered me in a red film of dirt from my ankles to my eyebrows. I tasted grit and did not give a damn.

I rode the same road, from my house to Germania Springs, over and over and over again. Back then, Germania Springs was a beautiful, crystal-clear stream full of crawfish and watercress and lined with oaks. People used to picnic on the ground—sometimes the younger ones would sneak in a little smooching—and enjoy the peace and quiet of it. At least, they would have, if a red-dirt-encrusted demon boy had not been slinging sand and dust into the air and chasing the serenity from the trees with the noise of his, well, they were not real sure what it was. I guess I was a distraction to them. Anyway, somebody called the law.

I was about a mile from home when I saw the sheriff's cruiser turn on its flashing blue lights, and I headed straight for Momma. I was almost home when I realized that bringing the law into her house might make her cry. I decided, as the dust flew and the siren wailed, that I had to escape justice on my own. I went rocketing down the dirt road and right on past the house, under the clothesline, around the barn, past the apple tree and straight into the cotton field, slewing around in that soft dirt, the green bolls of cotton beating my hands bloody, but I was free. I looked back over my shoulder and saw one of the deputies out of his car, bent over, laughing. I was eleven going on twelve. I reckon, if caught, I wouldn't have done much time.

Life was sweet, often, and the crises were small. There was the time we all loaded into my aunt Nita's Chevrolet Biscayne—Sam, Mark, me, Momma, my grandma, Aunt Nita, my cousin Jeffery and our mean-spirited little dog, Barnabas—for a trip to Pensacola, and forgot the dog somewhere south of Montgomery when we all had to go into the woods to pee. We were twenty miles down the road when somebody said, "Where's that damn dog," and we rushed back, to find Barnabas looking bewildered at the side of the road, where we left him. He never did trust us much after that, and refused to get in a car at all.

There would have been no crises at all, if we had just had a slightly better understanding of the broader world. On that same trip, I was sitting in the bathroom of the $12-a-night Castaway Cottages, reading the Pensacola Visitor's Guide, and I heard a siren and then, immediately, a pounding on the door. "Fire, Fire, Fire!!!" I heard my momma and Aunty Gracie Juanita scream, in harmony. Before I could even put my britches on my momma and Aunt Gracie Juanita had jerked it open, ripped me out of the bathroom and shoved me, naked as Marlon Brando, out into the hotel courtyard, where people stared in obvious wonder at why those two women had hurled a naked eleven-year-old boy out of their Castaway Cottage. I tried to cover myself and looked around for the blaze and the fire trucks. But all I saw was a mosquito sprayer on back of an old pickup, which blared its siren every few minutes to warn the old people with lung ailments that it was comin' through.

We were poor, but we were not dull. Momma and the kinfolks and the welfare made childhood sweet and warm. Uncle Ed even bought us a pony, a mean-spirited little midget of a horse named Buster, who ultimately ran away and got hit by a transfer truck. When Sam and I made the basketball team at Roy Webb, we had new high-topped sneakers, Converse. Our aunts hauled us to the games and, after a while, we stopped wondering or even caring if our momma came.

The basketball games were the event of the week in the community, if you discount church. Our uniforms were purple and gold, and having one meant that you were part of something important. The floor was dark wood, waxed so many times that the planks seemed to float under a blurry haze of ice, and I can still remember the sound the rubber-bottomed sneakers made as we shifted direction. One boy, nicknamed Chewey because he was always getting caught in back of the lunchroom with a jaw stuffed with Red Man, didn't have any toes, so his sneakers made a different, more muffled sound. I think it was the old sock he stuffed in the toes of his sneaks, to account. All I know is, if you weren't careful Chewey would sneak up on you from behind and steal the ball, because you couldn't hear him coming.

I was a shooter. I saw little point in defense, so I rested then. I saw little point in any part of the game that did not involve the ball in my hands, heading for the hoop. It might have been the single most significant reason why I didn't get to play too long in any given game. "Don't give it to him, he'll shoot it," my teammates would yell out to each other. But what got me into trouble most was the backing up. Because there was more glory in it when you knocked the bottom out from twenty feet than from two feet, I would dribble *away* from the goal. I would look over at the bench, all full of myself, only to see Coach Orville Johnson crooking his finger at me.

I think one of the proudest moments in my young life was a big game my eighth grade year—I believe it was Websters Chapel—when the coach looked down the bench, said, "I need a shooter," and motioned to me.

I took the pass from way, way, way out, beyond the top and to one side of the key, and let her fly. The ball couldn't arch very high—the damn roof was too low—but it swished so sweetly, so softly through the net that, I am certain, grown men in the bleachers had to wipe their eyes at the pure beauty of it. It was before the invention of the three-point shot, so they only gave me two, but if that shot wasn't worth three I'll eat a bug. I missed the next one clean, a brick, a rock, air-ball. I guess the first one could have been luck.

Naw.

Life was rich. On Fridays, in the lunchroom, we had hamburgers and chocolate ice cream. I had a new girlfriend every year from first grade on—I was a smooch 'em and leave 'em kind of boy—and one year, I was crowned King of Second Grade, or Third, I cannot remember, at the Roy Webb Junior High School Halloween Carnival. My queen was Debbie Grantham, who thought I was cute and didn't care that we were on public assistance.

I turned twelve in the summer of 1971. I was what I had always been, the son of a woman who did all she could do on her own, and needed a little help. I had given very little thought to being poor, because it was the only realm of existence I knew. The lives I read about in books or saw on the black-and-white TV were disconnected somehow, not real. We were never invited into the nicer houses, never shopped in nicer stores. The ritziest place I had ever been inside was the dime store on the old courthouse square. It was run by two ancient sisters. I would walk the aisles, looking at the toys and worthless knickknacks and magazine rack, which I was not allowed to touch. The old women tracked me with their eyes, every step I made. At ten-minute intervals one of the old women would ask if they could help me. "No ma'am," I would say, "I'm just lookin'."

Once, at Christmas, I was looking for a present for my momma. They had some ceramic angels to hang on the wall, spray-painted gold. They broke easy, I guess. I picked one up and turned to the counter and one of the old women met me, saying, "You ain't got enough money for that." To this day I don't know how that old woman knew how much money I had.

I got a lesson in who I was at Christmas, I believe in 1971. A fraternity at Jacksonville State University threw a party for the children of poor families. They bought me a coat, a pair of shoes, a football, and a transistor radio. They held the party in their fraternity house, all the sugar cookies you could handle, and the 7 Up flowed like water. Mark and I sat together, surrounded by strangers, and I drank it all in. I was twelve, but I remember everything about that night. I wasn't old enough to be ashamed about being the charity these glowing young people had gathered around, like a Christmas tree. But I was beginning to realize the difference between me and them.

The men, who called themselves Brothers, drove up with their dates in fastback Mustangs, Camaro convertibles and cream-colored Cougars, high school graduation presents, for sure. The women were all pretty— I cannot remember a time when every single woman in sight had been so damned pretty—and they all smelled very, very nice. They wore sweaters over their shoulders and they kept wantin' to reach out and mess up my crookedy haircut. The men all had on penny loafers and blue jackets with ties, more ties than I had ever seen, and smelled strongly of High Karate. It was like they had a big bottle somewheres and passed it around.

I did not understand the concept of "fraternity," but I knew that these were the rich folks. They were not rich folk by Manhattan standards, merely by Possum Trot ones. They were nice rich folk—they had to be to empty their pockets for children they didn't know—but were as alien to people like me as Eskimos and flying saucers.

These were the sons and daughters of small towns around Alabama and Georgia, the offspring of real estate brokers, insurance barons and English professors. They were members of their town's First Baptist Church, give or take a Methodist or two, and just because they had a six-

pack after the JSU Fighting Gamecocks whipped Troy State's ass in football didn't mean they did not love the Lord.

Their Christmas tree was the biggest one I had ever seen, even bigger than the one in church. It was piled three feet high with presents,
and after singing "Silent Night" and sipping punch they handed them
out to the sons and daughters of pulpwooders and janitors and drunks,
who all sat perfectly still, like my brother Mark and me, afraid to move.
The jacket they gave me was gray plaid wool, and the transistor radio already had batteries in it.

They were Southerners like me, yet completely different. I remember thinking that it would be very, very nice to be their kind instead. And
I remember thinking that, no, that will never happen.

We were part of it, of that night, because we were poor and because
we were children, and I like to think that the frat boys and their Little
Sisters still do that for the poor children in and around town. But you
simply outgrow your invitation into that better world, as your childhood
races away from you. You reach the age, ultimately, when that barrier
slams down hard again between you and them, and the rest of the nice,
solid, decent middle class. Perhaps it wouldn't be so bad, if it was a wall
of iron instead of glass.

You see them every day on their side. On their side, the teacher calls
their name in homeroom and they walk with their heads up to her desk,
to leave their lunch money, and pay their own way. On your side, the
teacher calls your name and you stare at the tops of your shoes, waiting
for her to check the box beside your name that says "Free," wishing she
would hurry. On their side, the summer glows with bronze beauties in
bathing suits at the beach. On your side, people step away from you as
you wait in line at the hamburger stand, because you smell like sweat
and fertilizer and diesel fuel.

On the other side are cars that don't tinkle with the sound of rolling
beer bottles, and houses that don't have a bed in the living room. But
what really kills you on that other side are the people—the smiling, care-
free people—who can just as easily look over into your side, and turn
their face away.

Only the oxygen is richer on your side. It has to be. Because your childhood burns away much, much faster.

All I had to do was look across the Formica-topped kitchen table to my brother Sam, to see my future. At thirteen, he had done a man's job, shoveling coal, pushing a wheelbarrow loaded with rocks, mucking out hog pens, loading boxcars at Dixie Clay with an endless line of fifty-pound bags of clay and lime. Some nights he would go to sleep sitting in that hard-backed chair, and Momma would lead him to bed. The work was his birthright. It was what he got instead of a Mustang.

11

Under a hateful sky

You begged the sky for a single cloud.

The sun did not shine down, it bored into you, through your hat and hair and skull, until you could feel it inside your very brain, till little specks of that sun seemed to break away and dance around, just outside your eyes. It turned the shovel handle hot and baked the red dirt till you could feel it through your leather work boots, radiating. Your sweat did not drip, it ran, turning the dust to mud on your face, soaking your T-shirt and your jeans, clinging like dead skin. The salt in it stung your eyes, until your lids were bright red and the whites were bloodshot, like a drunk man. Every now and then you or some man beside you would uncover a ground rattler, and you would chop it to little pieces with your shovel or beat it to mush with rakes, not just because it could bite you, kill you, but because it got in your way, because you had to take an extra step, to raise your arms an extra time, under that sun.

We did the hand labor in clearing land and building roads and grading lots for construction, digging out rocks and stumps and sawing down the pines, making room for new three-bedroom brick ranch houses with two-car garages and above-ground pools, working mostly for our uncle Ed. We scurried around the big, loud yellow International Harvester bulldozers and battered Chevrolet dump trucks, like worker ants scrambling around their fat queens, trying to keep our feet from being crushed under the trucks, looking out of the corner of our eyes for Mr. Bivens, the truck driver.

We did a lot of work, for a lot of people, but this was the hardest, the most regular, the dirtiest. We all did it at one time, Sam, me, finally Mark, and we were glad to get it. Our uncle treated us decent, paid on time and bought us, twice a day, an ice-cold RC. The sun burned down on him, too, he just didn't give a damn. I have known a lot of tough men, men who seemed immune to the elements, even to bullets, but no one ignored the pain like Ed Fair. As a child, his legs had not just been broken but shattered by a speeding car. Yet he worked twelve-hour days on those legs, pieced together with iron rods and fragments of bone, working the pedals of the big tractor, moving mountains, ignoring the pain. It was impossible to whine about the hard work to a man like that. We just did it, every summer, on weekends, after school, if he needed us. We started when we were in junior high, as soon as our momma decided we had sense enough, as soon as we were big enough to realistically do the work.

Our uncle Ed expected us to work as hard as anyone else in the crew, but the fact is he looked after us, trying to make sure we didn't get hurt. He looked after us in other ways, too.

One summer day, I think we might have been laying sod, I went into a country store to get some cold drinks and other junk food for the crew at lunch. I was covered head to toe in grime and sweat. For some reason, maybe because I didn't have enough money, maybe because I had forgotten what I was supposed to get, I had to turn around and go out again, and when I got back inside the store the man behind the cash register was glaring at me. "You gonna pay for the Coke you stole," he said. There were other people in the store, and they stared at me.

I told him I didn't steal anything. Then my uncle Ed, wondering why I was taking so long, walked in the door. He faced down the man, and I had little doubt he would have fought him right then and there.

"I know the boy. I helped raise him. The boy don't steal," he said.

"He don't have to steal, if he wants a cold drink. I got enough money in my back pocket to buy your whole damn store." Then he walked out, me in tow, leaving the man red-faced and shamed behind the front counter. I hope he realizes how close he came to getting a no. 9 work boot up his behind, one with a built-up heel, to compensate for Uncle Ed's worst bad leg.

I appreciated the work, but I dreaded it. I dreaded the last day of class, the beginning of summer vacation. The next morning our momma would wake us up, feed us a biscuit and some fried eggs and hand us a brown-paper bag that contained two skinny, white-bread, potted meat sandwiches—a pink paste made from ground pork and preservatives—and a cookie. She never sent chocolate. Chocolate melted to mush in the cab of the dump trucks, and you had to lick it off the wrapper. You rode to the job in an insidious mix of diesel fumes and gray cigarette smoke, the big trucks moaning, bouncing, jerking along the roads, and before you had done even a lick of work you were wishing the day was over, the sun was down.

If we were clearing a lot that day, we followed the bulldozer into the pines and, with chain saws that vibrated so hard you had to be careful to keep your tongue out from between your clicking teeth, we chopped up the trees that the machine pushed down. Then the work really started. The logs were cut in six-feet lengths—the only way they could be sold as pulpwood—and we had to heave them over the side of the dump trucks, which stood about eight feet high. Some of the logs weighed fifty pounds and some weighed two hundred. Sometimes, all you could do was get one end of the log over the side of the truck and try to shove the rest of it over, trying to keep it from knocking your teeth out if you failed and it fell back down on you. The sap, sticky as gum, coated your arms and face and the chips of bark gored into your eyes, and every step you made you expected to feel the needle-sharp fangs of a copperhead or rattlesnake sink into your calf, because there was no way to tell where you put your feet in that tangle of broken limbs.

But the worst of it was when we had to get a house ready for its yard, which meant every rock and root and clod of hard mud had to be dug, picked or raked away, and piled in mounds for "the trash man." Sam and I were the trash men, because we were always the youngest in the crew. We used giant forks, half as tall as us, big enough to hold forty pounds, to shovel the trash up and heave it, over our shoulder, into the back of the dump truck. Sometimes we couldn't get the truck between the trees— some yuppie was always afraid of getting a dogwood scratched—and we would load it into a wheelbarrow and, straining our guts out, push it up a two-by-eight onto the back of the flatbed truck, and dump it.

"Someday, you gonna get a good job," my uncle Ed told me. "You ought to take that fork and hang it on the wall, so you'll remember what this was like. You'll never gripe about that good job. You never will."

I knew this was not forever. It was the just the way, the means, by which we had things. Sam had caught the worst of it; I guess the oldest, by nature, always do. He worked, as a boy of twelve and thirteen, to help our momma, for nickels and dimes and quarters, trading his labor for a pickup load of coal. He would help a man cut hogs—the bloody castrating and nose-ringing work—for meat. By the time he was fifteen, his arms were corded with muscle, his legs hard as a pine knot. I saw him as indestructible, so much so that, one time when he accidentally ripped into his leg with the power saw, I was surprised to see him bleed.

The work was a hard and temporary thing that, I hoped, would pass in time. For me, it was a purification by fire, a thing that would make every other job, every other thing I ever did for the rest of my life, so laughingly easy by comparison.

For Sam, it was the first step in a long, long walk, where the scenery seldom changed.

Roy Webb Junior High School is a red-brick, one-story building on Roy Webb Road, and sits in the middle of the Roy Webb Community. I never bothered to ask who Roy Webb was, but if modesty was one of his virtues in life, he is twirling 'neath the red clay now. There were a few rich kids, but most of the children were the sons and daughters of working people. Even within a society like that, there are classes. I remember, when I was in the elementary school, having to answer questions about why we lived in our grandmother's house. The word spread. "They ain't got no daddy."

The principal and teachers, when they recognized who we were, where we ranked, told Sam that he could sweep the narrow halls, clean the bathrooms and shovel coal into the school's furnace, to earn his free lunch. He took out the trash and burned it and unclogged the toilet. They never bothered to teach him to read very well; he learned that on his own. They never bothered to tell him about the world outside his narrow, limited one. They forgot to show him maps of the universe or share the secrets of history, biology. As other students behind the class-room doors read about about empires, wars and kings, he waxed the gymnasium floor.

12

Getting above your raising

My momma did not lecture much, but when she did it was about false pride. My daddy had it. It was what made him sit for hours and shine his shoes or sharpen his knife, and forget to care about things that were really important, like whether his wife had money for groceries. She said, now and then, that I had my daddy's pride. I cared too much about appearances, about the façade that faced the rest of the world. I would have paid more attention to her if I had not known for some time that it was precisely that same kind of pride that kept her a prisoner in that little house. But I guess being a momma has little to do with logic.

The really sad thing is that I let that false pride—that pride, and a fourteen-year-old girl—make me ashamed of who I was. Worse, I let it make me ashamed of who my momma was.

It was the summer before I started high school, and even though I had long since discovered the differences in my family and others, no one had ever put it into words, until her.

I was, in my own mind, a dashing figure. I had played on the basketball and baseball teams and I owned a motorcycle, a white-and-red Honda. The chain was prone to come off at high speed, locking up the rear wheel at sixty miles per hour, but it was still a motorcycle, paid for with money I earned working for my uncle Ed.

The girl was my first steady one. She was tall, taller than most of the boys, with wavy brown hair, a vision in cut-off blue jeans and a T-shirt tied in a knot around her waist. She was a cheerleader, made all A's, went to church every Sunday and liked to talk about going to college.

She was the daughter of a respected family in the small community where I went to school, which was not—by luck—the one where I lived. She did not know anything about me, beyond what I told her. I did not invent a life, did not concoct a more respectable history. I would not have sunk that low. Instead, I told her nothing about my background. We sat in a swing in her backyard and talked and talked about everything except me, and I thought I was safe.

Then one day there was a knock on my door. It was her, flanked by a covey of her girlfriends. They had gone to the nearby Germania Springs for a picnic, and came to see if I wanted to go.

I will never forget the look on their faces as they took in the tiny living room with its ripped Naugahyde couch and the worn-out rug and the bare bulb hanging from the ceiling.

And I saw the way they looked at my momma, in her flip-flops and old pants cut off at the knee. I told them I had to work.

A few days later she told me that we had to break up. She said we were too different. I asked her what she meant and she said it was because I was poor and she was not. It never would work, she said. She made it seem like we were grownups, instead of fourteen. She made it sound like she was the lady of the manor lamenting her romance with the garbage man.

I should have told her to go to hell. Instead, I just said, "You might be right," and rode away on my motorcycle, noble.

I knew then there was no use in pretending, in hiding. I was still ashamed, but from that moment on I wore my poverty like a suit of mail. I brought my girlfriends home, and if I saw that look, that horror in their eyes, I took them back to their house and never came back. It, the look, was almost always there. It never even occurred to me that I was destined to lose. The only girls I had any interest in were the ones who represented the world I wanted to be a part of, the ones above my station, and in my part of the world class is damn near as strong as color. Luckily, a few of them liked slumming. They liked being on back of that motorcycle, being free of respectability, for a while. That was enough, then. Someone else could take them to the big dance. I didn't mind. I didn't mind.

My momma just kept trying, just kept pulling.

My favorite Bible story is of the widow's mite, of the poor woman who gave two small coins to the Temple. Rich merchants gave much more in tribute, but God saw her gift as greater because it was everything she had. So God blessed her.

13

Fine qualities

When he died, I don't remember any grief. It would have been artificial to grieve, like bending over plastic flowers laid at a gravesite, and expecting to smell their scent.

You never know how brave you will be when you die. You may cry and you may cuss. You may shake your fist at God, or, with the last ounce of energy in your body, try to steeple your fingers. But I know one thing: when I see it coming, if I see it, I will not reach out to the people I hurt in life, and ask them to care. It is not that I will be so noble, so considerate. It is only that I would be afraid they would react in the same way I did, at the end of my father's life. That I could not stand.

My daddy had been sick for a long, long time by my fifteenth birthday, and by the time I entered high school, in the fall of 1974, he was near death. He sat in that little house and coughed out his life, day after miserable day, getting weaker, becoming more afraid, searching for God with no experience.

We dreaded the phone calls. We had just gotten a telephone of our own, and we should have been enthralled by it, should have run to an-

108

swer it. Instead, when it rang we just stared at it, as if death itself was on the other end, and in a way it was. We just stared at it until our momma picked it up, and listened, without speaking, to his fears. Sometimes she would just dip her head and close her eyes and sit, not moving, and I knew she was praying with him.

There is little more to say about my last visit to him, that day he gave me the precious books and the new rifle and told me the stories of his war. Except maybe this: if it had never happened, if he had not bothered to tell me, then I would have hated him until my final breath. Instead, when his suffering was finally done, I truly did not know what to feel. But I know it was not hate. I know hate. There is nothing remotely like hate.

He died on January 29, 1975. He was forty-one. He was sober, I believe.

We did not go to his funeral, but Momma thought it was fitting that we at least go look at him in the funeral home. She laid clothes out for us on the bed, but Sam refused to go. In one of those few times in my life when I intentionally sided against her, with anyone, I said I would not go either. Maybe I was trying to repay Sam for that time he hurled himself at my father, to protect me. To Mark, he was a stranger. His death meant nothing. We all stayed home.

Momma went by herself. She didn't stay long, just long enough to pay her respects to my granny Bragg, and look one last time at his face. I never asked her what she saw or what she felt. That is between them.

Many years later, a man who had known him all his life, longer and better than me, said this: "If you took away the likker, Charles had some fine qualities." I told him I appreciated him saying that. I would like to believe it. I would have liked to have met him when he was a boy, before time had mutilated him so.

I wonder, sometimes, if I would have seen anything of myself in him, in his face, in his mannerisms. I have been told, now and then, that I got some of my character from him, but it was mostly bad things. Anger comes quick to me, like him. Forgiveness comes slow or not at all, like him. I rage against things I cannot change, and let things I could affect, I could change, just slide. As he had.

I would have liked to talk to him, before all that mess, all that terrible pain, all those gallons of whiskey, and search his face and his mind for something he had passed on to me. Something good.

14

100 miles per hour, upside down and sideways

Since I was a boy I have searched for ways to slingshot myself into the distance, faster and faster. When you turn the key on a car built for speed, when you hear that car rumble like an approaching storm and feel the steering wheel tremble in your hands from all that power barely under control, you feel like you can run away from anything, like you can turn your whole life into an insignificant speck in the rearview mirror.

In the summer of 1976, the summer before my senior year at Jacksonville High School, I had the mother of all slingshots. She was a 1969 General Motors convertible muscle car with a 350 V-8 and a Holley four-barreled carburetor as long as my arm. She got about six miles to the gallon, downhill, and when you started her up she sounded like Judgment Day. She was long and low and vicious, a mad dog cyclone with orange houndstooth interior and an eight-track tape player, and looked fast just sitting in the yard under a pine tree. I owned just one tape, that I remember, *The Eagles' Greatest Hits.*

I worked two summers in the hell and heat at minimum wage to earn enough money to buy her, and still had to borrow money from my uncle Ed, who got her for just nineteen hundred dollars mainly because he paid in hundred-dollar bills. "You better be careful, boy," he told me. "That'un will kill you." I assured him that, Yes, Sir, I would creep around in it like an old woman.

I tell myself I loved that car because she was so pretty and so fast and because I loved to rumble between the rows of pines with the blond hair of some girl who had yet to discover she was better than me whipping in the breeze. But the truth is I loved her because she was my equalizer. She raised me up, at least in my own eyes, closer to where I wanted and needed to be. In high school, I was neither extremely popular nor one of the great number of want-to-bes. I was invited to parties with the popular kids, I had dates with pretty girls. But there was always a distance there, of my own making, usually.

That car, in a purely superficial way, closed it. People crowded around her at the Hardee's. I let only one person drive her, Patrice Curry, the prettiest girl in school, for exactly one mile.

That first weekend, I raced her across the long, wide parking lot of the TG&Y, an insane thing to do, seeing as how a police car could have cruised by at any minute. It was a test of nerves as well as speed, because you actually had to be slowing down, not speeding up, as you neared the finish line, because you just ran out of parking lot. I beat Lyn Johnson's Plymouth and had to slam on my brakes and swing her hard around, to keep from jumping the curb, the road and plowing into the parking lot of the Sonic Drive-In.

It would have lasted longer, this upraised standing, if I had pampered her. I guess I should have spent more time looking at her than racing her, but I had too much of the Bragg side of the family in me for that. I would roll her out on some lonely country road late at night, the top down, and blister down the blacktop until I knew the tires were about to lift off the ground. But they never did. She held the road, somehow, until I ran out of road or just lost my nerve. It was as if there was no limit to her, at how fast we could go, together.

It lasted two weeks from the day I bought her.

On Saturday night, late, I pulled up to the last red light in town on my way home. Kyle Smith pulled up beside me in a loud-running

Chevrolet, and raced his engine. I did not squall out when the light changed—she was not that kind of car—but let her rpm's build, build and build, like winding up a top.

I was passing a hundred miles per hour as I neared a long sweeping turn on Highway 21 when I saw, coming toward me, the blue lights of the town's police. I cannot really remember what happened next. I just remember mashing the gas pedal down hard, halfway through that sweeping turn, and the sickening feeling as the car just seemed to lift and twist in the air, until I was doing a hundred miles per hour still, but upside down and sideways.

She landed across a ditch, on her top. If she had not hit the ditch in just the right way, the police later said, it would have cut my head off. I did not have on my seat belt. We never did, then. Instead of flinging me out, though, the centrifugal force—I had taken science in ninth grade— somehow held me in.

Instead of lying broken and bleeding on the ground beside my car, or headless, I just sat there, upside down. I always pulled the adjustable steering wheel down low, an inch or less above my thighs, and that held me in place, my head covered with mud and broken glass. The radio was still blaring—it was the Eagles' "The Long Run," I believe—and I tried to find the knob in the dark to turn it off. Funny. There I was in an upside-down car, smelling the gas as it ran out of the tank, listening to the tick, tick, tick of the hot engine, thinking: "I sure do hope that gas don't get nowhere near that hot manifold," but all I did about it was try to turn down the radio.

I knew the police had arrived because I could hear them talking. Finally, I felt a hand on my collar. A state trooper dragged me out and dragged me up the side of the ditch and into the collective glare of the most headlights I had ever seen. There were police cars and ambulances and traffic backed up, it seemed, all the way to Piedmont.

"The Lord was riding with you, son," the trooper said. "You should be dead."

My momma stood off to one side, stunned. Finally the police let her through to look me over, up and down. But except for the glass in my hair and a sore neck, I was fine. Thankfully, I was too old for her to go cut a hickory and stripe my legs with it, but I am sure it crossed her mind.

The trooper and the Jacksonville police had a private talk off to one side, trying to decide whether or not to put me in prison for the rest of my life. Finally, they informed my momma that I had suffered enough, to take me home. As we drove away, I looked back over my shoulder as the wrecker dragged my car out of the ditch and, with the help of several strong men, flipped it back over, right-side up. It looked like a white sheet of paper someone had crumpled up and tossed in the ditch from a passing car.

"The Lord was riding with that boy," Carliss Slaughts, the wrecker operator, told my uncle Ed. With so many people saying that, I thought the front page of the *Anniston Star* the next day would read: LORD RIDES WITH BOY, WRECKS ANYWAY.

I was famous for a while. No one, no one, flips a convertible at a hundred miles per hour, without a seat belt on, and walks away, undamaged. People said I had a charmed life. My momma, like the trooper and Mr. Slaughts, just figured God was my copilot.

The craftsmen at Slaughts' Body Shop put her back together, over four months. My uncle Ed loaned me the money to fix her, and took it out of my check. The body and fender man made her pretty again, but she was never the same. She was fast but not real fast, as if some little part of her was still broken deep inside. Finally, someone backed into her in the parking lot of the Piggly Wiggly, and I was so disgusted I sold her for fourteen hundred dollars to a preacher's son, who drove the speed limit.

I tell that story to show just how effectively I wasted high school, and came so close to wasting my mother's sacrifice. I had dreams but no ambition. I cut class and shot twenty-foot jumpers in the gym. I made a solid C average. I never, ever did any homework. I read things I wanted to read, but I never studied the things the teachers thought important. I was the master of ceremonies of the talent show, in a borrowed suit. I won contests in public speaking, because talking was so easy, and joined the school newspaper, because words didn't cost anything. I drank a little at parties and after ball games and on a road trip to Atlanta to try and get into a topless bar—which failed. I never, never danced no disco, unless some young lady wanted me to. I pitched for the Ed Fair Landscaping Dirtdaubers in the summer, and in one game I hit back-to-back home runs. If I needed money for dates, and there was no work because of the weather, my grandmother gave it to me from the change purse she hid under the mattress.

Because I worked, I paid for my lunches now. I had two pairs of blue jeans, which got me through the week, but nobody had to know that but me. I had a class ring made from fake gold, but nobody had to know that either. I was, if not bright, at least not bad-looking.

I should have studied hard and tried to win a scholarship to college, should have seriously prepared myself for the future, should have focused on dragging myself out of poverty, the way so many people do. But of the varied weaknesses in me, the strongest is a desire to live for the moment, and let tomorrow slide. That is fine, if you are a Kennedy. It was dangerous for boys like me, or at least, it should have been.

But I had a charmed life. The wreck had proved it, as other things would, all my life. Even then, I was smart enough to know that when you perform without a net, you by God better not fall.

When I took the girlfriend of the biggest and baddest ol' boy in town to a football game, and he came after me with a carload of goons, I just out-ran him, first in my car and later on foot. The noble thing would have been to stand and fight him, and if honor had been at stake, I would have. But honor was not what was at stake, but a girl named Allison who was just a friend, anyway. If you are going to get beat to death, do it for love.

My senior year, I borrowed money from a friend—I still owe him a hundred dollars come to think of it—and bought a bright-orange Suzuki 750, water-cooled. It would run 125 if you could hold on, but people called it the Water Buffalo because it was so heavy. In the summer I rode it bare-legged in tennis shoes, which was suicide. A wreck on pavement or gravel would have skinned me to the bone, so I could not wreck. I laid it down only once, at a red light in Lenlock, Alabama. I was talking to some girls in a car beside me and, not paying attention, let it lean a little too far to one side. It fell on me, pinning me down like a bug under a brogan shoe.

On the weekends, purely because my uncle Ed had no one else to drive the big dump trucks to and from the jobs, he closed his eyes and said a prayer and gave the job to me. His regular drivers were always losing their licenses to DUIs, or else he would never have let me anywhere near one. A fool in a dump truck is more dangerous than a fool in a Camaro. I would shift through that Georgia Overdrive like I was Richard Petty at Darlington, and take curves on two balding tires. I would look over at the aging workmen beside me and laugh, like the devil himself, until finally they would ride in back of the flatbed truck with the fertilizer, to keep from riding with me.

I enjoyed my life as much a I could, and excelled at nothing in it. The only thing I was ever any good at was in the telling and hearing of stories, and there was no profit in that. I cannot truthfully even say that I went to work for my high school newspaper because of a love for writing. Writing was hard work. It made your hand cramp, and I couldn't type a lick. Telling stories was something you did on your porch. Journalism seemed too much like work, like digging taters.

I took journalism at Jacksonville High because it was supposed to be easy. The press badge, safely protected by the First Amendment and lamination, gave me freedom to roam the halls, shoot baskets in the gym, stray over to Jacksonville State University to chat up college women, and just generally goof off. The journalism department consisted of one bespectacled teacher named Edna Baggs, who must have seen promise in me or she would certainly have kicked me off the newspaper for my flagrant abuses of power. My junior year, I was named sports editor of the paper because no one else wanted it. I probably was not very good, but I liked to see my name above the stories. It made me feel important.

I had no way of knowing, then, that it would be my salvation.

As I graduated from high school, the odds of continuing my writing were slim. I went back to work for my uncle Ed. I remember thinking that I could drive a truck for a living. As that summer died and I sweated with that fork in my hand, lifting and cussing rocks, I could feel that nonchalance begin to crack, replaced with regret, and finally with an increasing desperation.

The friends I had made, all the girls I had dated, were going to college, away from me, from my place in the dirt. I remember thinking, is this where I belong?

I had never pretended to be a rich kid, but I had pretended, for three years, that I was just as good as them. I was. Me, my brothers, my mother, we were as good as anybody. My mistake was in believing that other people had come to think so, too.

Nineteen years ago this summer, I was reminded, in a sickening and soul-killing way, of just how wrong I had been. There had been a killing, close by. I was a murder suspect, for an afternoon.

15

The usual suspects

For years, every time I thought of it, I found myself in a rage, eaten up inside. It was over in just a few minutes, the questions, the suspicions, routine police business. But it terrified my momma, purely because she believed the police would hang the crime on one of us. Because they could. Because we were who we were.

The gunshots were so close, less than a mile away. I should have heard them. I still don't know why I didn't. It could have been the crickets, or the rattle of the electric fan, or the canned noise from the television. I went to sleep that night, a Sunday, sunburned and wore out from swimming in the backwater of the Coosa River, peacefully unaware that murder was being done so close outside my window.

Germania Springs had been an idyllic place, before that night. The water was cold as ice but only a few inches deep, meandering between old trees. It bubbled straight out of the rock, as if by magic. Even before I was born, young people came to lie on blankets on the grass and plan lives, or live for the moment. Donna Tucker and Mark Martin, sweethearts, spread their blanket out beside the stream the night of July 17, 1977. They had graduated from Springville High School that May. Donna, a smart and pretty girl who wanted to work as a lab technician, was a freshman at Jacksonville State University. She had enrolled in col-

118

lege right after graduation, so that she could get her degree in three years instead of four. Mark, a popular all-around athlete, pumped gas part-time and planned to join her at Jacksonville State in the fall. Every Tuesday, he came to the campus to help her study. Every weekend, she went home to Springville. On Sunday nights, every Sunday night, he drove her back to the campus. They just assumed they would get married someday. They just assumed that everything, so perfect, would stay that way.

A man, all but invisible in the dark, sat at a picnic table a few feet away. He approached them once to ask for a cigarette, and again, later, to ask for a match. The third time he walked up he held a gun. He ordered them to stand up, then ordered both of them to take off all their clothes.

His name was John Sparks, described as a sexually obsessive man, addicted to alcohol, who had failed at everything he had ever tried, junior college, jobs, relationships. He was kicked out of the Air Force. He felt he never fit in anywhere, in anything.

The two young people were at his mercy. He fondled her, then him, then her again. When she screamed, he slapped her, hard, across the face. Mark, trying to keep his temper under control, trying to stay alive, finally lost control. He told Sparks that, before he touched Donna again, he would have to shoot him. It was not foolish bravado, but genuine fury. He expected Sparks to shoot him. Sparks did.

The first bullet drilled into his jawbone, the second sliced through his neck and his spinal cord. Then, Sparks turned the gun on Donna, shot her twice in the head, and ran.

Police found them about two hours later on a routine patrol. She would die. He lived, but now he turns the pages of books with a stick in his mouth. He is paralyzed from the neck down.

The next day, I awoke to see the springs acrawl with police, not just the locals but the county and the Alabama Bureau of Investigation. Word spread from house to house, the neighbors describing in detail the violence but leaving out, for decency's sake, the other details. It was the next afternoon when the officers came to the house.

We were not alone. They rounded up everyone who lived close to the scene who was either poor, black, had a criminal record, or was retarded. I remember seeing some poor fool with Mongoloid eyes sitting, confused and frightened, in the lobby of the building at Jacksonville State the investigators were using as a command post. It is a point of fact that they did not question the rich kids who lived near.

It lasted just a little while. They asked me where I was and what I was doing. I told them I was watching television. They wanted to know exactly what I was watching, and what it was about. I said I was watching *The Deadly Game*, with Lloyd Bridges, I believe.

Then, they pissed me off.

They asked me who else had been around and I said my brother, Mark, and they asked me what kind of car he drove. And I said a Nova, burgundy red with a white stripe and a white or black top. I couldn't precisely recall. "What is it, black or white?" the investigator said, thinking he was Starsky or Hutch. "Don't you even know the difference between black and white?" It went on like that for a few minutes, but I guess I didn't fit the pervert profile, and they let me go. Mark had to go through the same thing, but it was nothing like what our mother was going through.

She was frantic. She knew we had not done anything, but for a woman who had grown up at the mercy of rich folks, that did not mean a damn thing. It terrified her because she thought the police would hang the crime on one of us purely because they could, purely because we were who we were.

That Sunday, I had worn a pair of old sneakers to the river to swim in. The backwaters of the giant man-made lakes of Alabama are made by dams, which flood the low country and cover over everything from barbed-wire fences to whole houses. Only a fool walks on that bottom barefoot. I came home with my shoes filled with muck and gravel, and left them on the front porch.

My momma saw them, and panicked. She had heard that the killer, when he ran, crossed the stream. She was afraid the investigators would see my shoes, and think it was me. She buried them in the backyard, under a pile of trash.

❖   ❖   ❖

John Sparks found Jesus in prison. He preaches about hell and salvation at the tiny Uriah First Baptist Church in Monroe County, way down in south Alabama. People say he preaches a good sermon down there. He tells his congregation that he is living proof that religion can save anyone.

I reckon so.

I knew I was never in any real danger of being blamed for that terrible thing. But it still makes me mad enough to shake, sometimes, because it was so evil, so vile, because I was forced to have any connection to it all. But, it did one thing for me. It confirmed, fiercely, my notions of class, and power. It was not so much a matter of having power to do a thing as it was having the power to stop things from being done to you. My momma never had that power, not one day in her life.

I would have it.

I had blown most of my money that summer on cars and girls and drive-in cheeseburgers, but I had enough left, as September came, to enroll in one class at Jacksonville State University, which I passed every day on my way to work. It would be the first step, the first act, in a series of moves and machinations—most of them involving dumb, blind luck— that would give me what I was searching for.

For my one class, I picked feature writing under the formidable Mamie B. Herb, a woman with flaming red hair piled a foot high on her head. She told me, after reading my first few assignments, that I had talent, and promise. She gave me only a B, but it was a talented and promising B.

I was a college student. No one had to know I was just taking one class. No one ever even asked. At registration, I listed my major as "undecided," since there was no box for "barely there at all."

I wandered over to the office of *The Chanticleer*—the school newspaper named after the rooster in that poem—and volunteered to write. I told them I had experience from high school, and they took me. They would have taken anyone breathing. I covered the Fighting Gamecocks on beautiful Saturday afternoons, and got the facts right, mostly. I still worked every day for my uncle Ed, still stacked the pulpwood and forked the rocks and killed the snakes.

A few weeks later, the editor of the local weekly newspaper, the *Jacksonville News,* called my house and asked if I wanted a job writing sports, for money. They had called the college paper, and someone had told them I was halfway literate. The editor said I could even write a column if I wanted to. I would have not only my name above my stories, but my face, too. I would be an instant somebody.

The job only paid fifty dollars a week, more or less, but that was unimportant. They gave me a desk and an Underwood typewriter that wouldn't type a Q, but I learned to write around it. I learned to type with two fingers, which was about as fast as I could think, anyway. My momma cut out my first story and put it in a scrapbook, as she would every story I wrote that she could find.

To most people, it would not seem like much of a job, hunched over a typewriter late at night, writing about games. To me, it was a blessing. I went to a press conference and got to wear a tie. It was a clip-on, but no one knew. Unless you tugged real hard on it, my new tie, like my newfound respectability, stayed safely in place. In time, it dawned on me that I lingered over that old typewriter longer than was healthy for an eighteen-year-old boy, that I lingered over sentences, searching my mind for the images and details that could make those disjointed words from that faded typewriter ribbon take on color and life.

I learned, a while later, that the *Jacksonville News* had first offered the job to another writer at the college paper. He already had a steady job at the Kentucky Fried Chicken, so he turned it down.

The Lord must have been riding with me, still.

I had no idea where this writing business would take me. I did dream, then, that someday it might take me fourteen miles down Highway 21 to the respected daily newspaper, the *Anniston Star,* circulation 30,000. If you could get on there, you could get $114 a week, subsidized Blue Cross, Blue Shield and free roast beef at the Christmas party. I never dreamed, I never would have dared dream, of the great joy and despair that it would open up to me. I never would have dared dream it would take me into the temple of my profession, to that almost mythical place above the dirty sidewalks of West 43rd Street. And I never dreamed, to get there, I would run through the dark, twisting tunnels of other people's nightmares, that I would choose to do it that way because, in a foolish and romantic way, I believed I knew the way.

2

LIES TO MY MOTHER

16

In the temple

The newsroom and subway always seemed a lot alike to me. Both of them seemed barely under control, both rumbling, clattering, powerful things that people depended on to take them someplace. I sat at my desk in that crowded, busy place, and willed the words to come. I stabbed hard on a single letter on my computer keyboard, once, twice, again, harder. Nothing. It was broken, again. You can make it to the big time, make it all the way to the *New York Times,* but that doesn't mean you'll have a *Q* when you need one.

I walked home that evening to my little company apartment on 50th Street, through the cold of a Yankee winter, through the lights that people write songs about. It was after nine o'clock, but a river of yellow taxi cabs still ebbed and flowed down Broadway and Seventh Avenue, merging with a chorus of curses shouted in a dozen languages, unheard behind the tightly closed windows. The sidewalks still teemed, even at that hour, and I thought to myself, "Don't any of these damn people ever go home?" Some of them, the ragged ones who clutched at wrinkled garbage bags full of treasure and used plastic forks, were home already.

I walked past high art and low art, past the theaters where famous people played to packed houses, past theaters where anonymous people played with themselves. I passed up the delis with their eleven-dollar chicken salad sandwiches and stopped instead at the Popeye's Chicken and Biscuits, where you could eat enough to kill yourself for five dollars and change. It is the warmest place in Times Square. On a cold night, you can feel the glow from the deep fryer all the way across the counter. I got myself some chicken to go.

It might have been snowing before I stepped inside but I noticed it for the first time when I came out, little specks of white, murdered by the warmth of the sidewalk. A few blocks from home, a thin, unhealthy-looking woman with yellow hair and a pink plastic jacket stood beside a pay phone outside a dirty movie theater, not talking, just holding it, pretending, waiting for the police car to roll on by. She never solicited out loud, she just stared at you, hard, and smiled, slick and hard, like lipstick on the bathroom mirror, until you shook your head, no.

At 49th Street a beggar asked me for a little help, and I gave him a quarter, maybe two, because I had not been there long enough not to give a damn. The beggars could tell I was new, like horses can tell when you are afraid. They chased me for whole blocks sometimes, pleading. I was lucky this time. I got a Born Again, a man who did not blame God for leaving him on a freezing and dirty sidewalk. He only blessed me.

The doorman opened the door to my apartment building, and, as always, I felt funny about that. "How can you eat that stuff?" the doorman said. I told him my stomach was impervious to cayenne pepper and most forms of grease, and he smiled at my accent, like he did every night. He must have thought Gomer was loose in the Big City. He always told me everything twice, I guess so I would understand. I didn't mind that, either. He was a nice man.

I ate my chicken and biscuit out of the sack, on the couch, half-listening to the television that I had turned on for company, glancing out the window to the top of the Winter Garden, over to Broadway, to a string of headlights that stretched to the end of the world or at least to 110th Street. I had just finished a story about living and dying in New

York, and I looked at the front page, trying to keep grease and crumbs off the words.

Somewhere between one more killing in the inner city and the obscurity of the grave, is a wall in Brooklyn.

Khem Hubbard recorded her brother's name there last week, in big silver letters. Now Kyle Raseim Hubbard, 19, shot to death on Jan. 6, 1990, will be remembered in a New York neighborhood where the dead disappear in the crowd.

The memorial wall at the corner of Crown Street and Bedford Avenue in the Crown Heights section of Brooklyn is like the ones in the South Bronx, the ones in Harlem. They hold the names of dead children, innocent bystanders, stone-cold killers, untrue lovers and fallen angels.

They are remembered with elaborate murals that plead for a stop to the senseless killing, or just a few thin lines scrawled by a friend with a felt tip pen and a broken heart. They tell us that Papa rests in peace, that Kiki has found God.

No one is sure how many walls there are in New York, or how many inner-city victims have taken their place on the lists of the dead that decorate the sides of dry cleaners, clinics and corner stores. People who live beside the walls guess that there are hundreds scattered around the city, embroidered with thousands of names.

The dead have been carried off to cemeteries outside the inner city, but people here like to believe their spirit is still in the neighborhood, and that is where the shrine should be. People leave flowers in Dr Pepper cans. They touch the names and pray for souls. The murals, some with hundreds of names, are almost never desecrated. The respect Kiki and Papa, Rasheim and others couldn't find in death is now theirs.

"I don't have the power to save them," said Richard Greene, a community organizer in Crown Heights and a caretaker of the Brooklyn Walls. "But I can keep their spirit close.

"I had a friend who died in Vietnam. I couldn't go to his funeral. Later, I went to The Wall, the Vietnam War Memorial, and saw his name. That name, there was still power in it."

I read it to the end, and found a dozen things I wished I had written differently, like I always do. But there is no way to make that gigantic press run backwards once they turn the key, once the siren sounds, once it begins to tumble over and over and over again. Like time. Sometimes the warm newspaper in your hands reads clumsy and sometimes it doesn't even read right, but there it is. There you are. And it is much, much too late for the rewrite man.

I remember that night in New York, because it was every night in New York. I could have called my momma, could have whined to her about how awful it was for me here, the biscuit head, so far from home. But that would have been a lie.

I was not some poor Southern boy in run-down penny loafers and fashionably frayed khaki pants whining to his family about how much he missed the whisper of the river and the breeze on the veranda. I had been much further away from home than this, in places where they would kill you for your shoes. I could not even ask myself how in the fuzzy hell I got here, because I knew precisely how it happened, year by year. From the first time I tried to hunt and peck on that old Underwood typewriter, sitting behind that scarred desk in that little newspaper that smelled of ink and cigarettes, I had been searching for this, or something very much like it.

I was not even picturesque. I lived in Midtown, for God's sake. You have to live in the Village or SoHo to be picturesque, or Spanish Harlem if you have the guts and an angel on your shoulder. I was not a suffering writer, searching for inspiration. I worked in a city so rich in stories that I had to step over ten to get to the one I wanted, like stepping over the sleeping beggars to get to the subway. I was not eating canned soup and crackers, waiting for money from my rich daddy as I penned poetry no one would read until I was deader than Aunt Minnie's house cat. I worked for wages. Millions read the words.

I was not sure that this meant success, this New York, but I was pretty sure it didn't mean failure. For a minute I thought of Rudy Abbott, the baseball coach at Jacksonville State University, who had won two college world series. I had always respected Rudy, I suppose because he had started in the smokeneck section of West Anniston, in the shadows of the mills, and climbed out of it. He gave me some advice once, or maybe it was more of a warning.

"People like you and me," he said, "we can't fail."

No, I was doing fine.

It is true that there is something about the enormity of this city that forces you to be reflective, as if you have to constantly peek inside yourself to make sure your character has not somehow slipped away from you in the onrush of strangers. With so many rats in the box, you want to make sure that your rat is still unique, so you sit and think back to any place but here, any time but here. You find yourself in there somewhere, in that memory, and it comforts you. I do not know what native New Yorkers do. Maybe the New York in their memory is greatly different. I hear it was. Maybe they just make something up, and go there.

The only real regret I had, one I felt most acutely then and there, was that I had not been able to talk with my momma about what I did for a living, not for years and years. It was not because I was ashamed—I was proud of the work—but because it was what it was. I remember a young American soldier in Haiti, a boy from Mississippi who baked inside his bullet-resistant vest and wrote letters to his girlfriend and momma. He told his girlfriend the truth, mainly, of the filth and hate and cruelty without bounds, but he lied to his momma in those letters. "You only write your momma the good stuff," he said, and he didn't have to explain.

I wanted her to believe that everything I did was warm and safe and clean, just sitting around telling tales, waiting for room service. How could I tell her that I had spent the past two weeks, even the past ten years, searching out the homeless, the hopeless, the eternally damned? How could I tell her that her scrapbook was hopelessly out of date, that, just a few days ago, a streetwise photographer named Michelle Agins had told me to get my happy ass back in the van on a particularly vicious corner, not just because I might get myself killed, but get her killed, get everyone with us killed. How could I describe to her the look in the eyes of inner-city boys who paid for their funerals in advance, because they did not expect to live beyond their teens, who killed because someone stepped on their sneakers or looked at them hard. How do you go to a woman who lives at the foot of a mountain of sadness and shovel more around her ankles, the sadnesses of strangers? No. I left the phone on its hook.

I would call her Sunday, and tell her I went up to Harlem to eat turkey wings and cornbread at a place called Sylvia's, that New York was just one Big Rock Candy Mountain where the people talked slow so that I could understand, that they ran everything I wrote on the front page, both of them. That, I thought, was all she needed to know. When I wrote a happy story, I would send it to her with a hundred-dollar bill taped to the inside, and she would show the newspaper around and put the hundred under her mattress. She had three. Country people never throw away a mattress. They just stack 'em up on the bed, higher and higher, the new one on top. If you die in your sleep, you are that much closer to heaven, from Jump Street.

It was past ten o'clock by then, and she would have been asleep an hour, anyway. If it was this cold here it would be pretty cold down there, too. She would have let the dogs into the house, and left the water trickling in the sink, so that those patched-together pipes wouldn't freeze and burst again.

She would get up at five to put wood in the heater, which would have nothing but coals left by then. She would think about making biscuits and she might even get the lard can and the flour out, but she would put them back, because there is no need to fix a big breakfast to sit and eat by yourself. Sometimes she lets the fire go completely out, and has to start up again with a few slivers of pine and wadded up pages of the only newspaper she has ever taken, the *Jacksonville News*. It is a fine newspaper, she tells everyone, and good kindling. My son used to work there, she tells them. Maybe you remember him? He wrote about the ball games. He works in New York now, but I ain't real sure what he does. They don't sell it here. And he don't say.

❀   ❀   ❀

I watched the news at eleven, and the window for a while after that. I knew that across town, near the United Nations, the homeless would be spreading their blankets over the hot steam from the sewer grates, retiring for the evening. On Madison Avenue they would pull cardboard into the recessed foyers of the stores, and lie down just inches from the wealth that glinted on the other side of the glass. Down in the Meat Packing District, transvestite hookers would prance from car to car, nearly naked, their skin turning bone white in the cold.

I picked up the phone and called my girlfriend in Florida. I asked her to tell me that, where she was, it was warm. She said no, it was cold down there, too. They were afraid the orange trees would freeze.

17

Saturdays in October

In the beginning, I almost never wrote about killing, about misery. I wrote about violence, yes, about huge men trying to pound each other into mush and scattered teeth. What I wrote was football, which was short of killing, usually, even in the South. People have said it is what we do now instead of dueling. That is untrue. It is not so refined a violence as that. It is what we do instead of rioting.

I miss it, when I am away. Before the hot, wet air even begins to give way to the odd cool breeze, before the oaks and maples have begun to turn even the slightest bit red and gold, football banishes summer and announces, with crashing cymbals and an earth-quaking "Roll Tide," that it is now, officially, fall.

In that hurried season, on rectangles of ragged grass and wild onions and on the unnatural welcome mat of Astroturf, I have seen some things.

In Birmingham, I saw Charles White run for what seemed like a thousand yards against the Crimson Tide, helping USC beat Alabama like an ugly redheaded stepchild on a lovely fall Saturday in 1978. ABC telegraphed our shame to the entire nation, and grown men and women cried. To this day, I blame Charlie White for edging Coach Paul "Bear" Bryant a little closer to the grave.

In Athens, I watched Herschel Walker hammer the Auburn defense between the historic hedges, and then soar like some great red bird on third-and-short, the big men down below reaching for him like fat children leaping for a fist full of Sugar Daddies. Georgia fans, obnoxious in the first place, were unbearable for a long, long time because of Herschel.

In Auburn, the Loveliest Village on the Plain, I watched Bo Jackson run over pretty much everybody. He didn't do Bear much good either, I suspect.

But the greatest running back I ever saw was Boyce Callahan, number 33, listed at 160 pounds in the program at Jacksonville State University. He may have gone 145, with a pound of butterbeans in each pocket. He ran like a worm and got the mortal hell beat out of him almost every game, but he made Little All-American. My uncle John would take me to the home games once or twice a year, to see him put on a show. He would sweep the corner and get murdered. He would sweep the other corner and someone would knock his helmet off his head. Then they would run him up the middle and he would be stopped dead, and you would think it was time to call the ambulance. Then, all of a sudden you would see a single red jersey squirt out of the pile, free and clear. He would cock his head back, and everyone in the crowd would shout "It's Boyce!" and he was gone. He couldn't keep his socks pulled up and he had the scraggliest set of sideburns I have ever seen outside of prison, but he was a runnin' son of a bitch. We would even go to see him in the rain. People in front of us would raise their umbrellas and blot out the field, and Uncle John would grumble disgustedly that "we would see some football, if wasn't for all these doggone parasols."

My whole life I have wanted to believe that what I wrote about was important. I was not smart enough, as I drove from game to game in my native South, to recognize that I was doing precisely that. I sat in a thousand press boxes, ate a million bad hot dogs. On Fridays, it was high school football, under the lights. A poor boy was just as good as a rich one out there, as long as he could knock the tailback's front teeth out, and in the stands deacons shared space with men with beer on their breath. Men came straight from work in shirts that had their first name over the breast pocket. Women and men held their breath on every play, waiting for their sons to get up when bodies collided with a sound like banging two-by-fours.

I watched it all, night after night, on fields named for town doctors and dead coaches and benefactors, where parking cost a dollar and benefited the March of Dimes. "Press," I told the ol' boys at the ticket gate, and they let me in as if I had intoned, "Opennnnn Sesssaaaaammmmeeee." I watched it all from the press box, mostly, but that did not mean I had a seat. The press box was really reserved for the announcer, always a homer, and the announcer's buddy, and the buddy's feeble uncle, and the band director, whom they all secretly regarded as a sissy, and the band director's buddy, who was, the ol' boys believed, most definitely so. Either way, it was hard to find any room for the press in the press box. At Ranburne, I sat on a plastic bucket. At Vincent, I sat on a two-by-four. I shivered in warped plywood boxes and plugged my ears as fat boys with tubas wedged around the middle labored through a rendition of, well, something. I think it might have been "Saturday in the Park." I quoted coaches whose only comments were, week after week, "We gave 110 percent," and I never thought to ask how that was possible. I kept terrible statistics, causing coaches the next morning to shake their heads and go, "125 yards rushing, my ass." In the rush of deadline I misspelled the names of linemen who recovered fumbles, boys who would never, ever get their name in the paper again, unless they got married or died.

On Saturdays, after a few hours sleep, it was college game day. I flew a million miles in single-engine planes with pilots who learned to soar in Vietnam but were prone to doze at the controls in the boredom of a Mississippi sky. I got food poisoning from a box lunch in Starkville, got run over on the sideline on an end-around in Tuscaloosa. I stood like a jackass and waited for some nineteen-year-old to speak a truth that I could include in my story, which would have been unbearable if I had been much older than nineteen myself. I was deafened by that damn cannon they shot off after every touchdown in Mississippi, and strained to hear Bryant mumble out of his post-game press conferences to a small army of reporters who would cut their wrists before they would ever write one negative word about that old man or the institution he represented. We worked eighteen-hour days, got paid twenty-one cents a mile to drive our cars to Martin, Tennessee, and Philadelphia, Mississippi, and stayed in hotels where you found palmetto bugs belly-up in the bathtub and Cheetos on the bedspread.

God, I would love to do it all over again.

Football is a cliché, down here. I do not believe that sport is the very essence of Southern life—I know God and work and family precede football, except perhaps on Alabama-Auburn game day—but what it really is, is the grandest of escapes from that life. For me, that escape took on a whole other meaning.

I would never have been a writer if not for it. I never, ever would have gotten into a journalism school, what with me having a C average and all. I am sure I would never have gotten a job. Some newspapers see sports as the toy factory, not serious journalism, so it can be trusted to those who did not go to Harvard, or even to the dentist regularly. All I know is, it was my way in, and looking back I realize that I never realized how lucky and blessed I was.

I wrote of heroes. The most popular man in Alabama most of my young life was not George Wallace but Bear Bryant (or, if you lived in the flatland to the south, Shug Jordan of Auburn). Even now, if you go to a bar or restaurant in Birmingham, you will eventually hear the water joke:

Saint Peter welcomes a man into heaven. The new arrival spots an old man in a houndstooth hat walking on water. "Is that Bear Bryant?" he reverently asks.

"No, that's God," Saint Peter says. "He only thinks He's Bear Bryant."

He had his own television show, sponsored by Coke and Golden Flake potato chips. You knew that because at the beginning of every show he opened up a bag of potato chips and set an open bottle of Coke on the table in front of him. He would mumble about how proud he was of this boy or that boy and what fine parents his momma and daddy were down there in Opp or Enterprise or Sylacauga as the game highlight film played across the screen. Then, in mid-mumble, one of his linebackers would separate some ball carrier from his spine and Bryant would shout out "Bingo!" like someone had jabbed him with a fork.

He was one of our legacies that we could be proud of, in a state hurting for them. What he died, my newspaper sent me to interview the man who dug his grave.

Until I was twenty-three, at progressively larger papers that never reached more than 30,000 in circulation, I wrote of sports. I dropped out of college because I had accomplished what I wanted from it—a coat-and-tie job—and lent my meager talents to the *Talladega Daily Home* and then the *Anniston Star.* They did not care that I did not have a college degree. I could spell, sort of. I worked cheap. I needed the work and loved the work too much to ask for overtime.

At nineteen, working for the *Talladega Daily Home,* I went on a road-trip to Atlanta to cover a stock car race with the immortal Tommy Hornsby, who was the sports editor and a drummer in a country rock band. He took me to my first topless bar. The dancer—there were only two and one was drunk—had long, pink scars on her wrists, and her breath smelled like Marlboros. I learned a lot from Tommy.

At twenty, I was working full-time for the best small newspaper in Alabama and one of the best in the country, the *Anniston Star.* The sports editor was a talented writer named Wayne Hester, who told me once that I could write some, and let me. I came to work the first day in a white pair of pants, a white shirt and a white slip-on tie. I looked like I was selling ice cream.

I wrote about everything from high school wrestling to country club golf, but what I loved was racing. Our newspaper office was a twenty-minute drive from Talladega International Motor Speedway, the world's fastest enclosed speedway, but the spirit of the sport then was strictly backwoods. Most of the drivers had learned it running likker in the mountains of the Carolinas, or had learned it from people who did. I wrote about Fireball Roberts, Richard Petty, Bobby Allison, Cale Yarborough, Buddy Baker, Junior Johnson. Even the names were grand. Coo Coo Marlin. Lake Speed. And, of course, my all-time favorite, Jimmy "Smut" Means, the one who was prone to hit the wall at Talladega, and live.

They ran bumper to bumper and door to door at two hundred miles an hour, and now and then one of them would die. Usually, but not always, it would be some no-name driver in second-rate equipment who just could not handle the speed, that fantastic speed. He would wobble a little on the turns that were banked so steep it was hard to even walk up them, and spin out, and meet Jesus on the wall, or on the bumper of a car that hit him broadside, what they called "gettin' T-boned."

They would be, unless they were famous, only a footnote in the story, because the race was what was important, and the winning of it. We always wrote them the same way, those stories. In the third or fourth paragraph would be: "The race was overshadowed by the death of (insert name here)." I didn't know any better. I should have done better. I should have written, in the first paragraph: "A man died here today, and a race was run."

But Lord, it was thrilling. The sound alone would rock you, like a billion angry hornets in a giant bucket, and every time the cars flashed around the track, death was just a twitch away.

I was slowly beginning to realize that the only thing that was worth writing about was living and dying and the trembling membrane in between. I have never been a ghoul. I have been so sickened by killing and dying that sleep was just one more dream in bed at 4 A.M. But even then, I was drawn to those stories. There was something about the rich darkness of it, of that struggle by people at risk, people in trouble, that made all other stories seem trivial. They were the most important stories in the newspaper. I wanted to write them, only them.

The managing editor of the *Anniston Star* let me move to the state desk when I was still in my early twenties, into a newsroom dominated by Harvard, Yale, Columbia and assorted other pointy heads who came South for the invaluable experience they would glean from writing about people that some of them held largely in contempt. The *Star* drew them down here because of its reputation as a great place to learn. The paper's owner and editor, H. Brandt Ayers, got some good stories out of them before they moved on, because while some of them treated the South as if they were on safari, some of them did great work. They caught people doing bad things. When some grinning crook on the county commission tried to abuse his power and line his pockets, they wrote about it. They did about two years on their tour of duty in the heart of darkness, living in the pool houses and basement apartments of the well-off people on the East Side, and then moved on to the bigger but not always better newspapers. People like me, without any academic credentials on us, would stay behind. It was the system, or at least it always had been, and I did not even try not to be bitter. I had long talks with the sage senior editor, Cody Hall, who made it plain that I should be proud of who I was. "Life is too short to dance with an ugly woman," and my ugly woman was my own envy.

But the fact is, on hindsight, the Yankees were mostly okay. I ate barbecue and coconut pie with them, and beneath their Yankeeness, I found genuine concern for people who were poorer and weaker. The *Star*'s founder, Colonel Ayers, had believed it was a newspaper's responsibility to be an attorney for the least influential, the weakest, of its readership, and there were many, many people who passed through the doors of that place who read those words on the editorial page and took them to heart. I worked for the state editor, a young man named Randy Henderson who had the patience not to fire me, a smart and decent man with ethics you couldn't dent with a wrecking ball. But mostly, like I said, he was patient. It is a great virtue, where I am concerned.

The first story I wrote as a news reporter, I wrote about deer hunters who were killing themselves in the woods by accident, at a record rate. I described a man's attempt to drag his friend out of the woods, bleeding to death, after he shot him. It was hard, harder than anything I had ever done. The managing editor, Chris Waddle, told me it was a fine newspaper story, and I had my first taste of that odd mixed emotion, of pride in the work, of seeing your story at the top of the page, and of that terrible sadness that the words contained.

Because I was a working reporter, I did a lot of other, less dramatic stories. I covered the county commission in Cleburne County, and city council meetings at Anniston, where my favorite politician of all time, Pink Junior Wood, a barber by trade, sat on the dais. It was one of the grand things, of being a newspaperman in the South: just being able to write at least once a week the words "Pink Junior Wood." I wrote about speed trap towns and cockfighting rings and accidents on the lonely, twisting roads. I interviewed the mayor of Montgomery, Emory Folmar, who was so conservative that he compelled black people to vote in droves for George Wallace.

I continued to swap notions and stories and make friends with the Yankee reporters, and made fun of them even as they made fun of me. The experience of working shoulder to shoulder with so many educated and privileged young people was good for me, I am sure, but the chip I had carried on my shoulder for a lifetime grew in those years to about the size of a concrete block. To me, they had everything, and I am sure I resented it, foolishly, childishly. I could only write, a little bit.

After the *Birmingham News* hired Randy Henderson away, I worked for a metro editor who didn't think a lot of me. I am sure he had his reasons. But one meeting still sears me whenever I think about it. The managing editor had offered me the city reporter's job, about the best job on staff, because he thought I was good and because he did not care that I had never been to Princeton. The metro editor had another reporter in mind, a talented young woman who went swimming naked at pool parties. The metro editor took me for a drink after work, and told me, to my face, that I was not sophisticated enough to be the city reporter. I should have cussed him, but instead I just sat there and let it pass, hating myself for it. The next morning I walked into the managing editor's office and told him that, yes, I would like to be the city reporter, thank you very much.

The fact is that, in some ways, the metro editor was probably right. I had no business being a reporter. I had six months of college and four years sitting in press boxes trying to get the quarterback's name right. All I knew how to do was tell stories on paper, and didn't have even one dollop of what one respected editor, Basil Penny, called "jelly." Basil

explained "jelly" as a concoction of a lot of things, but the main ingredi-
ent was pretension. Me and him, we were just plain biscuit.

But the main reason I took the other editor's insult was because I had
no choice. I needed the job. By then I had a house payment, responsibilities. I had a $250 electric bill.

I had, by then, a wife.

18

White tuxedoes

She was as pretty as sunshine on roses. She was small, delicate, and her hair was almost black. She had huge brown eyes, and a big red Pontiac Le Mans she used to drive me around in when my rolling junk, third-hand muscle cars were dead on the side of the road. My girl cousins said she looked like a porcelain doll, that she was perfect. She was smart—made all A's in high school and college—and nice, too. I'm pretty sure she still is.

Her daddy read Rex Stout novels and her momma made the best macaroni and cheese casserole I've ever had. They raised their only child in a middle-class neighborhood of brick houses and well-fed cats. The dogs all had collars, and didn't bite.

We met in Jacksonville, when I was working for the *Jacksonville News*. She was a sophomore at Jacksonville State, training to be a social worker and working part-time at the Weaver City Hall, answering phones. Her daddy kind of liked me, I thought. Her momma kind of didn't, but that is often the way of it, cliché or not.

Not long after I got my first good full-time job, at the *Anniston Star*, I proposed. I got the ring at Service Merchandise, on credit. When I gave it to her, she cried.

I proposed standing up. I would have gotten down on my knees, but they were tore up on the inside so bad from playing ball, I knew that if I ever got down there, one or the other of my knees would lock and she would have to help me up. She didn't mind.

I was not afraid of getting married. Getting married was what you did if you were any damn good, at least in that culture I grew up in. I was not my daddy, I kept telling myself. I would not be him.

I was in my early twenties. I had a good job. I had done as much of what we tactfully refer to as "runnin' around" as a man can, without being shotgunned to death climbing out of someone's bedroom window. It was time, I believed.

I was no kind of playboy. It was just that, unlike a lot of my brethren, I learned early on that there is no way to make someone want you if they don't. You can either waste time fantasizing about how to win your woman back, or you move on. It might not be the stuff of love stories, but in the time it takes to dive to the depths of misery in a bad relationship, sulk on the bottom, and then come clawing out for air, I could have thoroughly enjoyed being dumped three or four more times, as bad as that sounds. I was not a heart-on-your-sleeve kind of boy. I did not write love letters, did not sit and wonder why they left me or I left them. They came and went by an average of about two a year, often—you could time it by a clock—when they found out who I really was, where I came from.

She did not seem to care about my shaky reputation or the fact I was what some people would have called, but only behind my back, white trash. She treated my momma with respect. She did not seem to think she was better than her, than me, than the other people I cared about. She had a good heart, an open one.

We got married at Weaver First United Methodist Church, a fifteen-minute drive from my home, in July. I wore a white tuxedo, and more erudite people might think I looked like a fool. At the time, I thought I looked damned spiffy.

When she walked down the aisle it took my breath away. I had heard of that happening my whole life, and I thought it was just something people said. But it really did. It took my breath away.

My brothers and Uncle John and one of the best men I ever knew, Tony Estes, stood up with me. Tony was married to my cousin Jackie and used to loan me clothes to date in, because I didn't have any. I would have asked my uncle Ed to stand up with me, but I thought he didn't want to. I should have asked him. Then all the men who had ever meant anything to me in my young life would have been there, in one photograph.

My momma came and sat in the front row, the first time I had seen her dressed up in my life. She wore a bright-colored dress that looked like it was maybe tangerine sherbet, and someone had curled her hair. I was proud of her.

I have given more thought to buying cars than I gave to getting married; it just seemed time, and she seemed like the right one. I had my last-second doubts; I wanted to cut and run. But I stood there and took it like a man. We drove down to Panama City, Florida, for a honeymoon at the Silver Sands Hotel. We came back sunburned, to set up house.

We lived in a three-bedroom brick house that was the nicest thing I had ever lived in. Her daddy helped us with the down payment, I think because I horrified her whole family by casually mentioning that maybe we should just get a trailer. We had brown wall-to-wall carpeting, three ill-tempered, ill-mannered Siamese cats, which I secretly despised, and a huge Saint Bernard dog named King, who I loved. She went to school and worked, and I just worked. She got her degree, and I was proud for her.

Every summer, we went to Panama City with her parents and grandparents and stayed in their time-share condominium. Every winter, we had finger sandwiches, punch and divinity candy at their house on Christmas Eve. They were nice people, her family. I was grateful for it, all of it. All you had to do to become a part of the middle class, I now knew, was work hard, act right, and sink roots so deep that you can never, ever budge.

In 1985, when I was in my mid-twenties, I got a job offer from the *Birmingham News,* the biggest newspaper in Alabama, at almost twice my salary. It was only seventy-three miles down the road, but the journey and the new job took all my time. I worked for my old editor, Randy Henderson, who wanted me to do big stories. He called it swinging for the fences, and suddenly I didn't mind working until midnight or getting home after 2 A.M. I won some awards, covered a wall in them.

It was about that time, one night sitting in the living room, that she told me she might be having a baby. I tried to shape a smile even as something that felt like hot lead seemed to course through my chest, and I thought that I would surely die.

We had talked about having children, someday, but someday had seemed like such a great, safe distance away. The thought that it was happening did not just frighten me, it terrified me, consumed me. And I couldn't say a word. For days, even after that hot-lead feeling had cooled, it lay like a weight on my chest.

It was several days before we found out it was a false alarm. She looked at me, not accusing, just knowingly, and said, "Aren't you disappointed, just a little?" I lied to her and said I was.

I withdrew from her then, or maybe we just withdrew from each other. She said we lived more like roommates than husband and wife, and she was right. I told her it was only because I worked so hard, so long. She was smarter than that. The months went by. One night, early morning, actually, I came home from working on a story about a prison riot. I was exhausted and hungry. I was standing in the glow of the refrigerator, making a bologna sandwich, when she came out and said that we needed to talk.

I just nodded my head. The next day I took my clothes and my dog and left. I was my father's son, after all.

I was not mean like him. I got drunk twice a year, three times at the most. I had never done violence against her, in any way. It was not in my character. We never yelled, we seldom fought. I often worked overtime and did magazine stories on the side to make a decent living, and was determined, absolutely, to surpass my father's sorry standards for being a husband. Still I failed. I failed in thinking that was all there was to it.

It ended, I have told myself and told others, because the only thing I had time for in my life was the work, that the only passion in me was for it, those lovely words. That is partly true. I love writing the way some men love women.

But the greater truth is that I could not bear the thought of someday having a child, of having that child depend on me, rely on me, need me. I would have, I am sure, dragged myself through hell to give that child everything I could, but somewhere, deep, deep in the place we keep our greatest shame and fear, I was still afraid I might, just might, be like him. Not mean. Only weak.

It is a funny thing. I have been hurt doing my job. I have stood in a crowd of massed bodies, knowing that at any second the mob's mood could turn and they would tear me apart. But I cannot remember being so afraid as I was that day in that living room, sitting on the Naugahyde couch by the console TV, pictures of cats on the wall.

She married again, several years later. I heard that she had a baby girl. I am sure she is a smart and pretty child, if she takes after her momma.

Some year or so after the divorce, she walked up behind me in a grocery store parking lot. She kissed me and smiled at me, and that made me glad. I know she does not hate me. I was only wasted time.

You do not hate the time you waste; it evokes a much more passive emotion than that. You only wish you had it back, like a quarter in an unlucky slot machine.

19

The price tag on heaven

Some things, growing up in Alabama, you just know. If you need a
house moved, you call Drennan Smith, who can jack even a Victorian off its foundation, put it on a big truck and haul it wherever you
want it if his tires don't blow: there is nothing more pitiful than a house
broke down at the side of a road. If you need to catch enough crappie to
feed a family reunion, you go to Cherokee County and fish the backwater with minnows. If you need a drink, bad, on a Sunday, when all the legal whiskey is locked away, you can go to Aunt Hattie's in backwoods
Calhoun County, where the calendar has no meaning if you have the
cash. And if you need a new set of false teeth and you don't have a whole
lot of disposable income, you go to Pell City, the affordable denture cap-
ital of the world. Ask practically anyone where I grew up where they got
their dentures, and they will say Pell City. Sometimes they will even spit
out their set to show you the craftsmanship.

We all try to buy our way into heaven, one way or the other. Some use
the genuine currency of faith. But others, like me, try to barter, as if the
great Hereafter was a swap meet in the clouds. Me, I'd always figured
that if I did right by my momma, I had a shot. I tried to buy my way in
with a set of dentures.

148

By 1986, I had not lived in my momma's house for a long time, yet I had never truly left home. I was always close, always within a few minutes' drive if she needed me. Any embarrassment I ever felt of being the son of a woman who took in ironing and scrubbed floors was long, long gone. I was ashamed of myself now. I tried to make up for it.

I was making enough money now to help her with little things, like groceries and doctor bills, trying to bribe my way into Glory a fifty-dollar bill at a time. At Christmas I filled shopping carts to the brim with hams and cakes and other delicacies, things I knew she wouldn't buy for herself, couldn't buy for herself on the income she had from the ironing and the few dollars she made canning jelly, hot peppers and watermelon pickles. She loved the cakes. She is the only person I have ever met who actually eats fruitcake.

I bought her what she needed, from electric heaters to new televisions, and I gave her money even though she never asked, not once in her life. She always said the same thing when I handed her some bills: "I feel like a bum." I told her she was being silly; I thought I was a big shot, knocking down a fat four hundred dollars a week, looking after my momma and all. But now and then something would happen to bring me back to reality.

I remember the time I saw her squinting at her Bible, holding the pages so close to her eyes that it almost bumped her nose. I told her we would go see the eye doctor over in Gadsden. A few weeks later, as she sat in the examination chair, the doctor asked her how long it had been since her last examination, and since her last prescription for eyeglasses.

"I believe it was 1963," she said.

The eye doctor looked at me like I was the lowest form of life on the planet.

Most of my life, she had been seeing and reading with those magnifying glasses, the kind you buy in dime stores, and going half-blind. I never even noticed.

We got her two pairs of new specs and she asked if she could get one pair that didn't have bifocal lenses, a pair just for reading. I asked her why, since the bifocals were for reading, too, and for at least a full minute she wouldn't answer me. Finally, she fessed up to me that the reason she didn't want the bifocals was because they made her look like an old woman. I smiled inside at that. Even after so many years, after she had been through so much, there was still an ounce or so of vanity there.

I saw it again a few years later, when I tried to get her to go to the dentist and get some dentures. She had always tried to take care of her teeth, but what money there was for a dentist went to us. By the time she was in her fifties her teeth were so bad she could eat only mush, another thing I failed to notice when I came home on the weekends from Birmingham. I told her she had to go to the dentist—if you cannot eat what you want in the South, life is not worth living—and she told me she would just as soon as the weather got cool. It got cool for ten years or so before she finally gave in; maybe the pain just got too bad to stand. (It is a peculiarity of my people that they refuse to undergo any kind of surgery—that includes tooth-pulling—in the spring or summer, when it is hot weather. Or maybe it is not a peculiarity at all. None of us had air-conditioning, most of my life. If you are going to be laid up, bedridden, it is best to recover in winter.)

The dentist pulled every tooth in her head. But instead of letting the dentist who pulled her old teeth order and fit her false teeth, she went to Pell City to get herself a set of cut-rate dentures, to save me money, she said. Pell City, being world famous and all, was the logical choice. She got a shiny new set that looked mighty fine sitting on a shelf.

They didn't fit. They made her gag. On the way home, she got so sick at her stomach that she had to get my aunt Edna to pull over to the side of the road. She retched and the new dentures, top and bottom set, went sailing like two porcelain birds into the weeds. I know it was not a bit funny then, two aging women searching through the weeds for my momma's new teeth, but when I think about it now, in the privacy of my own home, I laugh until my stomach hurts. I have this picture in my mind of what might have happened if a state trooper had pulled up and asked them, "Ladies, can I help y'all?" And my momma had said, "Yes, Officer, you can help us look for my teeth."

For months after that, I would call and ask her if she was getting used to her teeth, and she would say—I swear I am not making this up—that they hurt her too much to wear when she was talking or eating. But, she said proudly, she had learned to sleep in them. I told her she had it all backwards, that they were designed for daytime use, and it hurt her feelings. But the fact is, what good are teeth if you can't chew with them in your mouth, only dream.

I hope, sometimes at least, she dreams of pork chops.

I do not order my momma to do hardly anything—I have no authority—but I ordered her to go back and get some new teeth that she could wear without getting sick to her stomach. She said, "Okay, as soon as it gets cool." That was years ago, and we are still waiting for the temperature to drop sufficiently. It must be that global warming business.

She is not a stubborn woman, on most things. On some things, you cannot budge her with a pickup truck. The teeth issue, I know, might never be resolved.

Anyway, I did what I could. Every winter, I bought her a big, warm, fuzzy bathrobe, the men's size from Sears, because she was so tall. I bought her window fans, and a new toilet. I bought her a hot-water heater, and another one when it wore out. In a Christian bookstore in Nashville—I was killing time, waiting to interview a senator—I bought her a gold cross with a tiny Jesus on it. When someone stole it out of our living room, I bought her another one. They were tiny things, inconsequential things. I did them because I was supposed to, because it was my turn to do things for her, and because I was trying to make up for any wrong I had ever done her.

But the one thing I wanted most to do, to get for her, was beyond my reach.

All her life, as a child, as a young woman, as an aging one dozing in her new teeth, she had lived in other people's houses.

Sometimes through cheap rent, sometimes through charity, she had lived beholden. The closest thing we had ever had to a home of our own was a small trailer we lived in for only a few months, when I was a boy. I wanted her to have a house, a decent house, but I had chosen careers poorly in that regard. I had picked the one profession, except for maybe teaching, where you can climb and climb and pile up honors to the moon, and still be poor as field dirt.

But someday, I promised her, I would make it happen. We were sitting in the living room of that house where I could stand in the middle of the borrowed living room and touch both facing walls, and I told her: "Momma, one of these days I'm gonna buy you a house." She just nodded, as if to say, "That's nice, dear," and I shut my mouth. I know that, to her, I might as well have said that Jesus had just ridden down Quintard Avenue on a bicycle. She didn't believe me. She just thought I was dreaming again, like that boy in the field searching for four-leaf clovers. She is a woman who has learned not to believe in promises, or dreamers.

I do not want to sound ungrateful to the people who, through their charity, gave us a place to live. If it were not for them, I am sure we would have been the first homeless family in Calhoun County. For decades, my aunts and uncles helped pay her electric bill. My uncle Ed gives her twenty dollars a week, holding it out of the money he tithes to the church. He figures the Lord won't mind.

She never said she wanted a house. She never even hinted. But if you could have seen her face when we rode down the rural roads of our county, heard her talk about how this house is an A-frame and that one is a Victorian, about how this one will need painting in a few years and that one has just got a new covering of aluminum siding, you would know. For a woman who didn't get out hardly at all, she knew every house on Nisbet Lake Road, on Roy Webb Road, on Cove Road, any road. She knew who lived there then and who used to live there. She would look at the roofs and pass judgment on whether it was worn out or just stained by the sweetgum trees.

She is the daughter of a carpenter, after all, a man who lived his whole life building other people's houses and never owned one of his own, either. I guess she never expected to own one; maybe a little bit, before my daddy, when she still dared to dream.

When I was a teenager, she used to order catalogs from the Jim Walter Company, which was famous for building "affordable housing." These were not fancy double-wides made of tin and particle board, but neat, nice, small, real-wood houses, usually white, with porches. She would flip through them like a child flipping through a toy catalog, wishing. But there was no money for land, even if we could have ever saved enough to build anything bigger than a dog house. You can dream on welfare. You can hope as you take in ironing. It is just less painful if you don't.

I could have bought her one on credit, could have been careful with my money and made the mortgage payments. But like her, I am wary of things that seem too good, too much. I was afraid that I would get her in a decent house, and something would happen, taking away my ability to pay for it, and she would have it taken away.

Nothing that has ever happened in my own life explains why I felt that way—I had been lucky as sin my whole life—but if you really do grow up as what some people call white trash, you grow up knowing that it might all turn to shit at any second. The only way I knew to make sure of it, was to buy it outright.

I got started late, almost too late. I had never saved a dime. When I was married, we squeaked by like everyone else, month to month. When I was single again I wasted much of what was left from rent, bills and barbecue on 1966 Mustangs, anchor women and former Shades Valley High School majorettes. I have never lived lavishly. I still don't. My possessions, then and now, consisted of homemade book shelves, books, a couch, a chair, a TV, a stereo, a softball glove and just enough clothes to get by. I never owned a suit until I was twenty-nine. I owned two ties, then, but I'm up to four now. I didn't wear jewelry; still don't. My cars, never top-tier classics but rolling, pretty junk, seldom cost more than four thousand dollars, and I bought them on credit.

I seldom took a vacation, and then only to Fort Walton Beach, for a few days. I had never been out of the country, except one trip down to Mexico, when I was covering a football game in Texas. If it hadn't been for women, hell, I could have been a monk or at least a Hare Krishna, for all the money I spent. I already have the tennis shoes.

The problem was, I picked the lowest-paying profession in America.

Then I compounded it by waiting, I guess because I was selfish. I should have sold insurance, maybe, or worked in a bank, or maybe gotten on at Goodyear, or the mills in Birmingham. Instead, I wrote stories.

In 1987, I opened a savings account in Birmingham.

We were men by now, my brothers and me.

Sam, that indestructible object that the worst of life had failed to even nick, was building his life like a man laying brick and didn't need me or anybody. He had married Teresa, a thoughtful, quiet girl who made strawberry shortcake that would literally melt in your mouth. I went to the hospital to see their baby, Meredith Marie, named for my momma, Margaret Marie. She was so tiny I quickly passed her over to an aunt, afraid I would break her. Sam had life by the throat and was squeezing it. He would be fine until he gave out, and I knew he would never, never do that.

In many ways, Mark, my baby brother, was a stranger to me. I had known he had quit school, but that was not exactly unheard of in our world. I figured he would make a living with his own sweat, like Sam. Instead of trying to talk him out of it, I put on a bad tie and wrote stories for strangers, about strangers.

I heard about him only through my momma's worries. He drank too much, but considering our heritage, it would be remarkable only if he did not drink, and cuss, and fight.

Only the years would determine whether he would reach some uneasy peace with life, as some of us had, or whether it would burn him up.

I should have seen the signs sooner that there was no peace in him at all. He had a souped-up Chevy Nova he bought from our cousin Charlie Couch, and every time he took me for a ride he pushed it as hard as it would go without blowing up, not just driving fast, but punishingly so. I noticed there were always beer bottles in the back floorboard, always, and not three or four, but piles, and a six-pack of warm beer. He didn't give a damn that it was warm. That should have told me a lot.

But I always drove home to Birmingham more or less assured that, unless he broke down on a railroad track some night, he was fine. My uncle Ed gave him steady work. My uncle John helped him buy some land over near Websters Chapel, and he began to build a house.

I wrote stories and played softball and spent time with a twenty-one-year-old Catholic girl on long, sweet weekends in New Orleans. Some of the big papers started to notice me. They sent me letters, asking me if I had ever considered exploring the opportunities of journalism outside Alabama.

When I finally bothered to pay attention to my little brother again, when I finally bothered to halfway give a damn, I couldn't find him. The boy had vanished, swept away on that same river of alcohol that carried away our father. Just looking into his eyes, those unfocused, too-old eyes, broke my heart right in two. And for the next ten years I would hold out empty hope that he would change, quit, find Jesus, do anything except destroy himself, a swallow at a time.

I have never had a drink by myself in my life.

I drink in crowds. When I was younger I thought whiskey made me charming, and bulletproof. Once, in a bar in Birmingham when I was twenty-five, and stupid, I drank so much of it that I took a pistol away from a man who was waving it around at the clientele, convinced that no harm could come to me.

But I never, ever drink alone. I am afraid I will like it too much. I am afraid it will numb me and warm me and soothe me and ultimately seduce me. I am scared to death that it will take the pains and the doubts and the fears away, that it will make me like myself just too damn much.

I fear, mostly, I would find in it the absolution that people on both sides of my family have found, for generations. It is a thing in my blood, in my genes, like blond hair and blue eyes. And once you embrace it, behind some closed door, you will never escape it.

I believe it made my daddy not care, that it made him leave her without milk or money or a way to live, or to see a doctor. I believe it. Because whatever weakness he had in him, whatever devils rode his back, a man just don't do that sober.

I remember a time. I was in a hotel room in Miami, late at night, dog tired, keyed-up and sick. I was just back from a few months in Haiti, from writing about killing, mostly. I couldn't sleep, my head hurt too much to read and the television just jangled my nerves.

I sought distraction, if nothing else, in the mini bar. I slipped the key into the little refrigerator and it swung open to reveal a wonderland of liquor, in neat rows of tiny bottles. There was amber Scotch and yellow tequila and clear gin, and a vodka that seemed almost silver. They were pretty. I reached in and got a baby bottle of Wild Turkey, cracked it open and poured it in a water glass. I distinctly remember raising it to my lips, and the smell, like smoke and brown sugar and something stronger, The Spirit in it. And I gagged. I poured it into the sink and rinsed the glass.

Then I got me some jelly beans and a glass of water, and I watched *Rat Patrol* and infomercials until the sun finally fought its way over the dark line of Biscayne Bay.

20

Under Vulcan's hammer

By the time I got to Birmingham, its great story was already frozen in stone. Kelly Ingram Park is a place of statues now, quiet, peaceful, unless you are one of those people to whom history screams. Old black men sit on the park benches to feel the sun on their face, and discuss whether or not that statue of the Reverend Doctor Martin Luther King Junior really looks like him. It stands on ground, what many people in this city see as holy ground, where civil rights marchers were pummeled by batons, blasted with fire hoses and gnawed by dogs, on the orders of a one-eyed little man named Bull Connor. A few feet away is the venerable old Sixteenth Street Baptist Church, where a Klansman's bomb killed four little girls. History might not scream to a white man here, but it whispers.

It is a yuppie town now. At lunchtime, 20th Street is a parade of black wingtips and sensible pumps. The sky has not been darkened by the steel mills for a long time. A world-class medical school, not the furnaces, defines this green and pretty city. The very name Birmingham will always be shorthand for the worst of the civil rights movement, I suppose, but when I was there, in the last part of the 1980s, the city had abandoned even the memory of men like Theophilus Eugene "Bull"

Connor, as I wrote then, "like a gun left behind at the scene of the crime."

When I worked for the *Birmingham News,* I wrote a story about it, twenty-five years after that tumultuous time. I described the serenity of the park, the significance of the monuments to black people who suffered there.

"For Connor," I wrote, "there is no memorial, no sign he was even here. If the intersection of 16th Street and Sixth Avenue North is a shrine to the civil rights movement, it is Connor's unmarked grave."

The night the story ran, I got a call from a man who only said: "You the one wrote that article on Bull Connor?"

"Yes," I said.

"Well," the voice said, "you can kiss my ass." Then he hung up, like he had accomplished something.

Sometimes in this world, you don't get the whole dog. Now and then, you have to settle for the tail.

I would have loved to have had some part in covering the events of 1963. I know few real newspeople, of any color, who would not have wanted to be part of that story. But I was born too late for it. Instead of seeing it, describing it, I am awakened twenty-five years too late by some jackass who wants to turn back time. I laid the phone back in its cradle thinking that I may as well be living in Cleveland.

But the fact is, I learned to do the big story in Birmingham. The big story is the one that anchors Page One, the one that can make careers. I wrote them and they put them in the paper, and you cannot ask for more than that in this business. I wrote about the slow deaths of coal mining towns with a business writer named Dean Barber who had a dog named Teton and would one day learn to play the banjo. I wrote about the state of Alabama's shameful funding of social programs that allowed thousands of children to go neglected and be abused, sharing the byline with a reporter named Mike Oliver who had a good fallaway jumpshot and damned good sources. With Mike, I went into a prison to write about the ill-conceived design plan that made it a house of glass, that allowed prison employees to be trapped, stabbed, raped. I wrote about an Alabama preacher wrongly convicted of killing his young wife, and cleared his name.

The stories were important, serious, in a time when the word *reporter* did not conjure images of some doofus asking a woman with a ring in her nose why she professed love to a man with a giant safety pin through his eyebrow and claimed that he once glimpsed Elvis in a plate of scrambled eggs. My education in serious journalism that was born at Jacksonville and Talladega and nurtured at Anniston was, for more than three years, applied here. I did not expect it to last for long—I was a fairly liberal minded young man with a short temper, working for a conservative newspaper where at least two of the high-ranking editors considered me a smartass and a showoff—but I made it hard for them to fire me.

This was a midsize daily where many people came expecting to work out their careers and retire. Most of my colleagues came from the journalism schools of Alabama and Auburn, not Harvard and Yale. I was more at home here, even though some of them hated my guts eventually, which is the sad nature of our business. That chip on my shoulder was still there. I could feel it every time some reporter with "Roll Tide" on his breath asked me where I went to school, but it was not nearly so heavy now. I was proving myself on the front page of the newspaper every few Sundays.

I had fun. I made lasting friends. I stood up with Greg Garrison when he married Tracy from the art department, and threw a bachelor party that ended ignominiously when he, drunk as Cooter Brown on the one night of a man's life when it is more or less acceptable, bit a nudie dancer on the behind and got us tossed out of the bar by one of the biggest men I have ever seen. Greg is the religion writer. I ate enough barbecue with Mike Bolton, the outdoors writer, to kill a normal man. He got some sauce on his shirt once, and used Wite-Out to repair the damage. I admired Mike.

I rode with Jeff Hanson in a Volkswagen minibus to cover a tornado, and the wind blew so hard that the van swerved unnervingly over the highway. To keep our courage up, we sang every bad country song we had ever heard. He sang off-key, or maybe I did, but our harmony was so bad I had to keep yelling, "Shut up, Jeff, I'm tryin' to sing."

I had talks about the value of collard greens to the male digestive tract with a great man, a nightside editor named Ben House, who lamented the loss of the old-fashioned bathrooms that used to serve the historic *News* building. To hear him tell it, they were marble-lined palaces, an escape from the rigors of the newsroom. They were torn down, eventually, and replaced with bland, modern facilities. Purely because, Ben said, "some people just can't appreciate an elegant shithouse."

I rented an apartment on the fashionable Southside—in Birmingham, you could be pretty fashionable for $245 a month—with a view of Vulcan from the bedroom window. Vulcan was a massive cast-iron statue atop Red Mountain, the god of the forge, a relic from the days when the blast furnaces still smoked. He was supposed to point, I believe, a spear to the heavens, but a long time ago someone figured that he should hold a beacon that would shine red when there was a fatality on the highways and green when no one had died. For a while, I believe, he held a giant Coke bottle. Maybe that is just legend. I don't know. I do know that there was talk once of dressing him up in a giant pair of blue jeans, because people in the neighboring city of Homewood were sick and tired of being perpetually mooned by a mythical Greek deity. Vulcan, it is true, had nothing on under his apron, which was all that prevented him from scandalizing the downtown as well.

I didn't have much of a home life. I didn't have much furniture, and for six months I made it just fine with a bed and a cast-off recliner. I never, ever cooked a meal. I had no pots. Once, I heated a can of peas in the can, and made such a mess I never turned the stove on again. I would have young ladies over and they would look with bald suspicion on the bare apartment, and I would explain that I was just too damn busy lately to shop for antiques.

This is one of those places where it would be better to lie, but the truth is that in those three years and change I was there, I was not always a nice man. I was just good-looking enough, and maybe just smart enough, not to be lonely. I spent time with very nice and smart and pretty young women who knew going in that I was a poor bet for anything permanent, and I lived up to their expectations.

I was not much better with my friends. Joe Kiefer, a reporter who lived down the hall from me, gave me a key to his apartment so I could "look after" his place when he was gone. Instead, I stole all his ice cream, one bowl at a time.

I pitched and played a lead-footed left field for the *Birmingham News* softball team, and cussed out Greg, one of my own teammates on the softball field, when he fumbled a ground ball. He responded by throwing the ball at my head as the players in the opposing dugout stared in wide-eyed wonder at what was certainly the first time two players on the same team suspended play to contemplate kicking the mortal hell out of each other.

I guess I was having too much fun.

One day, after a small argument with my editor, Henderson, he sent me a simple note over the computer screen.

"Some people are beginning to say you are a prima donna," was the gist of it. I reckon so.

The *News* educated me and put up with me and I will always appreciate that, just as I appreciated the editors who stood beside me at the *Star* in the face of such enormous pretension. But in the end I just didn't fit in, again. I could have tried to alter my character—people do that— but I was afraid to start, because I thought it would never stop. I was too damn dumb to know that a swagger is a silly walk for a man with yet a long way to go.

I sent out résumés to several papers, and, in the end, I had some choices. The *St. Petersburg Times,* the best midsize paper I had ever seen, flew me down for an interview. A few days later they offered me a job, but my plans on moving there, in trying to prove myself, had to wait.

Personal reasons, family reasons, brought me home. My momma was sick, listless, tired all the time. It would turn out to be nothing serious, but I turned down what at the time was a dream come true and went home, to work again at the *Anniston Star,* to be close to her.

A lot had changed in those three years I'd spent in Birmingham, things I had not noticed coming home for a few hours on holidays and the occasional weekend. My momma looked washed out, helpless. It was as if, without children to raise, to provide for, she had lost her purpose, and just given up. She had grown accustomed to fighting upstream for us, for so long, and now there was no battle left. She went almost nowhere, spending weeks, months, without going farther than the mailbox. She just sat in the little house, day after day, reading the Bible, worrying.

But I was wrong about what threatened her, mostly. I do not know if there is a clinical definition for what afflicted her but I learned what it was over time. She dreaded hearing the phone ring, once again. She dreaded the crunch of tires on gravel in the driveway, once again. She was sick at heart, and scared so badly that there was little joy in living and every day just brought a new round of trouble, angst, fear, once again.

What she was, was worried half to death. She was not afraid for herself, at least not in any physical sense. Sam and I would have killed almost anyone who hurt her. We would have burned their house down and shotgunned them in the legs as they came running out. I wore a necktie, but I was not so civilized yet. Everybody loves their momma—there is nothing even remotely unique in that even in this dysfunctional world we live in. But not everybody owes their momma so much as us. We would do anything to protect her from the outside world, Sam and me.

But there was nothing we could do about this, absolutely nothing, except sit and watch and feel the anger claw away at us, inside.

21

Running hot

He was running from the law again, in a flatbed pickup that wouldn't outrun a riding lawn mower, but on the narrow and twisting roads of home, speed is less important than nerve. A man who can live with the fact that he will almost certainly sooner or later drive head-on into a tree can almost always outrun a man who expects to live to see his children when he clocks out that evening. The man who doesn't have any fear, who has so little to lose, hell, he can almost fly.

It helps to have a little bit of liquor in you, and Mark did, even on a Sunday. I only heard about it after the fact, but I can see him hunched over the steering wheel, cigarette in his mouth, rumbling between the ditches in a cloud of blue smoke, the engine running red-hot, about to come apart under his feet, slinging rods like shrapnel. He had a good head start and was already well out of sight, but to get away he needed a hidey-hole, a place to duck and cover for just a little while, until the deputy gave up. (One of us, it seems, is always running from the law, or something.)

That was when he saw the little church, the Church of the Nine Gifts, and saw the cars pulling up in the parking lot for the Sunday service. He hit on a plan. He whipped the truck in among the sheep, and together they filed inside, for the worship. Mark sat drunk in the back row.

"Welcome Brother," they said to him, and he stayed for the entire service, the preaching, the singing, the altar call, everything.

They are good people, there at that church, my momma told me. The
preacher told her, when he came to visit her some time later, that the sinners are the ones he wants to find in God's pews. The Saved are doing alright already. They treated Mark so good that he kept going back for two
years.

But, like me I guess, he never heard the call.

I could not make that story up if I tried. At best, it sounds like a scene
out of the whiskey-running days of the 1950s, like pages ripped from my
own ancient family history. It was just a few years ago.

Time doesn't mean much to Mark. In many ways he is frozen in a
generation he never even saw, and all his adult life he has lived life pretty
much like he wanted. The price, from time to time, is jail, and every time
he goes in my momma dies a little more inside. I know it is a cliché to say
that, but if you had ever seen her sit in that living room and talk to him
on the phone when he is in jail, knowing there was not one thing she
could do to help him beyond a little cigarette money, it would be clear to
you what I mean. It's not the shame of it. The shame she can stand. She
has experience at it, at standing before judges and bailiffs, pleading. She
learned to do it with my father.

No, what kills her is the helplessness, the worry, the fear that someone will hurt him while he is in there, separated from her love and protection by razor wire and iron bars. I have seen her, a dozen times, stare
at the ringing phone like it was a coiled snake. But I never saw her not
pick it up, because company was the only thing, I guess, she could give
him.

Maybe it is because the boy is my brother and I am blind to some
things, but I do not believe, not for one minute, that he is cruel, that he
is inherently mean, the way that my daddy could be. But at times it
seems like he is possessed by the same demons that drove my daddy, as
if he inherited them, the way some rich man passes down a silver pocket
watch. Sam escaped them. I escaped them, except on some particularly
bad nights. In a way, I guess Mark was just a victim of odds.

I know he is a decent man, when he is not drinking. I also know that there is nothing he would not do for me, sober.

I have seen him almost cry over run-over dogs, and seen him gently lift them in his arms to care for them. I have seen the pride that he takes in building things—like the house he built with his own hands—and I have marveled at how there is nothing he can't do, given the right tools.

There are times, many times, when he makes me laugh, like with the story of the church visit, and times when I want to drive my fist through a wall. Mostly what I do, just like my momma, is worry. Unlike my father, whose story came to me in time, I have no idea what he is trying to wash away. I only know that he hurts my momma, and doesn't seem to know.

He would never hurt her intentionally, never. There is only the worry he causes from the drinking, fighting and recklessness. I know how close he has come to dying so many times. He carries one bullet in his arm, between the bones, and his back is crisscrossed with knife wounds from a man who cut him up from the backseat of a car as he tried to fight his way out the front. I'm afraid of what it will do to her, if he is hurt much more.

She told me, once, that the reason it hurt her so to see him so angry, so unhappy, was because it made her feel as if she failed, as if she did something wrong, or didn't do enough.

"I know you can pass hate on," she told me. "And when Mark was being born, I was so angry at your daddy. I'd write him letters, and I was so full of hate, I think maybe I give it to Mark."

I told her she was acting crazy, that if my brother's life was a result of genetics, we all knew where it came from.

Our family is patient with drinking men. I hope, someday, that I will be surrounded by so much love, so much loyalty and patience, as that boy engenders. Kin, angry over insults, butt-kickings, over being used again and again to pay off his bails and debts, still help him, protect him. I begged him, once to change, for her. He only grinned.

My momma has grown old beside him, afraid.

My father took her youth, boy.

Let her have her old age.

✿　　✿　　✿

My momma had been hoping again for a girl, when he was born. He had light brown hair, darker than mine or Sam's, more like our daddy's hair. She used to let it grow a little too long, when he was a baby, because she thought it was pretty. He was the only one in the whole family who ever had a curl—mine and Sam's and even her hair hung straight as a board, but not his. When she finally cut it, he was almost a year old. She put the curls in an old envelope, and saved them.

We called him Freckles when he was little. You could take one look at him and know, in that half-joking way, that this boy is going to be trouble. In his school pictures he is not smiling so much as he is grinning, grinning like the devil. Our barbers had improved at the time, so his bangs were cut more or less straight across his forehead, and the eyes underneath were alive with mischief, and you knew he was going to get into something as soon as the photograph was taken and he climbed down off the stool.

He was not spoiled any more than Sam or me, because there was nothing to spoil him with, except attention. After the fourth son had died, Mark was still just three, and maybe it is true that Momma made him the baby again, making him her greatest responsibility, the focus of so much of her attention, her life. In her eyes, he is still "the baby," still her greatest responsibility on this earth. When Mark was sick, especially after her baby died, she was frantic.

He grew up thin as a rail, and stuck on one speed: wide-open. When we played football in the schoolyard, I was the quarterback and Mark was the only one I ever threw to, because he would catch it and knock anybody down who was in the way. The only way to fight him was to sit on him, carefully. He bit.

He was also the best rock thrower I have ever seen. After that time he hit me in the hand with a rock from so far away I didn't even see him, we put him to work in right field for my uncle Ed's softball team. He was the youngest player there. If the outfielders inched in on him, grinning at the skinny boy at the plate, he slapped it over their heads and they would chase it, cussing and red-faced, to the fence.

He didn't care much for school, but he was a wizard with tools. When he was still too young to drive, he could take a car apart. He was a brick-layer, a plumber, a roofer, a carpenter who could sight down a board the way some people sight down a gun, and tell you if it was true or not.

When he was sixteen, he had a job that was hard but steady, a nice car and nice clothes. And that was all I knew about my little brother for a while, because it was about that time that the road in our life frag-mented, that I stopped riding to work with him in those huge dump trucks, that I began a life that only faintly included him.

I heard, once, that he had found a girl, but that she was mean inside and ultimately left him, and broke his heart. People tell me he was never the same, after that. I don't know. I can't believe one woman can wreck a man. Maybe I've just never met the right one.

Out of sight and mind, he built a house with his own hands, far back in the woods, and used a handsaw to cut the boards. When I finally made it to see him, I was amazed. It was no shack, it was a real house. He was proud of it. He dug a catfish pond. He planted a flower bed. He filled the yard with dogs and chickens. When I went home on Thanksgiving, we would take my shotgun up into the woods behind his house and, with Sam, take turns throwing Purex jugs into the air and blowing them into scraps of white plastic. I guess I fooled myself into believing everything was fine; maybe I just wanted my new life to be free of any reminders of the old days.

But every now and then when I called home, I would ask Momma how she was and she would say fine in a way that told me she was lying. Always, there was some news of Mark, a wreck, a run-in with the law, and she would always say the same thing. She didn't call me because she didn't want to worry me. Once they sent him off for a year, and she suf-fered every day of it, afraid for him. You hear people say all the time how someone ages ten years in one. I have seen it.

I should have gone to see him. I told myself it was because I couldn't bear the thought of it, seeing him in a cage. The truth is a damn sight uglier than that. That was a time in my life when I was so conscious of who I was, working hard not just to survive but succeed, and a brother in prison did not fit in.

I should have gone. I should have taken him a carton of Camels and some money for the prison store, and talked to him as long as the guards would let me. Instead, I gave the money to my momma, and let her take it.

I didn't do right by him any more than I did right by my momma all those years I was content to let her live in the background. There is time, I tell myself, to make it right. But while I know what I have to do for her, I do not even know where to begin with my baby brother. There is an anger in him so much like my father, but I cannot tell how it developed, where it came from in his own life. It is enough to make a man believe in ghosts.

He calls me sometimes, usually when he is drinking, and tells me he loves me.

22

What if

My brother Sam grew up to be a good man. He works at the cotton mill in Jacksonville, unloading the big trucks outside that massive old red-brick building. It's a good job, compared to the work he has done before. The pay isn't a whole lot but it allows his family to have decent health insurance, and that eases his mind. It's hard to put a price tag on peace of mind, he says, and that's all he's really working for. So he always comes to work on time and works as long as they will let him, and like any man who works with his hands in America today, he wakes up wondering if this morning might be the last time they let him in the gate. Still, his loyalty to the people who give him his check, his livelihood, his life, is boundless. The plant awards hats, shirts and jackets for bonuses for perfect attendance. I have seen him when every single piece of clothing on his lanky body read "Fruit of the Loom."

In the slow times—no one likes to say the word *layoff*—he cuts firewood and loads it on his old '63 Chevy pickup to sell to people in town. He will work on your car for five dollars and sometimes for nothing, but somehow he always manages to keep just a little ahead of the bank on his little wood-frame house with the rose garden in back and the state flower of Alabama, the satellite dish, off to one side, even if that means working

169

with a drop-cord light and a fistful of tools until 1 A.M. under a broken-down tractor, and getting up just a few hours later to pull a twelve-hour shift.

Teresa, his wife, works at the Food Outlet: we still just have two supermarkets. She has been good to him, and good for him.

The education he didn't get so many years ago, as he fed that school's coal furnace and plunged the toilets to earn his free lunch, doomed him to manual labor. When he was thirteen he was working full-time for my uncle Ed, pick-and-shovel work, loading those boxcars with fifty-pound bags of clay and lime that left fat blisters on his shoulders and arms.

He is not ashamed of work. If he is bitter about it, about any of it, he has never said. He built a decent life from absolute nothing and is content, and does his dreaming in a healthy way, forward. He rarely drinks and only cusses in moderation. (I respect him, in case I haven't made that clear. I always have.)

Much of my young life he spent coming to rescue me, with his fists—on the playground—or just his hands. He is one of those men who can fix anything. I would break down on the side of the road and sooner or later there he would come, shaking his head, calling me a "chucklehead," but he always got me running again, or pulled me out of the ditch, or at least wrapped a chain around my bumper and towed me out of the embarrassment of the middle of the road.

Sometimes I wonder what will happen if Sam and I are called to stand before Saint Peter on the same day, and my sins include everything from trifling with loose women to sleeping in church, and Sam just says, "Well, Pete, once I did fish on a Sunday."

It is what Sam does if he is not working. He has the patience of Job and I like to watch him play his lure across the pond, so easy, smooth, peaceful, waiting for the tug on the line and an explosion of water as the fat bass climbs into the air, mad, shaking its head left and right, its jaw big enough to stick your fist in. "Son!" he always hollers, then pulls him in, slow and steady. He looks the fish over a little, not gloating, but admiring, and eases him back into the murky water, free. He is damn near a genius at fishing. When I was a little boy he would hook a fish, then hand the pole to me so I could pretend I caught it.

He watches over my mother, giving me opportunities to roam, to discover things. He cuts her firewood, and patches her water pipes when
they freeze. He is the one who always comes to see her on her birthday.

All he demands is that once in a blue moon I will sit with him in the
barn where he stores his pickup and bass boat and tell him about where
I've been, what I've seen.

In return, he brings me home, all the way home, telling about layoffs
at the mill, about who died and where the funeral was. He tells me about
babies born, about how his new saw can cut through a green pine in
nothing flat, and how ol' Chuckle Head in Websters Chapel got locked
out of his trailer again. He is a grand storyteller, much, much better than
me. Sometimes I laugh so hard I have to go lie down.

We plan, every time we talk, to go fishing. Me, him, Mark, if he will.
We plan it and I always ruin it, because of work. He never gets mad at
me, he just nods his head.

Work. He understands.

Funny, where boys find their heroes. We find them in wars, on football
fields in Tuscaloosa and Auburn, on the hot asphalt at Alabama International Motor Speedway. I wanted to gallop with the football like Johnny
Musso; I wanted to crash and live, like Jimmy "Smut" Means.

But the one I wanted to be just like for the longest time was the one
who beat me up every other Thursday, who chased me around and
around the house with a slingshot loaded with chinaberries, who lied and
told me that a sunk-in septic tank outside the house was really an unmarked grave, who rigged up a trapeze in the barn and let me go first, to
test the ropes, and who hid with me under that bed in that big, hateful
house, and, as the tears rolled down my face, put his arm around my
shoulders.

I wonder a lot if Mark would have been different, if he had just had me,
like I had Sam. Maybe not. Probably not. I guess we'll never know, and
in a sad way, that will be my salvation.

❀   ❀   ❀

We finally got to go fishing, Sam and me. Mark was nowhere around.

We fished in Paul Williams's pond, about a mile from home, using bright-colored worms to compensate for the murk of the water. "Look," he told me, pointing to where a water moccasin, thick as my arm, moved in slow undulations across the still water. "There's fish in here," he said, "that can eat that ol' boy."

But as usual, he was catching them and I wasn't. I cranked the bait too fast, he told me, but I've never had any patience for anything. Any bass chasing my bait would have had to have been on roller skates. The hours slipped by and he caught six. I lost half a rubber worm.

I told him I reckoned I needed to be getting home. We fished the next few minutes side by side. One of his casts hooked a fat, four-pound bass, in the shallows near the bank. I could see its gills expand as the huge mouth, like a bucket, scooped up the lure.

Then he handed the rod to me, so I could reel it in.

23

Paradise

Those few months I was home in Calhoun County in the winter of 1988 and 1989, back at the *Star*, back with my family, run hot and cold in my memory. It was clear now that I had made a mistake, in believing I could somehow fix everything in my momma's life by my mere presence, in thinking I could just click into place again in that world that had changed without me. In the meantime, I had placed my ambition on hold, but it would be wrong to say that it was wasted time. A wealth of good things happened in those few months. I wrote stories again for people who knew my name and face, which is always more rewarding than writing for strangers. I even got a letter from my ex-mother-in-law, saying she liked a column I did about King, my dog. He had gotten old, weak, and walked around stiff-legged, like an old man with rheumatism, and when he finally passed away I was relieved because I knew he wasn't hurting anymore. I buried him in the goat pen, because the goats kept the weeds cut down.

I covered a high school football game again because the sports desk was shorthanded, and I got the names right, mostly, although the numbers still evaded me. I did get the score right, which is important. For the first time in years, I was home for Thanksgiving and Christmas and

New Year's Day, and ate my momma's black-eyed peas, for luck. I even went bird hunting, but all I shot at was the sky. I saw three puppies born, and one of them, to be named Gizzard, would become both the ugliest dog on this planet and my momma's cherished companion. He was a sickly as well as a remarkably ugly puppy, but Momma kept him alive, feeding him drops of milk until he was well.

I ate breakfast again on Saturday at my momma's, got to know my kinfolks again. When my car broke down, Sam came to get me, again. "Ricky, if I didn't buy no better cars than you, I sure wouldn't move away from home again," he told me, once, from under the hood of my car. "I ain't comin' to get you in Florida."

But after a few months, it was time to go. I was twenty-nine, and while that seems young to me now, I felt like I was standing on the dock, watching the boat leave without me. I might have been content to stay there the rest of my life, if I had waited fifteen, twenty years. I just came home too soon.

I had a girlfriend, a good woman, who pointed out that I was pacing in the living room late at night like some circus elephant in a pen that was way too small. "Go," she said. She was about tired of me then, anyway. It had something to do with my attention span.

I called the *St. Petersburg Times* on the phone and asked if they would still have me. The St. Pete *Times* was not a big newspaper in circulation—though it was twice as big as any paper I had ever worked for—but it was big in reputation. It was, consistently, year after year, one of the top ten newspapers in America. I would normally have been a little scared of it, of proving myself there. But the editor who hired me, Paul Tash, told me that it takes all manner and texture of people to make a good newspaper, and he would be glad to say he was hiring a reporter from Possum Trot, Alabama. Randy Henderson, my editor at the *Birmingham News*, had told me that, too. As long as there was at least one such person in every newspaper I went to, I knew I would be fine.

But it was the interview down there that sold me. The managing editor, Mike Foley, had a bust of Elvis in his office. I thought I might fit in, in a place like that. From some floors in the building, you could even see the bay.

On a chilly, rainy afternoon in March, I said good-bye to my momma with two hundred dollars in an envelope. I made sure she knew how to find me in case of an emergency, and told her to call me collect. I told her that Florida is just a quick plane ride away, that I could be home in a few hours if she ever needed me. That might sound silly to people who vacation in Europe and ride planes every week. To my momma, who had never been more than three hundred miles away from home in her life, who had never been anywhere close to an airplane except for the crop duster that swooped down over our house to get to the cotton fields, Tampa Bay was a million miles away. She cooked me some stew beef with potatoes and onions, which is my favorite, and tried not to cry. Before I left she gave me an envelope with a card in it, and told me not to open it until that night. It had a ten-dollar bill in it.

I said good-bye to my girlfriend with some roses and a promise to keep in touch that we both knew was more civility than anything else, and headed south. I got into St. Petersburg about four-thirty, too late to get a hotel room. I went straight to the beach at Clearwater and watched the sun come up, which was stupid because I had forgotten which side the water was on. It only sets over the water, genius, I said to myself, as it rose over my shoulder.

It was an odd place, in many ways. Pinellas County was paved from Tampa Bay to the beaches, pretty much, with all manner of people living elbow to elbow in little pastel tract houses, rambling brick ranchers and bayside mansions. To find the reasons why people ever came here in the first place, you had to live on the edge of it, by that beautiful water, or drive inland, through the sugar cane, to the heart of it. I rented a small apartment near the bay that was perhaps the most peaceful place I had ever lived. At night, when the water in the little inlet I lived on was smooth as glass, you could sit on the ground and watch the mullet jump, and egrets and other wading birds would take pieces of peeled orange out of your hands. I heard the other reporters complain about how slow it was and dull it was, how life was just one big Early Bird Dinner Special, but I loved it. The editors hurt my feelings sometimes, by sending me to do stories that I thought were frivolous, but it was hard to be miserable living by the beach.

The highlight of my time there, at least in the first few months, was the story of Mopsy the chicken. The little bayside town of Dunedin, north of Clearwater, had been the target of a serial killer. It seemed that a bobcat was, night after night, slaughtering the chickens of the retirees. The editor walked up to me, straight-faced, and told me that there had been a bobcat attack the night before but the chicken had miraculously survived, clawed but still clucking. The chicken's name, he told me, was Mopsy. I said something to the effect that he had to be kidding. Two minutes later, I was motoring to the quiet and peaceful city of Dunedin. I was twenty-nine years old. I had won a whole wallful of journalism awards and risked my life in bad neighborhoods and prisons and hurricanes. I was going to interview a goddamn chicken.

The chicken had indeed had all the feathers raked off its ass, but when I approached it, it went squawking off across the yard. I supposed they would have to get it some counseling. I interviewed its owners instead, drove to a little parking lot by the water, sat in the car for a half-hour and rubbed my eyes. At home, Mopsy would be covered in gravy about now.

I went back to the newspaper office determined to get even. I would write the most overwritten crap of my life, I decided, something so purple and lurid that the editors would feel bad about sending me on the story. I began it this way:

"Mopsy has looked into the face of death, and it is whiskered."

It ran in the paper that way. All the editors told me what a good job I did, and not too long after that I got a promotion that would, I believed, take me away from stories about butt-gnawed chickens for the rest of my natural life.

The moral, I suppose, was this: Do not, on purpose, write a bunch of overwritten crap if it looks so much like the overwritten crap you usually write that the editors think you have merely reached new heights in your craft.

They promoted me to the state desk covering southwest Florida, including the Everglades, which had an almost magical appeal to me, a boy from the foothills. My first assignment on the state desk was the kind of story that would make your usual well-groomed and well-spoken city hall reporter pop his suspenders, but to me, it was a dream come true. They sent me to cover an alligator hunt.

The state-sponsored hunt was intended to thin the gators out a little bit, and protect a few tourists and dogs that strayed too close to the condominium ponds and pristine rivers. The gators had done well all those years they were protected, so well that the state of Florida decided to hold a lottery that would give a limited number of hunters permission to take them for their hides and meat, and for the sport of it, for two weeks in September. The gators had to be harpooned first, and dragged to the side of the boat, jaws snapping, tail thrashing, before being killed with a bang stick. "By God," I thought, "that is fishing."

I arranged to meet with three ol' boys from south Florida who, having rigged the lottery, allowed us to come along for the ride. The paper sent a long-haired hippie-looking photographer named Joe Walles along, to record the death throes of the gator on film.

The hunters planned to cruise the rim canals of Okeechobee, the source of the River of Grass, the Glades, where the gators had been spotted sunning themselves side by side on the banks like hot dogs in a grill. I had been to Okeechobee before, to fish. Life is different there.

It is a vast inland sea, full of poison mud and fish you would only eat if you had a geiger counter on the end of your fork. At night, it was blacker than sin. Sometimes your boat got clogged in the mass of yellowish muck and duck weed and you had to jump out and push, conscious that it could suck you right down, conscious of the black cottonmouth water moccasins that squirmed along the top of the vile mess.

The people were different. Law did not quite reach Okeechobee. It was there, upon seeing a shoe lying in the middle of the road, I actually got out to see if there was still a foot in it. It was there that I met a fishing guide named Jimmy who never, ever wore shoes, who never noticed the mosquitoes that feasted on him, who talked only when he wanted to and that wasn't much. I will never forget sitting in a boat with him on one of those pitch-black nights, and hearing him clear his throat.

"I've et dog," he said, unsolicited.

"Why?" I asked.

"It was in my yard," he said, and that was it for a while.

I am not making any of this up.

But this trip, to kill a gator, was special in every way. It rained as we pulled away from the dock that night, black rain from a black sky on black water. I am not afraid of the dark unless there is something in it that will eat me if I give it a chance. There were countless reasons to be afraid that night. I will always remember the eyes. When one of the gator hunters flashed his light around the canal, there they were, hundreds and hundreds of glowing orange reptilian eyes. The boat suddenly seemed very small.

Then, for the next several hours, we proceeded to piss them off. We took two boats, gliding slowly down the canal as one man stood on the bow of the lead boat, hefting a harpoon. Time after time after time, he gouged, pierced, perforated and otherwise wounded gator after gator, but never got the barbed harpoon in deep enough to stick. The light was the problem, he said. They needed an extra hand in their boat to help, and I volunteered.

They pulled the two boats together so that I could easily jump from one to another, but either I pushed them farther apart when I made my leap or a ripple in the water did it for me, because I dropped like a sack of mud straight down into the black water of the eighteen-foot canal, and knew that I would surely die. I rose up to grasp the side of the boat, scared to death, waiting for one of those twelve-foot monsters to clamp down on my legs and drag me down. I tried to pull myself into the boat, but there was nothing to grab on to except the slick sides, and it was impossible for the little fellows on the boat to dead-lift a six-foot-two, 230-pound dumbass back over the side, to safety.

I know that gators prefer a nice piece of rotted turtle to human beings. I had read National Geographic, too. I know they usually will not attack human beings if there is a poodle anywhere near, but none of that went through my head as I hung there, helpless. It was only for a few minutes, but time has a different meaning when half your body is submerged in black water aswarm with alligators, the same gators your hunting partners had been jabbing with cold steel most of the night.

"Guys," I said, trying to sound calm, trying to keep my voice low. "Y'all got to get me back in that damn boat." It was about then that I heard the clicking noise, a *click-click-click* from behind my back. I arched my neck around in a panic, expecting to see a gator clicking his teeth together in anticipation, but what I saw instead was our photographer taking pictures of me. And I remember thinking, quite clearly, that if I ever got back on dry ground, he was a dead man.

Finally, someone suggested that I should work my way around to the side of the boat and climb up over the engine's transom, which I did, with the last of my energy. Everybody but me thought it was pretty funny. The photographer, Walles, later explained to me that he felt obligated to cover the news, and for a few minutes I was the story.

I could see the headline:

GATOR EATS REPORTER: ALL POSSUM TROT MOURNS.

Then, a year later:

WALLES WINS PULITZER PRIZE.

The editors demanded that I write two stories, one about the hunt itself, and a first-person story about what happened to me, one that could only make me look like an idiot. The next day at the Page One meeting in the St. Pete *Times* newsroom, this conversation was overheard and reported back to me.

Editor One: "That gator story didn't exactly work like we expected, did it?"

Editor Two: "Naw. It was fantastic."

That luck, that charmed existence that began with an upside-down convertible so long ago, still held. My momma didn't have any, Mark didn't have any, and Sam made his, but I could fall face first in a septic tank and come out smelling like a rose of Sharon.

I moved away from my little house on Clearwater Bay, to live on an honest-to-God island. It was called Anna Maria. The city allowed no houses over two stories and set the speed limit at twenty-five, as if it was determined to keep what was happening to the rest of the Sunshine State from happening there. I walked to the beach every morning when it was warm, and it was almost always warm, and swam in water that some mornings was as clear as moonshine. This was no rich folks' island with mansions and yacht slips, but a place where people came after they worked a lifetime selling insurance in Evansville and aluminum siding in Scranton. This was affordable paradise, and even a man on a reporter's salary could live close to the beach every evening and bob up and down the water until the sun went down. I remember that the sand had pine needles in it, which is unusual for Florida. Usually, the only shade you get is from the condominiums.

Home, and all the old and new miseries associated with it, seemed a long, long way from this place, where you could sit on Bean Point and watch the lights of the freighters glide under the towering, breathtaking Sunshine Skyway Bridge into the black emptiness of the bay, churning for the Tampa docks. In the daytime I worked in a tiny bureau with just two desks, sharing a rundown office with a middle-aged ad man who had one of the best names I have ever heard, Joe Romeo. On Saturday mornings he would come and bang on the door and take me fishing for trout on the saltwater flats of the bay, and at night he and his wife would cook them up with grits and beets and iced tea.

I lived in a two-bedroom apartment that was two bedrooms bigger than I needed, since I still didn't have any furniture, but the rent was right and it was less than a block from the beach and the only supermarket anywhere close. I drove a silver 1966 Mustang convertible with virtually no rust. It had a 289 V-8 that scared the pelicans, and a loose front end that scared me. But it was pretty, from a distance.

For supper, on those nights we didn't fry fish at Joe Romeo's, there were two choices: a rambling joint for the tourists called Fast Eddie's that served a good blackened grouper sandwich; and an equally touristy upscale joint called the Sandbar, where you could watch the sunset with your sweetie, if you could find one who was still speaking to you. For breakfast, there was a tiny place called Candy's right on the water, where you could get a gravy and biscuit and eat it outside. I thought, truly, I was in heaven.

The newspaper gave me time and opportunity to tell stories about everything from poachers in the beautiful, mysterious Everglades to the bizarre case of a woman who had been beaten and brain-damaged by an attacker seventeen years in the past, but it only became a murder case when she finally died from a seizure brought on by her injuries. I wrote about criminals who stalked the elderly, about the last Florida panthers on earth, dying slowly in the Everglades. I wrote about mercury poisoning in the swamps and wetlands, and interviewed a man who married his own daughter and swore, "I didn't know." (He also told me that once, when he worked at a bar in Vegas, he used a nail to punch a hole in the belt of Elvis's jumpsuit, to give the King a little more room to shake it.) But mostly, I was a serious journalist.

I did some stupid things. I believed that because I had grown up the way I did, I was just inherently tougher than my more urbane coworkers, and could get away with more. On the story on poachers, I needed to talk face to face with at least one, to give the story teeth. It is not hard to find a poacher in Florida, just look for a man with an airboat in his driveway. He will know somebody, if he does not have a dozen gator hides curing in his backyard, himself. I arranged not so much an interview as just a quick meeting, a chance to see them, ask a question or two, and then leave. The men I saw were not rustic heroes, just criminals, stealing from nature. They did not see what they were doing as anything wrong; their daddies had been free to take game when they wanted, however they wanted. But they knew they would be fined and maybe even go to jail if they were caught, and I was a risk to that. I was no risk, in my eyes. They did not give me their names. I did not look at their tag number. But as one of them reached behind the seat of his truck and slid out a .22 rifle— poachers like the .22 because it has a softer report and won't draw the game wardens to them—I thought for just a second that I might die there. I am not trying to be melodramatic. Reporters live for war stories, except the ones who have been so genuinely frightened in so many terrible places that they do not need to scare themselves all over again with their own memories. But for just a second, on that sand road in the middle of the scrub, I knew I had risked my life for five or six paragraphs.

But that was only a second of bad time, lost in the rest. Some people spend lifetimes looking for the perfect fit. I had it for a while, as the South Suncoast bureau chief of the *St. Petersburg Times*. I worked for an editor named Rob Hooker who defended his reporters and had a light hand when he edited a story, and for the first time in my life I felt like I had found a place where I could stay a while. My momma gave me my first home. The St. Pete *Times* gave me my second. The editor who hired me, Tash, had called it a place where people take their work more seriously than they do themselves. The work was what mattered, not where you went to school. I could do the work, and even as I did it I learned one agonizing lesson that would make me better at what I do.

I have said a few times that I try to lend dignity and feeling to the people I write about, but that is untrue. All you do is uncover the dignity, the feeling, that is already there. I learned to do that there.

In the spring of 1990, we learned that a woman in St. Petersburg had given birth to twins, joined at the chest, what people usually call Siamese twins. My editors sent me to try and convince the family to write about it. I made the mother a simple promise. I would portray her children as two distinct personalities, as little babies with a complicated medical condition, nothing more. I said I would treat the story, their story, with dignity. I kept my promises.

I spent months on what would be a tragic tale. I followed them from their birth, wrapped in each other's arms, and through their surgeries, and finally followed their young mother and father through two funerals.

It was as heartbreaking a thing, on a purely personal level, as I had ever done. I will always remember the day I saw them in the nursery's intensive care unit, the first time I had ever seen so many lives so near to death. To me, it seemed that anything, a faint breeze, a whisper, a loud sound, anything, could take them away. And in the middle of all those tiny, delicate, premature babies were the twins. I wanted to make perfect the way I described that place, those babies, and make other people see what I saw and feel what I felt. Almost all the time, you just paint a picture with the words and let people make up their own minds and emotions, but this time I wanted to force them to feel.

"Nurses on the late shift called the twins Miracle Babies," I wrote, "but there never seem to be enough miracles to go around. Most babies in the neonatal intensive care unit at All Children's Hospital are born too soon, incomplete. Some last for a while and then slip away, like beads off a broken string."

We are taught in this business to leave our emotions out of a story, to view things with pure and perfect objectivity, but that was impossible on this story. I learned that objectivity is pure crap, if the pain is so strong it bleeds onto the yellowed newsprint years, or even decades, later.

The momma and daddy and one of the grandmas thanked me for it, sometime later, and I didn't know what to say.

Florida really is a magical place, from the wonders of Disney World, where Goofy is really a sweating freshman from Clemson inside a mountain of plastic, to the dark sorcery of Miami, where the canals clog with the floating carcasses of sacrificed chickens and an occasional headless goat. You see some things there that you just don't see anywhere else in the world, ludicrous things and frightening things and amazingly sad things. I will never forget sitting on the hood of my car on a spring day in 1990, and seeing a swamp fly. (I do not mean that I saw an insect in a swamp, but that I saw an entire swamp, fly.) The DEA and Manatee County Sheriff's Office had overestimated the amount of dynamite needed to blast some little islands of ganja to smithereens, and when they pressed the button an entire swamp—trees, dirt, water, gators, snakes, turtles and frogs—rose up into the wild blue yonder. I sat there and watched it all rain down again, careful not to let any moccasins drop into my mustang, and went home and wrote a story about it. The next day I got a call from the Society for the Prevention of Cruelty of Animals, asking me if I was incensed by the inhumanity of it. I told him I felt kind of bad for the frogs and turtles but that, no, I felt no remorse whatsoever for the snakes and, to tell the truth, had once had a very bad experience with gators.

There was only one job in the world I would have traded my own for, and that was the one in Miami. It was a reporter's nirvana, a place where smash-and-grab robbers stalked tourists with chunks of concrete, where whole skyscrapers stood on foundations of drug money, where the Tontons Macoute of Haiti reached across the Florida Straits to kill political enemies, and old men with hatred infusing every cell of their bodies played soldier in the Glades, dreaming of the day they could kill Castro.

Our Miami job came open in my second year at the paper, and I begged for it. I didn't speak any Spanish or Creole, and what I knew about the complicated geopolitical situation I had read in books. I had never even been there. But the editors decided they would rather have a reporter who could write good stories for their newspaper than someone who could sound good at a dinner party and shift languages like a Lexus changes gears.

The editors put the announcement on the bulletin board in the newsroom, and a friend read it to me over the phone. It was written by John Costa, the deputy managing editor. It said, simply, that I was going to Miami.

". . . and one of them, Bragg or Miami, will have to give."

24

Miami, in madness

By Miami standards, it was a popgun riot, a little bitty thing. But I think about it from time to time and I still get a little sick. The terror is a vague thing now, but the shame . . . I guess it follows you into the clay.

I am not above attempting to enthrall an intern with tales of high excitement. I am not a romantic figure but I have not led a humdrum life, either. I have not done a lot but I have seen some things, right up close, and sometimes there were small risks in that. But one story I almost never tell, because it is personal in a way that leaps well beyond grief, love, hate. It involves fear, and that is nothing to be proud of.

It was June 27, 1991, a Thursday, about 10 P.M. It was hot, the way it can only get in Miami at night. Some places cool after it gets dark, but some nights in Miami it just feels like someone has draped a black cloth over the place. On South Beach, the wind blows off the water and cools it a little, but the ocean breeze never reaches Liberty City and Overtown. It gets hot there and stays hot till November.

My girlfriend at the time, Rachel, was a reporter for the *Miami Herald*, and said she had to work late that night on the big story of the day. The city was tense, more tense than usual. Black people—in many ways a forgotten people in Miami—were incensed by a court's ruling that had overturned the conviction of a Hispanic Miami police officer in the manslaughter of two men. In some cities, such a thing would bring out the preachers and pontificators. It would solicit signs and picket lines. Miami is different. In Miami, it meant that the start of the burning, the rioting, was just a matter of time. Riots had raged and burned across Liberty City and Overtown four times in the past decade after white officers killed blacks or were acquitted in killings. Miami was due for another. It was almost tradition.

People were dying in racial violence here long before anyone had ever heard of Rodney King. The most recent riot had been three days of burning, shooting and beatings in January 1989, after Miami police officer William Lozano shot Clement Lloyd, twenty-three, an unarmed black man who was driving toward the officer on a motorcycle. The motorcycle then crashed into a car, killing Lloyd and his passenger, twenty-four-year-old Allan Blanchard. In the rioting that followed the shooting, one person died, 11 were injured and 372 arrested. Thirteen buildings burned.

Lozano was eventually convicted of two counts of manslaughter, and the community was satisfied. But on Tuesday, June 25, 1991, when a higher court reversed that decision to set the stage for a new trial, it was a match scraped across the backs of many black people here. The court had ruled that the trial should have been moved out of Miami because the fear of violence in the black community contributed to the guilty verdict.

For one night, then two, nothing happened. Black leaders walked the streets calling for peace, begging for it, telling the angry people there how senseless it was to burn their own neighborhoods, again. The peace held, but it was a rubber band stretched just a little too tight. The *Miami Herald* reporters were on constant watch, and I told Rachel to be careful. Riots will hurt you, faster than anything.

The St. Pete *Times,* not being the local paper, did not have to be so vigilant. I know how coldhearted it sounds, but the fact was, I had the night off as long as the city did not burn. With my girlfriend gone, with time to kill, I did what any man would do. I invited my friend Sean Rowe over to eat a steak and watch *The Wild Bunch*.

I forgot all about the possibility of a riot until the phone rang, and an editor at my paper told me I might want to stick my head outside and see if I smelled smoke. He told me that the worst possible thing had happened. A Miami police officer had shot a black man, and if the city had not erupted already, it surely would.

By early evening, a crowd of people had stormed a city bus, dragged out the driver, a woman, and beat her bloody. A police officer was run over by a car as a film crew watched, and whole city blocks of people were hurling rocks and bottles as scores of police moved in, standing vigil in bulletproof vests and helmets. They stood back to back in some neighborhoods, frantically scanning the rooftops for snipers, deflecting rocks with plastic shields.

I am not a brave man, but I do my job. I had heard of reporters who covered riots from their television sets. I may lose my nerve someday and do it myself, but at the time I knew I had to get close.

My Mustang had died on me the year before—actually the brakes failed and I crashed through a parking meter and into a palm tree on Biscayne Boulevard—and I had bought a burgundy 1969 Firebird convertible that would run most of the time. It was a good car to cat around in here, but a bad car to drive into a riot. It would be a magnet for attention, and when you drive around in a neighborhood where people want to hurt anyone whose skin is white, you cannot afford attention. My friend Sean, a former reporter for the *Herald* who was now an investigative reporter for *New Times* in Miami, told me he would drive us in his wife Lois's Toyota. He grinned.

He is one of those rare people who thinks that the more absurd life is, the more it's worth living. But he is also what we call in Alabama a capable man. If you insult him, he will fight you. He once rode a tramp freighter from Miami to Haiti with a crew of cutthroats and thought it was amusing that the raggedy, barely seaworthy freighter lost power halfway through the trip and, its lights dark, went drifting broadside through one of the most traveled shipping lanes in the Atlantic. He had serious guts, and while I knew that he wanted to cover the riot for his own paper, the real reason he went with me that night was so I wouldn't go alone in a car that screamed, "Here I am. Hit me with a rock."

The police were handling this riot differently from ones in the past, when they just cordoned off large areas and let the violence and the fires rage. This time they seemed determined to quell the violence, and moved into violent areas. That created, instead of a well-defined line of violence and defense, pockets of it. Some blocks were safe, some were not. We were unlucky enough to drive through one that was not.

There is a feeling that comes over a place in a time such as that, or maybe it just comes over you and you project it onto the dark buildings and broken streetlights around you. You can get killed dead in broad daylight in Overtown and Liberty City in the calmest of times, by people who only want your car or your wallet. But I had driven all over those neighborhoods, day and night, and never felt this kind of menace.

That night, as we weaved our way through the neighborhood, I was afraid of it. Now and then we would see people running. I remember one man carried a length of chain. Sean and I didn't talk much; I guess we were afraid our fear would show too much.

It happened on Third Avenue Northwest in Overtown, in front of a small housing project. There seemed to be a lot of people out in the street, but they were quiet, lining both sides of the road. There were men and women and some children, and we slowed down to a crawl because some of the children were running back and forth across the street.

The next second, the air was full of rocks and bottles and curses. Some banged into the car, one smashed a side window and one hit me under my ear, where my jaw links to the rest of my skull, and for a second I didn't know or feel anything. Sean told me later that I screamed when I was hit. I just remember rocks and curses flying, as a young man without a shirt on came running straight up to the now open window and threw something inside, point-blank, but missing me somehow, missing Sean. As frightened as I was, I managed to mumble, "Whatever happens, keep moving, just keep moving." Then I saw something that made me sick with fear.

As we rolled slowly between the rows of people, trying not to hit any-body, I saw a long black car, a junker, roll out from between the buildings and block the road. There was no one at the wheel; people were pushing it out there to block the street. Instead of panicking, Sean whipped the steering wheel to the left, hard, taking the car up onto the sidewalk, off the road completely, and somehow missed the trees, the parked cars, the people. Somehow, we got around it, we got away.

I do not want to believe it, but I think we might have died there, if he had lost his nerve, if he had stopped, if he had stomped hard on the ac-celerator and run over someone. People say all the time, with trite and silly melodrama, that someone, by their actions and clear thinking, saved their life. It may be that this time, he did save mine.

We made it to a block that the police had more or less secured. Some jackass television reporter tried to interview me, and I said no, I don't think so. There were other people there who had been through the same thing, and they were black. In the dark, in their anger, people had thrown rocks at anything that moved. I was a little fuzzy-headed, but fine. I went looking for a phone, to call in the story.

It would not be much of a riot, by Miami standards, just that one night of anger. Once again black leaders like H. T. Smith, a prominent lawyer, stepped in and went neighborhood to neighborhood, calling for peace. This time it held, until the anger subsided to a low boil, which is about normal.

We found two rocks in the car, one beside my seat, the one that hit me. I put it in my pocket.

The next day I put it on my desk, as a paperweight, as a reminder.

The morning after, daylight revealed the old and new scars that covered Overtown and Liberty City, the burned-out and boarded-up hulks, va-cant lots with a stub of a wall left standing, weeds where there used to be a store. I drove through the neighborhoods and tried not to be afraid anymore. Once, a man walked quickly out the front of a store and I jerked the wheel so hard I almost ran off the road. I had to remind my-self that I was not weaving through a war zone but riding through a place where people lived. That was the story I tried to write for the next day's paper with a young black woman named Janita Poe, who came down to help.

I remember the hopeless words of Willie R. Colman, who had moved to Overtown with his wife in 1968. He had seen black and non-black businesses leave because of the riots, rips in the fabric of Miami that were never mended.

"Why they going to come back?" asked Colman, a seventy-one-year-old retired construction worker. "Ain't nothing to come back to but ashes."

But it was the anger and hopelessness in the words of one young black man, an eighteen-year-old named Tony Fox, that I remember most. To him, rioting was a way to get even, to make people listen. He said he would trash and loot with others, because in his neighborhood blacks owned nothing. They just lived in the hot houses with the two-inch-long palmetto bugs, almost in sight of the condos of the more prosperous Hispanics who came to Miami and flourished, leaving black people behind. In their eyes, they had been subjugated by the old Crackers, and now they were subjugated again by people who were not even born there.

"It ain't right. We ain't got no money. That's why they destroy the buildings. It's a way to get even."

This is a business, this journalism, that likes a good trend. We can examine it from four different directions and get some college professors to tell us what we ought to think, and we pass it on to the readers. Over the years, it became fashionable to talk about hope in Miami's black community, about growth. There has been some.

The years of violent public reaction to injustice are over, one black leader promised. Miami burned for the last time, and only a little, that night Sean and I took our ride in the unfortunate Lois's Toyota.

Sean Rowe and I were close friends for the time I spent in Miami. When I moved away we drifted apart, and when we did talk we seldom talked about that night. Men, especially where I was raised, don't like other men to see them so afraid.

I kept the rock on my desk for a long time. One day I looked at it and just didn't like remembering anymore, and dropped it in the trash can.

I called Sean some time back, after years. I did not apologize for not calling sooner and he did not apologize for not calling me. I told him what I was writing about that night, and asked if I could read him what I had put down. I needed to know whether I had gotten it right. He listened, and told me he thought that, yes, it was right, it was true. But he said I was too tentative in what it might have turned into that night. "I have no doubt that, if they had ever gotten us out of that car, they would have killed us," he told me. I guess so.

He told me some things I didn't know. He told me he had kept the other rock we found in the car, as I had kept mine, as a morbid souvenir. And like me, one day he just didn't like looking at it anymore, and he dropped it in the trash.

25

Eating life

Some places you exist. You live and die in Miami. In one month, when I was covering the place: a sixth-grader shot a homeless man over a slice of pizza; an Eckerd pharmacist shot and killed another pharmacist in the store; a trash hauler was shot in the spine when he refused to stop for a robber; a homeless man was doused with gasoline and set on fire; assorted tourists perished. I would drive to my stories on a pitch-black interstate, because the homeless and other poor like to strip the power lines for copper. On any given day, a hundred people stood in line for food in Bicentennial Park, in the lee of skyscrapers partially financed with cocaine money. I once rode around the city at night with a state law enforcement agent who stopped every few hours to call his wife and tell her he was alive. He made sure I knew how to use the pump 12-gauge before we pulled away from the curb. "We took a forty-five off a guy the other night. Six in the magazine, one in the chamber," he said. It was one of those good days in paradise. No one was killed, not even a tourist.

You could whiz by it all, of course, with your windows rolled up tight, and whip into your gated community and pretend to be in Sarasota. Most people did. It was irrelevant that they lived in a city where the corpses in the morgue had bar codes on their toes, to keep up with them.

I could have lived in Coral Gables with them, I guess, but that would be like tasting food without taking the Saran wrap off.

That one bad night in Overtown was with me for a long time. It still is, I guess. But I did not let it sour my love of Miami. If you were young, if you had any sense of adventure, then there was no better place in the whole world to live, to do what I did for a living. There were days when I would get my paycheck and laugh out loud, not because there was so much money, merely because they paid me at all.

I lived in Coconut Grove most of my time there, first in a concrete-block duplex where I lost three car stereos in the initial three months, then in a little house, on a less crime-ridden street, surrounded by giant oaks and palms and assorted crawling vines. The trees sang with birds, even parrots—escapees—and I forgot for long weeks to feel guilty about running even farther away from home. My momma worried about me in such a sinful place, but I assured her that, unless I forgot to put on my sunblock, I was just fine. Once, she sent my aunt Edna down to check on me, and I took her to a yard sale in the rich folks' part of the Grove to throw her off the scent. We found some nice saltshakers.

I called my momma on Sundays and told her I was writing about the models on South Beach—and I actually did, once—and promised not to go anywhere near Cuba. I told her I was getting fat on chicken and yellow rice and croquetas de jamón, which is about as much fun as you can have with your clothes on. I told her I wrote about art shows, and forgot to mention that the only reason I went there was because a rabidly anti-Castro group had condemned the gallery operators as dung-eating communistas and planted a bomb. I told her I was in mad, never-ending love with this place, with the café con leche that was like melted Hershey bars, with the music, with the excitement. But I made sure that I made it sound like it couldn't hurt me, unless I died of joy.

The truth was that I was elbow-deep in some of the darkest stories of my life. I spent long days under an Interstate overpass with homeless men and women who had created an alternative culture, with laws and punishments. They would gang up and beat a man if the accused was caught taking someone else's stuff or messing with someone else's mate.

They had no court, just laws and punishment. Daytime existence was a constant merry-go-round of begging, napping and begging some more, for a dollar, a dime, a little attention.

They dreaded the setting sun. I talked to a thin man with a raggedy cat who said he went to sleep every night afraid some crackhead would crawl into a refrigerator box he called "my condominium" and cut his throat for pocket change. After midnight, as people gathered around big fires made from trash and tires, women who looked freshly dead filed into surrounding streets and Interstate exit ramps, selling sex for three dollars, one dollar, less. One woman offered herself in exchange for a ride in a car.

There were roving bands of homeless transvestites—six-foot-tall black men in blond wigs and high heels who slept on the ground—and an old man the other homeless called the Invisible Man because, in mid-conversation, he would just announce, "I am not here," and pretend he was invisible. You could shout in his ear, but he stared straight ahead. Most people under that overpass were afraid of becoming invisible— many people already treated them as if they were—but he had embraced it.

Walking the shantytown, even in daylight, was like walking through some Baptist Bible Camp's film show of hell. The dirt, pounded into powder, was dotted with evil-smelling mattresses. A skeletal man stared up at the trembling highway above him, still as marble. On another mattress, two teenage girls in their underwear, both pregnant, motioned to you, beckoned, offering.

A very normal-looking homeless man, Ed Washington, pulled back his blankets to show me a long, thin knife. He had never been hurt and he had never hurt anyone, "but the only reason it ain't happened is the right fool just ain't come along. Things happen here. Things you wouldn't believe. There was this one guy got cut up real bad one time, and this cop comes up. He looks at the guy and says, 'Look, if you die here it's my problem.' So the guy walks on down the road. We never did see that guy again."

One man, Rollo Williams, had just become a father. "My woman had a baby here last week, the prettiest thing you ever saw. But I don't know about keeping it. Not here. If I had a place I would. All I got is a box. But it is a pretty baby."

There was a young man Alex Wright, a tall, thin guitar picker from California, cool as the other side of your pillow. He said he played for Carlos Santana once in San Francisco, but had to pawn his guitar. When I asked if he was homeless he seemed insulted. "I'm a musician, an artist. I'm not homeless, I'm just here until I get my guitar. I'm not homeless. I'm just camping out."

They were the first thing the tourists saw when they exited the Interstate in the downtown: Welcome to paradise. Do you want your windshield washed? Sure you do.

But the closest to chaos I had ever been, except for that one bad night in Overtown, was in a little migrant workers' town on the edge of the Everglades. In the mornings the legals and illegals queued up to beg for work. The crew bosses picked the strongest and the youngest and loaded them, a United Nations of cheap labor from Guatemala, Haiti, El Salvador, on death-trap buses that had a bad habit of running off into the canals. The bosses worked them for twelve hours, then sometimes neglected to pay them at all.

They lived somewhere outside the basic decencies of America. Babies came to the county health department with ant bites that looked like measles. Others came with TB. Then they just disappeared again as their migrant parents moved on, chasing the seasons, leaving doctors to wonder what ever happened to the sick children. Twelve men lived crammed into a trailer meant for two. Prostitution was allowed, out of mercy. There had to be some relief. The people, fresh from the rain forests and death squads and endless slums, did not mind it so much. The town was called Immokalee. It means "home."

I got there as the season died, as the rains started to fall. The Haitians, who knew something about suffering and survival, had a beautiful phrase for it. The translation is not perfect, but the nut of it was: "The season of pain is never over until the sky begins to cry." One night I sat in my car and watched a man stagger out of one bar—there was no name on the door, no sign, just a line of drunks inside—and begin cursing the air. He flicked open a pocketknife, waving it insanely through the air like a sodden Zorro, and then sat down in the dirt to weep into his hands.

Another man, a man named Gallo I found staggering dog drunk from a whorehouse, told me a joke. In it, he dies in the field and a crew boss tells his body to go back to work.

"But I am dead," his spirit shouts down, from somewhere in the clouds.

"You cannot die," the boss says.

"Why?" the spirit asks.

"Because God is too busy with the living," the boss answers.

"Not in Immokalee," the spirit says. "God don't know where that is."

But it is easy to write about suffering on that scale, because it is less personal. A story north of Miami, in Fort Lauderdale, tested my objectivity.

It was about a little boy named Dirty Red, who lived with his momma in a treeless, hopeless housing project just outside Lauderdale. His saga began on May 20, 1990, when a police car came and took him away for a dirty little crime he didn't do. He was six, but the Broward County deputy said he had sexually assaulted a seven-year-old girl. They said he had poked her between her legs with a stick. All his momma could see of him as they drove away in the police car was the top of his head.

They fingerprinted him and took his mug shot, and scared him to death. Red just kept shaking his head, NO.

It would turn out to be a lie, the accusation, drummed up by a man who had sexually abused the little girl, but somehow the Broward deputies never bothered to come back and tell people in the housing project that Red was innocent, that it was all a mistake. The people in the project treated him like a pervert. They made him an outcast. Most of the children wouldn't play with him, and chanted "Dirty Red, Dirty Red, Dirty Red," whenever he walked by. Grown men slapped him when he came close.

His momma had started calling him "Dirty Red" long before that, but it was a good nickname then. She called him that because his skin had a red tint, and because he was always going out in the yard to play and getting dirty right after she gave him a bath. But after his arrest, the people turned it into something dirty, something mean, and the little boy, the one who roamed the project free as a bird and wrapped his momma's dish rag around his head for a turban, was lost.

The boy became almost catatonic. He refused to leave his momma's side. He sat beside her or at her feet and followed her around like a puppy, his fingers entwined in the hem of her dress.

The day I went to talk to them she needed to speak to me a few minutes alone, and had to pry the boy's fingers away from her dress, and told him to go outside. "Baby, it's okay to play."

But Dirty Red couldn't face the neighborhood that day, any day. To please his mother he walked down the steps, then quickly doubled back and sat on the steps, his thumb in his mouth, just outside the door. I know this because our photographer, Ricardo Ferro, took a heartbreaking picture of it.

"They told me my boy fell through the cracks," said his momma, a woman with those defeated eyes you usually only find in the terminally ill. "I wanted somebody to write a letter, maybe, to the people who live here. I wanted somebody to tell them my boy is all right. But nobody has done, maybe because they just don't care about him. If this had been a rich white family, do you think this would have happened. Do you think they wouldn't have fallen all over themselves, saying they were sorry."

She tried to spread the word that her son did nothing, that it was all a mistake, but the people believed only what they saw that night, the night they came for the child.

For months after that, he screamed when his momma turned loose of him even for a second. "Finally we got him to go outside by himself, but that's when the people get him."

I wrote the story of Dirty Red in the Miami bureau of the St. Pete *Times,* a peaceful place on Coral Way shaded by banyan trees. At the very worst, I promised his momma, I wouldn't do her son any harm. They ran it on the front page, with a big, heartbreaking photo. The next week, I sent his momma a bundle of them.

She took them door to door in the neighborhood, as I knew she would, and shoved the story in the faces of the people who had abused her son, and said, "See. I told you."

Seeing it written down, they began to believe. The story drew the aid of ministers and other do-gooders who helped spread the word, who made sure the word got out. Counselors called and offered to help free of charge. People sent money. People sent toys. He became a sort of mascot for the Miami Heat basketball team. He got better.

I didn't get into this business to change the world; I just wanted to tell stories. But now and then, you can make people care, make people notice that something ain't quite right, and nudge them gently, with the words, to get off their ass and fix it.

The fact is, I did very few happy stories in Miami, and the vast majority did not change a damn thing. I wrote about Castro selling relatives to Cuban Americans in Miami, and the hopeless story of a man who had been choked into a coma by Miami police. Friends have told me I did too much of it, that I dwelled on it, that I should be careful not to let it build up inside of me. One reporter, a friend, christened me "the misery writer." But I have always been able to distance myself, to dance between the raindrops. Miami is a great place for distance. On a good day, you can stand on South Beach and see forever. I lived my life as full and rich as I could on a reporter's salary, and every month I put money away in savings, to keep my promise.

One day I just had too much of the bad news piled up in my head, and I guess I snapped a little. I wanted to do a happy story, anything that did not involve killing or meanness, and I flipped through the local papers, searching for something, anything. There was one, just one. A rare plant, the "deltoid spurge," grew only in a few places in Florida, and one of those places was to be developed. Environmentalists were trying to save it. Never mind that they couldn't save the panther or the manatee.

I called Bill Cooke, our free-lance photographer and my friend, but an ornery man even on his best days. I told him to join me in the bureau, that we were going to help save the deltoid spurge.

"What in the hell are you talking about?" he said.

"We are off to save the spurge," I said.

"Are you drunk?" he said.

"No. Come. The spurge awaits. It needs us."

He showed up a few minutes later, looking at me suspiciously. Bill had been in Vietnam. He had seen people drift quietly away from the piers of life.

Thirty minutes later we were standing in a grove of pines and scrub just off U.S. 1 in South Miami, standing over a little green plant that looked like a cross between a mushroom and a pineapple.

"Looks like it," he said.

"Well?" I said.

"Well, what?" he said.

"Take its damn picture."

"They'll never run it," he said.

"Take it anyway."

He took a few shots and we went home. That night, I wrote the prettiest story I could on the plight of the deltoid spurge. Faulkner couldn't have done it better. My newspaper ran it across the top of the Tampa Bay and State page, and Bill Cooke had to buy me dinner.

"You may be the only man I know who could get twenty inches out of the deltoid spurge," he said. "You are a poet."

"Thank you," I said.

The spurge lives, to this day.

For more than two years the newspaper left me alone and let me find good stories, except for one week when they sent me to cover Operation Desert-whatever-it-was, the part before they actually did any serious shooting and renamed it Desert Storm. I didn't even have a passport, when they told me I could go, but I was thrilled. "I will kiss a camel, if you will let me go," I told the editors. I wrote one good story—Jewish soldiers in Saudi Arabia were forced to pray in closets and had the Star of David removed from their dog tags—and about four truly bad ones. It was the first time I had ever gone outside the country to write a newspaper story. The next time would rearrange my soul.

I had come to believe that I was good at one thing, writing about people in trouble, about misery. As it turned out, I was a rank amateur. I didn't know what misery was, but I would learn.

26

Tap-tap

Port-au-Prince, Haiti,
October 1991

I had always wanted to go to Haiti, the same way I'd wanted to touch my mother's hot iron. The resilience of its people amazed me. But in truth, what drew me to this place was its capacity for evil. A bloody coup gave me a reason to come, and write of it.

"The dead disappear into the muddled minds of old caretakers," I wrote, "in a graveyard where roses rust. The funeral flowers are made from tin so they can be used over and over again. Vilason Dorvilier wanders the cemetery searching for his father, but there have been so many dead since September the caretakers can't remember where they put them all. The ground is full, one old caretaker said.

"Crypts rise from the old graves, four to eight caskets high. Dorvilier steps to the top of one and climbs the concrete cross, hoping he can find his father's crypt from there, but all he sees is his future. The cemetery stretches for five acres until it blends into the stink and swelter of the slums, where naked babies stand in sewage and old women hide from view because it is shameful to starve. He sees the yellow army barracks, where illiterate young soldiers play with guns the rich people bought for them, guns used to murder his father two weeks ago. Higher up, up into the cloud-capped mountains, are the homes of the light-skinned aristocracy, who live clean and have too much to eat. But Dorvilier can't see that far, even standing on the coffins of generations.

"It was less than a year ago that a savior came into the murk of Haiti, an angry avenger for the poor who warned the aristocracy to share the wealth or watch the peasants take it. He reminded them of the Père Lebrun, a car tire soaked in gasoline that the people use to burn their enemies alive. The poor loved Jean-Bertrand Aristide, but in the end all he brought to Haiti was a return to darkness. Aristide, the first Haitian leader elected in a legitimate democratic process, watches in exile as his divided nation edges toward chaos and Haitian soldiers enforce the status quo with bullets."

Nightfall of that first day in Haiti caught me sitting on a crypt in the biggest boneyard I had ever seen, waiting for the young man Dorvilier to locate his father. Here and there, between the old crypts, gray bones jutted out of the gray dirt, where grave robbers tossed them aside. I had told my momma not to worry if she tried to call me in Miami and couldn't find me. I told her I was on vacation "somewhere in the islands."

I was thirty-two and divorced, could have lost a few pounds—a few dozen—and I felt the beginnings of arthritis in my knees and ankles. The woman who said she loved me, at the time, was beginning to think that she might not be able to improve me sufficiently after all; the rest never had. I was not in debt but I didn't own anything, either. One good friend had said I was the only man he had ever met who just might glide all the way through life without leaving "one single lasting footprint in the sands of society." But I had a hell of a story to do, and I would be happy for as long as it lasted.

I was working with a towering Haitian named Daniel Morel, my photographer and interpreter and one day to be my friend. He had met me at the airport, standing a full head taller than the mass of gesticulating, shouting men who offered to drive, to interpret, to—I would later learn—try and sell me the location of dead bodies. A shooter for the AP, he had heard of my newspaper—"good, good photographs"—and agreed to show me Haiti, all that I could stand of it.

I was no kind of foreign correspondent. I begged the foreign desk at my paper to let me do it; I didn't know then that I had none of the qualifications to join the club. I didn't even look like one. You can pick an FC out of a crowd at a hundred yards. They can talk without moving their jaws—it is a genetic thing that, I believe, comes from generations of speaking through teeth clenched around a pipe stem—and they speak French a lot, even when they don't have to. I don't speak French—I know how to say, "Señorita, how beautiful you are" in Spanish—and the only Creole I had picked up in Miami was "Git mou mou," which I think is something dirty.

But I wanted to come here, because it was a story unlike others I had done. A whole country, ruled forever by despots and murderers and low-rent sons of bitches, had been promised something better, and seen it yanked away. I wanted to come here because I had read about it my whole life, not just as a place of misery, but magic.

The foreign desk let me do it, mainly because reporters were not exactly lining up to volunteer. I was barely better than nothing, but I was still better than a blank page.

I told Daniel what I needed. I wanted to talk to Aristide's people, and he just said, "Of course." I told him I also needed to speak to the rich, and a shadow passed over his face. When I was safely gone, he would still be living here. I should not have worried, though. He just said, "Of course."

Daniel, I would learn over days, over years, could fix almost anything.

That first day, the images of poverty and cruelty whirl through my head one after another after another, but the smell seldom changes. It is a mix of flowering plants, charcoal smoke, human waste, rotting garbage, crushed sugar cane, old sweat, death.

I had rented a car but, because I had no idea where I was and Daniel couldn't hold my hand the whole time, I took a long taxi ride. As the rusted, dented, smoking thing hurtles around a blind curve on the road to Pétionville, where the people with money live, the driver almost hits a little girl with a big bucket of water balanced on her head. She stumbles back, and the water spills. The taxi driver is not concerned. She is only a restavik, a slave for one of the middle-class families. Her life is an after-thought, a pothole, a speck on his bumper.

In Cité Soleil, where people live in huts the size of outhouses with sewage creeping between their toes, a boy with a distended belly sits with the flies. Vedlin Severe's two naked babies play in muck near the docks as her son, Presnoc, begs. An old woman who looks like she hasn't eaten in weeks sits half-hidden in the door of a tin shack. She hides her head when people pass. Aristide's symbol, a red rooster, is painted on the wall. These are Aristide's people.

"God sent him to us," said Celeste Georges, who sells chicken cooked in hot oil on the street. She won't say where she lives because sol-diers are killing people who talk. She said it broke her heart when they made Aristide go. "Titid will return to us," she said, using Aristide's pet name. "He won't leave us like this."

They waited two hundred years for him, and they got less than a year of relief, respite, before the return to darkness.

The more I read about Haiti's history, the more fascinated I became. I learned that Haiti was rich once, a lush French colony with 95 percent of its people in chains. "In 1791," I wrote, "a voodoo priest named Bouk-man drank the blood of a sacrificed pig and led the first slave rebellion. When Haiti finally seized independence at bayonet point in 1804, slav-ery ended, but oppression was only beginning. The poor stayed poor and the upper class stayed rich under a succession of cruel, inept leaders. People starved as Haiti's resources vanished, turning it into what would be called the Hell Side of Paradise, the poorest nation in the Western Hemisphere. Then, in a questionable election in 1957, Haiti found its man to rule over hell: François 'Papa Doc' Duvalier, a doctor and dab-bler in voodoo who once tried to converse with the head of a dead enemy, who sought the future in goat entrails, who beat an enemy to death and then had his doctor perform emergency brain surgery in an effort to revive him. (We didn't know what cruelty was, back home. When we buried somebody, at least we made sure they were dead. Duvalier put them in the ground alive, wrecked their minds, and left them to wander, as a lesson.) He declared himself president for life, and unleashed the Ton-tons Macoute, named for a mythical giant who walked the mountains stuffing unfortunate children in his sack. They crushed resistance until Papa Doc died in 1971 and his son, Jean-Claude 'Baby Doc' Duvalier, took over. Food riots became so violent that he fled Haiti in 1986. One leader after another tried to stay in power by terror. The Duvaliers were gone, but the Macoute lingered on, under other names.

"Hope manifested itself in an unlikely savior. In September 1988, thugs walked into Mass at St. Jean Bosco Church and killed 12 people and wounded 70. They missed the man that military president Gen. Henri Namphy most wanted dead: the troublesome young priest named Aristide. He had been heard speaking of a Haiti where the soldiers didn't slaughter civilians and the poor shared in the fat of the wealthy Creoles' pocketbooks. Haiti must be reborn, he said. A speech is a powerful thing in a place where 65 percent of people can't read. When caretaker President Ertha Pascal-Trouillot set up a transitional government to oversee fair elections in 1990, Aristide was on the ballot. He won the presidency on Dec. 17 with 67 percent of the vote. On Dec. 18, soldiers fired into a crowd of supporters, killing a pregnant woman. On Jan. 7, before Aristide's inauguration, thugs seized the government in a short-lived coup. Aristide, a small man with glasses too large for his head, finally took over. The poor danced in the street as the aristocracy stared down from their mansions."

I had seen him just once, in Miami. He had come to be feted by the Haitians who had escaped their homeland and settled there. "We meet to celebrate a victory," he said in a speech to thirteen thousand Haitians. "Come home. The terror is over."

Aristide tried to govern the nation of seven million on popularity alone. The soldiers feared him, afraid he would take away their small privileges even though he promised a marriage between them and the people.

On September 30, just three days after his speech in Miami, Haitian soldiers mutinied and opened fire on his home. The savior went into exile.

And that gave me an excuse to see firsthand if the stories, the horrors, were true. I had no idea.

"The soldiers who guard the city hospital carry Israeli machine guns," I wrote, "in case some one-legged man should hop out and try to kick them to death." There is little else to fear within the walls. Half the patients have been shot to pieces and the other half are dead, they just haven't been moved yet. I walked up to one man, lying on his side, and noticed too late that he was beyond talking ever again. The distance from the hospital to the morgue is only a few yards, so the old nuns don't have far to push the gurneys. In the morgue, the bodies are piled haphazardly, to no particular scheme or order. The air conditioning and coolers have broken down, and the smell of rot is so strong it chases away all other living things, except a man called Presnel, who has no money and family. He squats in the dirt of the courtyard, waiting to die.

"Crazy man," Daniel explains, but not unkindly. The man is truly dying, and waits there, to be expedient.

Hearses—really station wagons with the windows painted black—wait near the hospital. The people in the morgue are the ones no one wants, so hearse drivers wait near the front entrance of the hospital for a fresh body. "One will be ready soon. No problem," a driver says. He is eating a Popsicle.

Inside, the hospital stinks from the fouled sheets and the smell of the morgue, which wafts in through the window. The afternoon slips by, and no doctors, medicine or relief come to this dormitory for the poor, only the nuns, who take a dead man off one bed and place a new patient there without changing the sheets.

The row of beds has one horror after another. One man's face is missing. Flies peck at twelve-year-old Inus Lundi's leg, shattered by bullets three weeks ago. His parents are missing, so he has no food. He will surely starve, surely die, surely walk on sticks the rest of his life if by some miracle he does live. His brother, younger, older, I can't tell, sits beside him, silent.

Jean-Claude Flankin was shot in the knee by soldiers. "It was a little boy who shot me," a smiling teenager with a machine gun, he says. He says they shot him for sport, for practice. They had been told to shoot anyone in known Aristide neighborhoods.

These are Aristide's people, too, I learn. They are the poor that the army knows it can slaughter without repercussion. They shot women and children. I stood in the middle of it, and tried not to cry like a baby. At one point, a young soldier with a rifle slung low, the muzzle pointing at my stomach, steps so close to me that the tip of the gun bores into my ribs. He is not threatening, only playing, the way the soldiers had been playing when they shot Franklin's leg. I hate this. I hate this place.

We are told we are not supposed to be here, and leave, but Daniel motions to the boy, the one with the shattered knee. "You can give him something," he tells me, but at first I shake my head. We don't pay for stories. He just looks at me. I gave the boy fifty dollars, enough money to feed him for months. "Merci," he said, but his expression didn't change.

Up in Pétionville, where the air smells better, people concede that they gave the army money, food and even new guns, at least partly financing the coup. They say it was necessary to head off the chaos that Aristide encouraged from the pulpit. Pétionville is a place where restaurants serve lobster pizzas and pear sorbet and fancy beer, where people drive European sedans and have other people scrub their floors. The refrigerators are full.

"Aristide told the poor people, 'If you are hungry, then eat. If you are thirsty, drink,'" said one woman. "Why shouldn't we give the soldiers money to protect what we have?"

In a jewelry shop in Port-au-Prince, a rich man sits surrounded by gleaming gold. The store is small, but there are three men with pistols in the front room.

"Aristide thought he could rule without us," the rich man said. "You heard what he said, about the Père Lebrun? 'I like its color. I like its smell.'"

What a life, to cruise a city searching the sky for plumes of smoke. Men had been burned alive in the past few days, and Daniel has told me we will likely see it happen again, before I am done. The joy of the story has been beaten out of me by what I have seen. I know it will return, when I sit down to write. It always does. But for now, I am tired and a little sick. The meanness of the place does not jab at you, now and then, it hammers, constant.

We see a column of smoke rising from a hilltop slum and we rush there, to see a crowd circling some kind of commotion in the center. But there is no fire. They have gathered to watch a three-legged dog try to keep company with another dog, which is as good a show as you're gonna get in Port-au-Prince, between killings.

The Père Lebrun, I thought, was some exotic name for the "flaming necklace." If I had known any French, like a real FC, I would have known better.

It was named for a man who sold tires. Jean-Claude Lebrun used to run radio and TV commercials, calling himself "Père (Father) Lebrun." So when people thought tires, they thought of him.

After Duvalier fell, the people burned Macoute wherever they found them, soaking a tire with gasoline, wedging it over their shoulders and head and setting it on fire. Aristide supporters had revived the tradition, but now the soldiers are cruising the slums, killing again. Killing. Someone. Always killing.

There is no stark line between good and evil here, I learn.

On October 23, hundreds of middle-class Haitians gathered for the funeral of the Reverend Sylvio Claude. He had talked badly of Aristide, and a mob of the poor attacked him. He fled to a police station, which was surrounded. The two policemen did not have to weigh the odds for long. They gave Claude to the mob, which hacked him to death with machetes.

His funeral, which I saw, told me much about this place.

The middle-class Haitians, friends and supporters of Claude, mill around under the protection of a company of soldiers outside the service. From inside comes the wailing of women. The casket is open, and the undertaker has not been skillful. Middle-class mourners file inside and come back outside with flame in their eyes, shouting to each other. And all around us, for I am standing in their midst, is a circle of poor Haitians in rags, looking on in hatred.

"Aristide is an assassin," bravely shouts one man in the crowd of the middle class, in English, so I can write it down.

A barefoot young man in the group of poor stares at him. His English is not good, but he makes himself clear to me, later. He came to watch the crowd, to catalog their faces in his mind. He would remember them, if Aristide ever came back. He would remember.

I was warned by one of the foreign editors not to predict in my story a judgment day acoming for Haiti. It would be premature. But it is hard not to expect some cataclysm. How can it go on and on like this? But like I said, I was ignorant of the place.

"The black market can supply what the wealthy people need. They keep their assets in U.S. banks," I wrote, "and they can wait out the crisis in Miami or Santo Domingo. The corrupt military has its own sources of income, contraband, drugs and protection rackets. The embargo only inconveniences the rich. But a missionary said he had seen the number of people in line for food double in just two weeks at his mission. The army shoots people who break in line for gasoline. The migration already has started in Port-au-Prince. The people are walking out of the city, into the mountains, to get closer to the food. From the air, they look like a caravan of rags, with buckets on their heads and babies in their arms. Trucks that carry food from the docks and fields don't reach the poor of the cities because the trucks don't have fuel. Aristide wants a complete embargo to force his return, but the hungry and the well-fed agree it won't happen that way. The embargo already has cost an estimated 5,000 jobs, as plants close. Another 10,000 were lost over the past year as the political tension grew. Many people with jobs can't get to their work because there is no gas. Stalled cars block the roads. Blackouts silence the music in the bars. Sirens sound at 10 and 11, warning people to go inside. At 11:01 sharp, gunshots break the silence, and people hope it's only the soldiers firing warning shots into the air. Haiti's society is disintegrating. Aristide waits. The soldiers play with their guns. Ask Haitians what they think will come of all this and they shake their heads. Haiti's story, the religious say, is pulled straight from the Book of Exodus. The poor Haitians wandered in the wilderness for 200 years, and found the man who promised to lead them out. His exile is just part of their wandering, their suffering."

I hint—against the editor's advice—that surely something profound is coming, some great change.

"Louis Bolivar, a woodworker in the downtown, knows the future," I wrote. "He turns rough lumber into sturdy tables, chairs, whatever the people want. The tap-tap-tap of his hammer has been constant, seven days a week, well into the night. He is making coffins."

I chartered a plane and flew to Santo Domingo, and from there, home. When I got home to Coconut Grove, it was Halloween night. People filled the street, in rubber masks, covered in fake blood, waving toy knives. People might have wondered why I was laughing.

27

Snow in a can

I came home for Christmas that year, like every year, to tiny houses ablaze with Christmas lights, twinkling islands of red, green, yellow and blue separated by acres of pine barrens and dark, empty miles. People who know they don't have enough money in their coffee cans or bank accounts to pay even their usual electric bill will string them for fifty yards across rain gutters and peach trees and hog-wire fences, lighting my way home from the airport in Atlanta. I smiled every time I passed a particularly garish neon garden, happy and proud that my people had not given in to the pretension popular among people in town, who called such displays tacky.

I love this time. The air, after the balm of Miami, was chill, delicious, but it would be stretching it to call it really cold. It just felt like home, like Christmas. Christmas does not mean snow to me. I have never seen it snow on December 25 in my life. Snow came in a can. We sprayed the tree with it before we put the lights on. If we didn't have the store-bought kind, Momma just used spray starch.

Momma never strung a lot of lights on the little house we lived in. But through the window, all my life, there has been a weak glow from a single strand of lights on a simple, small cedar tree. I looked for it as I pulled into the driveway, and it was there.

Momma was the same, still worried to death about Mark, but otherwise solid. I asked her when she wanted to go back to the dentist and be fitted for her new dentures, but it was a warm winter and so I had little hope. Mark was the same, still oblivious to the pain he caused her. I told him I wished he would try to do a little better, but he only grinned at me. He said he planned on coming to see me, down in Miami, maybe live with me. I told him it would be fine, but I knew he would never come. It was just as well. Miami would have consumed him, like a puddle of gasoline consumes a lit match. Sam was the same, still working, days, nights, weekends. My aunts and uncles were the same, still asking me when I was getting married, still two or three girlfriends behind.

Only my grandma was different. She was quiet now. She had never been quiet in her whole life.

I know there is nothing special about getting old. Everyone gets old. But you had to know my grandma, had to see the child in her that grinned when we were bad, that would have created the mischief with us if her old bones could have stood the strain, to understand the pain of it, seeing her that way.

If I had been coming home more regular, more often, I would have seen the change coming over years, as she grew older, more frail. As it was, it was as if she suddenly just got very tired. She had never been tired before, either. I would stick my head in the door and she would squeal out my name, year after year, and jump to her feet, or at least she would come as close to jumping as her age and slowly healing broken hip would permit. In minutes, she would have out her harmonica or banjo. She would announce to me, like she was calling a tune on the stage of the Grand Ol' Opry, that we would now have a little bit of "Boilin' Cabbage Down." She plucked the strings a little clumsier every year. It still sounded sweet to me. She would tire of one instrument and grab up another, and sometimes I would sing if I knew the words.

When I was a child, we would sit on her bed and sing "Uncloudy Day," or at least as close as we could come to it, at the very top of our lungs. We sang so loud that the kinfolks would come rushing in, and she would cackle a little, because she just liked to get a rise out of folks, sometimes. But as we got older we sang it loud to make up for the fact we still didn't know the words, or had just forgotten them, or didn't give a damn, because the noise was the thing. Just an old woman and a young man making noise.

Oh they tell me of a home
Where no dark clouds rise
They tell me of a home
Far away
Oh they tell me of a land
Of cloudless skies
Oh-h-h-h they tell me
Of an uncloudy day

It was different this time. She sat in her little room, surrounded by the tokens of love that we bestow on the old. There were pictures and dolls and stuffed animals and more knickknacks than I have ever seen in one room. There were her instruments, the guitar and the banjo and the harmonica, but they lay silent, unused. She did not play for me that day. She never played for me again.

I was so very afraid, as I walked into that room, that she would not know who I was. Her eyesight was not good, so I leaned in real close. I saw a grin spread across her face. "Rick?" she said, and I said, thankfully, "It's me."

I only sat with her a few minutes. She asked me how Lisa was, my onetime wife, and I told her that she was fine. She asked me if she had come, and I said no, she was at home. I know that she knew we were not married anymore, but that it just slipped her mind. She had always loved her, and I saw no need to hurt her now, for the sake of clarity. I could stand a lie better than she could stand the truth.

I told her she looked good. She said, no, she looked bad. I told her she looked young, but she dropped her head at that, and said, no, son, I'm old.

I asked her, as I always did, if she had "a feller." That always got her grinning. This time she just said no, she was too old for that, too.

She had seemed ageless to me. The sun and wind had scoured and grooved her early in life, and as long as I knew her, she was gray. The years tumbled past and seemed to have little impact on her, at least on the outside, but on the inside she was beginning to weaken, to fail.

Both my grandfathers were long dead, and I had never really known my daddy's mother beyond a quick visit every few years. My grandma Abigail, for all my life, had been my only real lifeline to the distant past. That Christmas, as I sat in the little room and held her hand, I felt more than her hand tremble.

The kinfolks gathered on Christmas Eve, as always. As always, they gave me presents that I needed. Momma, as always, got me nine pairs of white Fruit of the Loom underwear, size 36. Others got me towels, socks, T-shirts, a pocketknife. Sam got me tools, to make up for the fact I had moved so far away he couldn't come and rescue me. When I am seventy, I hope I am getting a gross of underwear and a dozen pairs of socks, and tools. With presents like that, you can ratchet yourself firmly into place, and remember who you are.

The next day we had Christmas dinner, and I don't reckon I've ever had food as good as we had that year, every year. There was a ham as big as a five-gallon bucket, and mashed potatoes, and pans of dressing (you might call it stuffing), and pinto beans with the ham hock swimming in the pot, and cabbage slaw, and biscuits that were hot and crisp on the outside and soft inside, and cranberry sauce because you can't have dressing without cranberry sauce, and sweet tea, in a gallon pickle jug.

I ate too much and let Sam beat me, badly, in a game of Horse. The basketball goal had been at the regulation ten feet when he first tacked it to the tree, but over time it had grown a lot, and I claimed that was what had thrown off my shot. He called me a chucklehead again. I noticed his hair was getting thin.

He asked me, as he swished through a perfect twenty-footer, if I was ever coming home to live again. I told him I did not reckon so, at least not for a long, long time. He told me he was sorry about that, and I saw no reason to say what I always said, that I lived away from home because

I was doing good, because my career was taking off, not because I was being punished. I lived in Miami because I wanted to, because I could. But to Sam, no one lived away from here, away from these pines, by choice. I am still not sure who is right and who is wrong, or if there is even a right and wrong to it.

I went in and said good-bye to my grandma, and made her say my name again.

I told Momma to call me collect. I didn't see Mark. As I left for the airport in Atlanta, Sam gave me a last gift. It was an orange plastic hard hat with a plastic screen to protect my face. It was a logging hat, what you wear to keep the falling trees from knocking your brains out and the limbs from gouging out your eyes. I looked at it, then at him, puzzled.

"For them riots," he said.

28

The interview for the
Ivy League

Except for that pesky hurricane, Andrew, the summer of 1992 was magic. I had made something almost like a home for myself in Miami. I roamed the place, searching for stories or just diversions, just living. I ate grouper sandwiches on the Miami River, roamed and fished and waded the Glades, floated on trade winds, stayed warm. My then-girlfriend moved on about that time, but I didn't feel much sting. We had been mostly just roommates for a long time. Passion is something you really don't miss, after it has cooled. It is like looking at an empty bottle on the side of the road and thinking, "Boy, I wish I had a Coke." The loves you miss are the ones that go away when they are still warm, even hot, to the touch.

This was a sweet time, even sweeter by the simple fact that this life now had a distinct horizon. I had been here almost three years, longer than I had stayed anywhere in quite some time. Even though I was happy, I was restless. I needed a change.

Lord, did I get one.

On the urging of some friends, I applied for a Nieman Fellowship for journalists to Harvard University, for nine months of study in 1992 and 1993. It is the most prestigious fellowship in the country, about the nicest thing that can happen to a working journalist who lives story to story. I had about as much business at Harvard as a hog in a cocktail dress, and the competition for the thing was fierce. But friends told me I was perfect for it, and it for me. How many journalists, my friends told me, had gone as far as me, but were as ignorant.

In essence, all you had to do to win it was write two essays about yourself, and convince a selection panel that you would make use of the time, give something back to the university, and not burn the place down. The truth, I would learn over the next few months, was that a lot of the people who got in it were not people filling gaps in their education, but people who had fancy educations already.

I felt like the lowest form of hypocrite. I did not need a fancy education to do my job. I was openly scornful of people who rode their school ties like some chariot. In fifteen years of writing stories for money, all I had needed was talent. I wore that chip on my shoulder like a crown. I hung my plaques on the walls, all of them, until my living room looked like a dentist's office and I had some left over to give to Momma. When I had finally proved myself, at one of the best papers in America, I came looking for, for what?

I told myself it was because the man in charge, the Nieman "curator," was one of the legends in our business, a Southerner, a former *New York Times* editor and reporter named Bill Kovach whom I had always wanted to work for, or at least talk to. It would be, as I said in a magazine story about Kovach once, like "shooting the bull with Moses."

But it was more than that. I applied to the place and the program because they had something I wanted.

I made the next-to-final cut and was invited up for an interview before a panel of Harvard professors and journalists who had been Nieman Fellows before. They held it in an elegant old white house that is the Nieman headquarters, a house that just looked like Harvard, somehow. The interview was held in a room where the selection panel sat gathered around a table. At least I didn't have to stand before a raised dais.

It would be a lie to say I was shaking when I walked in. I have never been afraid to talk, never been shy, always able to think on my feet. But

I was a little nervous here, because it was more than a test to see if I would get $25,000 in cash, a year off from work, free tuition and all the sherry and goose liver pâté I could handle.

It was a test of whether or not I really belonged among these people, in this world, even if only for a year-long visit. Nothing they would tell me would make me feel less than proud of who I was or what I had done, over years. At least, I sure hoped not. No, this was a test of whether or not I could make them believe that I was smart enough to give something in return, something of value, to the finest university in the land. I had spent a lifetime telling myself I didn't give even a little bitty damn what the smart people thought. Yet here I was, hat in hand to them.

It was worse than I ever imagined.

One of the first questions they asked me was if I was a fake, if "this Southern thing" this country boy image, was just my gimmick. It was not that I sounded Southern—Southerners are some of the most pretentious people on earth—but that I sounded country, or, since I was at Harvard, "rural." Southerners, a lot of them, work to rid themselves of their accents. They believe they sound slow, or at least unsophisticated, to outsiders. I guess now I know why.

I got mad then, but I just smiled through the heat in my face and said that no, I really was what I sound to be.

"I am not a phony," I said. "This is what I am."

Another person on the selection committee asked me how I could say, in one of my essays, that a respected black mayor in Alabama had failed the people who voted for him. His inference seemed to be that, me being a white Southerner, I was probably also a racist and a redneck.

I told him that when the mayor had taken office, blacks had owned less than one percent of all business in his city. Three terms later, almost time for their children to vote, blacks still owned less than one percent of all business.

"I don't expect anyone to correct in a few years a hundred years of good ol' boy leadership," I said, but the mayor had time to make a small difference in the pocketbooks of his constituency.

The questioner nodded his head, and I thought, "I dodged a bullet, there."

But the hardest question, the one that tripped me up, was from Kovach. It was simply: "Why do you want to do this?"

I told the truth. I told him that I had worked hard and taken risks— to my life, my career—to get where I was, but that this business of journalism has a bubble of pretension over it, one that I often found myself pressing against. Harvard would give me a needle, to burst it, to get through. I had proved myself. But, as my old editor Basil Penny had said, I didn't have enough jelly on me.

"To tell the truth," I said. "it's gonna mean a whole lot more to other folks than it will me."

Kovach wasn't buying that answer, which was just half an answer. I don't remember precisely what he said, but it was to the effect of: "So you're saying that painting a big 'H' on your chest will take care of all your problems?"

I said no, I wanted to learn. I told them what I wanted to learn and why, so I wouldn't be always winging it, so that I could write with some authority, instead of just seeming to.

When it was done, the man who thought he was fast on his feet, who was determined not to let the fancy people put him down, was raining sweat. It is one thing to be sure of yourself. It is another to have someone tell you to quit dancing, look them in the eye, and tell them the truth even if it hurts your pride.

I was certain I would never see this room again, this house. They asked me to please leave by a side door, so that I wouldn't come into contact with other hopefuls waiting in the lobby of the old house.

The plane ride home was the longest one I think I have ever had. I had gone to visit the fancy people, with my hand out, and left feeling like I had forgotten to clean out from under my fingernails.

The Nieman Fellows are apprised of their selection by an early morning telephone call, a few weeks later. If your phone hasn't rung by 9 A.M., you're probably screwed. I didn't sleep at all the night before.

The telephone rang at about 7 A.M. It was Kovach. He asked me if I would come to Harvard, that he was proud it had come true for me.

It occurred to me then that I wasn't wearing any britches—I wasn't wearing anything—and here I was talking to a journalism icon in my birthday suit.

I hung up the phone, hugged my girlfriend, and felt the guilty relief wash over me. I tell myself now that it should not have been important, so important. I can almost make myself believe it.

I called my momma and told her that her middle son was going to the most prestigious college in America. We had talked about it, from time to time, but it meant nothing to her until it came true. Like I've said before, my momma is weary of broken promises.

"Thank God," she said. Then, in a worried voice, "Where is that at?"

I told her it was in Cambridge, near Boston, in Massachusetts.

"Lord God," she said, "you'll freeze to death."

Kovach, whether he is proud of it or not, would turn out to be a guiding force in my life. I learned later that he campaigned for me, whom he had never met until that day. I guess he did it because he thought I had earned a chance to be there. Or maybe it was because he was from Tennessee, from a place below the gentry, himself.

Either way, I was by God going. My girlfriend, Rachel, bought me a duck hunter's coat for my birthday, the closest thing we could find in the mail-order catalogs to a freestanding shed. I bought a pair of insulated boots, and some long-handled drawers (long underwear), and gloves. I was ready.

I had a plan for leaving. I made a big payment into Momma's house fund—and planned to take the four hundred dollars I had left in my checking account and head south, on a seaplane. I would listen to steel drum music and act a fool for a few days, till I was broke, then kiss Rachel good-bye—we were still friendly—and head north. A puff of wind off the coast of Africa messed everything up.

Hurricane Andrew punctuated my life and times in Miami with winds that blew 180 miles per hour. I had been invited over to St.

Pete for a going-away party, and hurried back to Miami across Alligator Alley into a wall of black clouds. Everyone else was going the other way.

I had sold my old Firebird, and as Andrew swirled offshore I roamed the mostly empty streets in a rented Thunderbird, searching for people who were stupid enough to stay. Among them, I saw a single homeless man who seemed not to have gotten the word, and was unimpressed when I told him to duck and run. It was as if, after what he had lived through, a hurricane would be nothing short of cleansing. Finally the winds blew the car around too much to safely drive, and a falling limb crashed down and sheared off the left taillight. I tried to go home to my little house near the bay, but the police said no, it was too close to the shore. So I went to our office, just a quarter-mile inland, to ride it out. I had a paper sack full of junk food—Oreos, Cheetos, pork rinds, I believe—and some bottled water. I got a futon and put it on the floor. Then, as the windows trembled and the giant storm bore down on south Florida like the wrath of God, I rolled up in the futon like some big ol' burrito, and went to sleep.

I woke up to chaos, to sailboats in trees, to shredded houses and ruined lives. My own little rented house was wrecked, awash. The beautiful banyan trees that faced the office were in splinters. I had written a hundred stories, staring across at them, and for some reason the sight of them, in kindling, saddened me worse than any other structural harm.

Oddly, Andrew came to south Florida on precisely the day I had planned to leave it. I stayed on for three days, amazed at the power of it, and finally drove to the Miami airport with a ticket to Atlanta, then Boston.

As the plane lifted off, I took one good, last look at the city that had somehow suited my character, even though my Alabama drawl seemed so out of place in a city where the words were flavored with Cuba libres (rum and Coke), where English had long become a second language. From high up, it looked like someone had picked up one of those snow globes they sell in the tourist shops and smashed it on the floor.

❖   ❖   ❖

I spent a day or two at home, in Alabama, before heading north again. I know my momma was proud of me for going back to college, even though she was not real sure what a "fellowship" was. Fellowship, to us, was what you did in church when the preacher told you to turn around in the pew and shake hands with your neighbor, which, in this case, was not far from accurate. Even though it was not "real Harvard," as one *Anniston Star* buddy had felt compelled to point out to me—he had been to real Harvard—it was still a nice thing, I told her. I learned later that she told everybody who would listen that her son was going to Harvard.

She tried to give me some blackberry jelly and pickled peppers to take with me, and told me to dress warm. She said my blood was thin from all that time in Florida, so I would catch a lot of colds unless I wore long underwear and two coats, at all times.

I spent one last lazy evening down in Sam's barn, just talking. I didn't talk about Harvard. I felt sure that he, of all people, would be least impressed by this gift of free, fancy education. When two friends drove up, we walked outside to talk, to just stand around. It is something Southern men do, when they don't have anything to say. They will just stand around, quiet, shifting their weight from foot to foot, until someone finally feels moved to talk. This time, it was Sam.

"Ricky's goin' to Harvard," he said, and I swear to God he said it proud.

There was a long silence.

"Well," one of the young men said, from under the bill of his cap. "That's good."

Then they started to talk about the mill, about layoffs and slow-downs, and, for reasons I am not quite sure of, I was ashamed.

29

Perfume on a hog

I had just one bad day at Harvard, but only because I lived up to my own stereotype. It was the night I let my temper push through my paper-thin veneer of respectability, and I threatened to whip a man's ass during a white-tablecloth dinner in the Harvard Faculty Club, sometime between the chateaubriand and a stirring speech by a Native American newspaper publisher.

It was the dead of winter, which could have fallen anywhere from October to May. I had slipped into what I thought was a friendly argument with a man whose name I forgot as soon as we were introduced. I am bad with names. The argument had to do with President Clinton's search for an attorney general, and I had merely shared with him an opinion: that selecting an attorney general from perhaps the most ineffective justice system in the nation, Dade County, might not be the brightest thing to do. He didn't think much of my reasoning, and if he had just said so, things would have been fine. Instead, he insulted me.

"You embarrass yourself," he said.

He might as well have slapped me or spit in my face. It is a failing of pampered intellectuals that they assume everyone at their table is as civilized as they are. I had on a coat and tie and my socks even matched, but he had made a terrible mistake. My whole life I had wondered if I was as good, as smart, as clean as the people around me. Now this, this insult, hurt like salt flung in my eyes.

"I'll tell you what," I said, "I'll drag you out of here and whip your ass."

He turned bright red—I have never seen a man light up like that—and said again, insultingly, "No one's said that to me since elementary school."

I just stared at him, and then I laughed in his face. It scared even me, that laugh. It sounded a little crazy, it sounded like someone I hadn't heard from in a very, very long time.

He left not long after that, to an uneasy silence that made me feel like I had dragged my sleeve through the peach cobbler or committed some other terrible faux pas. Later, a very erudite journalist from South Africa, a young man named Tim DuPlesis, leaned over and said, "Excuse me, Rick. Did I hear you say you were going to whip that man's arse?"

I told him, yes, and begged him to forgive me for my rudeness at table.

I expected to be defrocked after that, or whatever it is they do to you up there. But when I told the curator, Kovach, about it, he only laughed.

But, to play it safe, I kept a low profile after that. It is easier that way. The pretension just slides right over you if you're hunkered down.

It is a fact that I am hypersensitive to it. It may even be that I saw the disdain in places where it didn't exist. It is more than possible, it is probably true.

But I had too much to learn, too much to do, anyway, to even think about it.

Harvard, to a man who had been in college precisely six months, was a gift, a glorious gift. I studied Latin and Afro-Caribbean history. I took every American history class I could. I studied diplomacy. I studied religion. I studied people. My whole career, I had been winging it. Here was a chance to know, to truly know something for a change.

I read all the books on the reading lists and went to class almost every day. In my spare time I rode the subway to Boston and took Spanish, building on the pitiful few phrases I could already speak. I soon learned that being able to say, "Señorita, qué linda tu eres," would not get me through life.

I had an honest-to-God knapsack, full of books, and I walked every-where I went. There was a peace in that place between those old build-ings, in the stacks of books in the massive library, in the classrooms that smelled in the mornings of old polish and still-wet hair. Maybe for some people it was like going back in time, but I had never seen or done any-thing like this.

I lived on the third floor of a Colonial house, and invited friends over to do nothing except talk, and talk, and talk. I made friends. I ate pâté, which is a lot like the potted meat sandwiches my momma used to make, and met some pretty fancy people. I went to enough seminars to kill a normal man, and sat in the back, so I could slip out if it got slow. It usu-ally did. If I got homesick, I called my momma, then went to Mrs. B's—a place with real food—and got some meat loaf and mashed potatoes. I bought a Harvard sweatshirt, then bought thirty more to take home as Christmas presents. That year, you would have thought the whole popu-lation of Possum Trot, Roy Webb Road and Germania Springs had lodged at Kirkland House.

In December, I watched the Charles River freeze over. I will always remember that first, deep, lasting snow. I went running through the house, trying to get somebody to go play in the snow with me, and they all just looked at me like I was crazy. I hurried down to Harvard Yard, where the freshmen hung out, and found them flinging handfuls of snow at each other. I did not join in right away—I was twice their age—but then some young woman caught me square in the eyes with a ball of wet snow and for the next few minutes I was a kid again, slipping and sliding around like an idiot. I would come to despise it, as the snow piled up waist-high from the snowplows and turned the color and consistency of crumbled asphalt, but I think I loved it for a little while.

The cold, I never liked. Maybe my blood was a little thin, like my skin.

The other Nieman "fellows"—I've always thought that to be a

twenty-dollar word and a little ridiculous—were ready-made friends, all journalists like me, and yet completely unlike me. Half were from this country, even Alaska, the rest from around the world: India, Albania, South Africa, China, Jordan, Vietnam. There was a fierce Russian woman who I am fairly certain could kick my ass. I loved to hear her talk, but now and then I couldn't help but think of Rocky and Bullwinkle's adversaries, Boris and Natasha. I would whisper to her, "So, vere is Moose and Squirrel?"

There was a mean woman from Italy who didn't think much of American journalism, but she was nice to me and I liked her. She pinched me on the cheek once and said, "Ciao bello," which even I knew was something nice.

The American Niemans, almost all of them, had already been to Ivy League schools. They were from Harvard, Yale, Columbia, Swarthmore, almost all of them, so I was prepared to dislike them on sight. There was one jackass who actually believed that because I was from Alabama I was stupid—this is not paranoia, this was blatantly obvious and even bothered the other people in my class—but I did not knock his teeth down his throat because it would have cast a shadow over my Nieman experience. But the truth is that most of them were good people, and couldn't help it that the worst day of their lives had involved wilted arugula.

I made some friends for life, the way I usually make them. Any jackass can be pleasant company, but if people help you when you're at your worst, that's a friend. I hurt one of my bad knees, badly, while I was there, and for almost two months I couldn't walk. Two Niemans, a Texan named Olive Talley and a New Yorker named Heidi Evans, hauled me back and forth to the doctor and demanded information about my condition that, as a boy from Alabama, I would never have asked. We just always figured doctors were too important to waste their time explaining things to us that we wouldn't understand. Another Nieman Fellow, Terry Tang, cooked me duck and turnips—we spent a good part of an hour discussing the virtue of the lowly turnip and decided that it is greatly underappreciated—and once she even brought me a banana split. It was 12 degrees outside, so the ice cream didn't even melt on the way home.

They, especially, taught me that you can't go through life not liking people because they didn't have to work as hard or come as far as you did. And who knows, maybe if I had bothered to get to know them better, maybe they had. Maybe they just didn't wear it like some bullshit badge of honor, as I did. Olive was from Texas, anyway.

The students, the ones who actually paid tuition and had to study—didn't quite know what to make of me. I was twice their size—Harvard students tend to run small—and some of them would walk all the way off the concrete paths in Harvard Yard to avoid walking close to me. I am not a scary-looking man, and I know I was better dressed than the homeless. A friend of mine told me that it is just the way most of them had been raised, that it wasn't me, it was them. "Don't make any sudden moves. If you throw up your hand and say, 'Hey, how you doin'?' you'll scare 'em to death or at least into therapy, and they might hurt themselves getting away."

In the classrooms, though, when I felt I had something to add or something to ask, it was different. It is a fact that some Harvard students will not ask questions in class because they are afraid they might appear as if they don't already know everything, but time and time again I found myself answering questions from them after class, about the South, about race in the South, about politics and food and relationships between the sexes and . . . after a while I realized what they meant in the Nieman program about giving something back to the university. I was, by my very presence, a walking lab, a field trip. I had seen the meanness and killing that they read about in their texts on the Third World. I had seen George Wallace, big as life.

Most of the professors were glad to have us in their classes, because we were there because we wanted to be, not as one more credit. One professor seemed less than happy to have me. The professor spoke about the legacy of pain and prejudice, in that Yankee accent, and I could tell that the professor was speaking from insights gleaned on long-ago field trips, from old safaris through the rural South, and had formed petrified opinions that no amount of new information could change. There is plenty of new meanness and new racism in the South, but it is more complicated now. Some of the bad men have public cable access shows. Others are more prone to wear swastikas than burn crosses. The new racists blur their messages of hate with anti-government sentiment more than religion. Harvard was a little out of date, on racism.

But there were so many others who opened doors in my mind. I remember watching one old professor speak long and eloquently on U.S. diplomacy and the legacy of mistrust this country had sown in the rest of the Western Hemisphere, and as he would talk he would reach up to clutch the lapels of his robe, a robe that was not there. When he had begun, professors had worn such things, and he still reached for it as his mind whirled from fact to fact. I would just sit and listen.

It is a cliché to say I learned something about other people and other cultures, but it is true; I had begun that process with my first interview as a reporter, of course, but Harvard was a Sam Walton Wholesale Warehouse of information and experiences. I will always loathe movies with subtitles, I will perhaps never own a pair of Birkenstocks, but I opened my head a little, in that place.

When I could, I talked about writing and living with Bill Kovach, one of those smart, decent men you would like to be like, if you had it in you. Through his intelligence and hard work and decency, he had proved himself. I did not have his arsenal, I couldn't be like him, and I am even reluctant to claim him as a friend because I do not want to suppose anything. But few people have been as good a friend to me as him.

A silver-haired, dark-eyed man whose parents had emigrated from Albania to Tennessee, he never thought it particularly funny when I asked him if they still had a football program at the University of Tennessee. When I would try to avoid a question, or use my Southernness as a shield, or try to bullshit him, he would call me a "mush mouth."

He told me I had a gift, which I guess anyone wants to hear even if it ain't noways true, but he also told me, more or less gently, that I could use some work. He told me I crowded too many pretty lines into my stories, that I needed space between them. I tried to fix it. He told me he thought I was a decent man, and I almost cried, because somehow he had seen something in me that made him believe it.

As curator of the program, you have to listen to a lot of whining from journalists who have it made and are too dense to realize it. Maybe one of the reasons he could put up with me was I woke up every day grinning.

One day he asked what I was going to do with my life. I told him I loved my job and might stay, but that the idea of a bigger paper, of proving myself at some writer's paper like the *Los Angeles Times* or one of the better magazines, tugged at me.

"How about the *New York Times*?" he asked me.

I shook my head.

"They wouldn't look at somebody like me," I said, and he looked at me like I had told him I couldn't do one more push-up.

"Don't be sure," he said. I dismissed it from my mind.

I was grateful to work at St. Pete. In many ways it was the best job I ever had. But I truly believed that there was a barrier between me and a place like the *New York Times*, a barrier that Kovach did not recognize— or refused to.

Of all the things I took away from my short time with him, one rests in my mind the way an arm rests around your shoulders.

An editor had asked me, sneering a little, who taught me to write. I told Kovach that.

"The next time someone asks you that," he said, "tell 'em it was God."

The year slid by, quick, like it was time, greased. As the winter finally gave up and the Charles thawed, I realized that much of a year had passed and I had not written a single story. I had not talked to a grieving mother or walked a hallway littered with crack vials or . . . I had just read and learned and talked and slept. What a gift.

I knew now why I had disliked those Ivy League kids so, for so long. It was like I was a dog on a kinked chain, a foot short of the water bucket, watching every other mutt drink. The time at Harvard took the kink out of the chain.

The last day, they gave me a certificate that had Harvard on it. I put it on my wall, where everyone could see it. Friends of mine who had gone to "real Harvard" said that displaying one's Harvard pedigree was "not the thing to do," as if people could tell you went to Harvard by your ambience alone.

I left it on the wall for a good while. People might not be able to tell, just by looking at me, that I am a Harvard man.

I had been ready to leave Miami when I left, but the more I thought about it, in those cold months in Cambridge, there was no other place in Florida I wanted to work when I returned to the *St. Petersburg Times*. I had known that the paper had closed its Miami bureau, which hurt my feelings but was nothing I couldn't survive. I would work out of my house, I figured. But the paper had other plans. The top editors wanted me to return to St. Pete. I thought they were going to make me pay for my year-off drinking sherry and eating goose liver pâté by making me do some distasteful, boring work.

I landed in the rose bushes again. The new executive editor, Paul Tash, the man who hired me, made me a sort of roving national reporter and told me to go to where the best stories were.

I found some. I spent time on the Navajo Indian Reservation, eating grape snow cones and talking to medicine men and women about disruptions in the life force that flows from Mother Earth. I went to a "sing," where people gathered to drum and sing under the biggest sky I had ever seen, not so some tourists could take pictures, but because a hanta virus was killing them. I walked in the desert and sat under a tree with an old woman who had lost her husband to cancer from the uranium he mined to make bombs. She invited me in for fried bread.

I wrote about racism in Vidor, Texas, and floods in Des Moines, Iowa, and casinos in Biloxi, Mississippi. In the meantime, I lived on the beach on Florida's west coast, in a second-floor apartment that had a view of the Gulf of Mexico from its kitchen sink. I had made a new friend, a lovely young woman who was going to college at the University of Florida, which I am sure I should have felt guilty about. It seemed like I had it made, again.

As if things couldn't get any better, I had job offers now, from the *New York Times* and the *Los Angeles Times*. I thought I was charmed, again. I thought I couldn't lose, again.

I flew out to Los Angeles and met nice people who thought I would fit in, who complimented my work and took me to lunch in the "Picasso Room." It would be a perfect marriage, they told me, a happy one.

I flew to New York and saw the Empire State Building shrouded in fog. I sat in a room with Max Frankel and Joe Lelyveld, men of legend in this business, and I admit to being a little nervous there. I kept dropping my little security badge that said "NYT." They would not try to change me, they said, except to maybe make me better. I could do the kind of stories I had always done, in the way I did them. Those stories had a place in their newspaper, they told me.

I felt like a blue-chip quarterback. Maybe, I thought, it was true. I couldn't lose.

Then, the charm must have slipped through a hole in my pocket and rolled through a crack in the floor.

I took the *Los Angeles Times* offer. It was the perfect job, a job I could not have designed any better myself, the perfect fit. The *New York Times* frightened me. Just reading it frightened me. There was great writing in it, but so many people had warned me that I would never survive there, that I was too different, that the newspaper would try to process me and my work. That would surely lead to disaster. In Los Angeles, I would get to write long, pretty stories. It was much more similar to St. Pete, and St. Pete had almost nurtured me.

I know some reporters will roll their eyes at this, but I hated to leave St. Pete. The editors there had not given a damn where I was from or how I talked or where I went to school. I was ungrateful, at best, to leave so soon. But the editor, Tash, told me as I shook his hand: "We got our money's worth out of you." I will always appreciate that.

I remember that my kinfolks were almost angry with me when I told them I was going to Los Angeles. Florida had been bad enough, but it did not seem so far, even when I was in Miami. My momma did not say don't go, but for weeks, when I would call, her voice was small.

She told me she had looked at Los Angeles on a map, and looked at where she was, and it scared her to death.

I left for L.A. in the fall. I got my feet wet in the Pacific Ocean for the first time. The color of it almost startled me. In the deep water off the piers, it was almost purple.

It was just a year after the L.A. riots, and the city was, as Miami had been, rich in the stories that I knew how to do. I rolled past them, cataloging them in my head. I took a stroll through Echo Park, ate a pig tripe burrito in the downtown, saw a man passed out with a needle dangling from his arm, chatted with a family of five living in a single room that had the fire escapes wired shut to keep out the "Chollos," the little shitheels who terrorized their block.

I arrived to sunlight still warm and strong in November, to traffic I could not even imagine, to Korean barbecue—it wasn't much like home but it sure wasn't bad—and an apartment building built on rollers, for when the earth moved.

I arrived, I quickly found, to a job that did not exist. The job that waited for me wasn't as good as the job that I thought I had accepted, and it pricked my pride so deeply that I let anger rule my reactions, and dictate the future.

Too many people there knew the job I had been offered, so, at least, I didn't have to doubt my own sanity when I challenged the top editors about the job I had traveled across the country to take. They told me to be patient, but patience is a quality I simply do not have, nor have I ever wanted it.

There was no one to even really get mad at. This was just an unlucky circumstance of crossed wires. To be fair, the editors worked it out and made good on the job I thought I had come to do—the bottom line—but when you begin a job by fighting with your bosses there is little future in it for you. Common sense tells you that. As it was, when people ask how long I worked there, I tell them three weeks, two days, four hours and twenty-seven minutes. An editor demanded my parking card before I left. It was a little like having your chevrons ripped off and being drummed out of the service.

It would have been a lot more noble if I had not landed so gently. I had called the *New York Times,* told them I had made a big mistake, and I would love to come to work for them if they would have me. I expected them to tell me to enjoy the sunshine, palm trees and unemployment. Instead, the hiring editor, Carolyn Lee, said I could start in January, start fresh.

My luck, my old friend, had not left me after all.

For maybe the first time in my life, I had tried to do the safe thing, and it had blown up in my face. Never, ever again.

I stayed in L.A. for a month or so, mainly because I had no place else to live and my rent was paid. I worked on my pitiful Spanish, read some books, even went to the beach. But it never felt right. The ocean was too cold, out there. It was the wrong ocean, entirely.

Now and then I would sing a few words of an old Tennessee Ernie Ford song, and it made me feel better.

> *I've been to Georgia on a fast train, honey*
> *I wasn't born no yesterday*
> *I got a good country raisin'*
> *and an eighth grade education*
> *Ain't no need in y'all a-treatin' me this way*

30

New York

It is late afternoon in the newsroom of the *New York Times* and I have just turned in the story that will make or break me. It is only my second story, but I have written it with no concessions, no second-guessing of what will or will not get in this newspaper. The story sounds like me. It is gothic, dark, personal. I think it is good. But it doesn't matter what I think, only what they think, the editors in that meeting, the mystical Page One Meeting, where stories are dissected by great minds. I watch the door like a doomed man watches a gallows being built. I cannot fail here. I cannot fail again. Finally it swings open and the editors file out, and I see Joe Lelyveld, the managing editor and soon to be the executive editor, walking toward me. He is not smiling.

He stops at my desk and leans against it. I do not remember exactly what he said but it was something to the effect of, "I know we said we would try to get you some gentle editing, but . . ." and my heart froze.

". . . but we had to change the comma in your lead." And now he is smiling, and I know I have been had. I do not mind at all. I only hope he does not notice that my laughter is laced with something not too far from hysteria.

This, I think, is the cold and austere *New York Times*? This is the cold and unapproachable Joe Lelyveld? All I know is, at that exact moment, the debacle of Los Angeles that I had carried around like some clinking leg iron fell away, and I thought I might be OK. I would not, I thought, have to go back to Alabama in shame. I might still have to, someday, but not now. Not now.

I don't know if he planned it that way, if he even knew how I felt. Maybe he did. People say he is a smart man.

It took me just a few weeks to learn that much of what was said about the *Times* was woefully out of date, or just plain wrong. Most of the editors I worked for had a simple mission: Go find the best and most important stories, and put them in the newspaper.

It was the directive that Mike Oreskes, the metro editor, gave me before I even began work. For the next six months, through one of the coldest, nastiest winters on record, I roamed that giant, confusing place, but to say I searched for stories would be a lie. I did not have to search. New York hurled stories at you like Nolan Ryan throws fastballs. All you had to do was catch them, and try not to get your head knocked off.

The newsroom, at the time, was a crowded, noisy, dusty dungeon of a place, where the reporters worked practically shoulder to shoulder. Some of them were nice to me and some of them treated me like I was going to get their newspaper dirty if I touched it with my pedestrian hands. I could feel the old chip on my shoulder pressing down, down, heavier than I could remember it being in a long while. But that was fine, too. Just because they let you in the school door doesn't mean they're going to invite you to the dance.

Instead, I found my friends on the photo staff, a collection of delightful, smart, cranky, streetwise and often fearless artists and weirdos who knew this city frontward, backward and sideways, and consented to let me ride along. If not for them, I would have surely floundered, helpless. Instead they dragged me along to good story after good story. I felt like a freeloader, but we did find us some tales to tell.

One sticks fast in my memory. With a long-haired, bearded man of

Puerto Rican heritage named Angel Franco, who referred to me almost fondly as "big, dumb white boy," I set out to report a story that carried me deep into the real New York, another story about living and dying and that fragile, shivering place in between.

At least once a week in the New York papers, there had been stories of chilling murders in the city's tiny groceries, what most people here called bodegas. In the past year, fifty people had died behind their counters, making it the most dangerous job in New York, more dangerous than fighting fires or fighting crime, even deadlier than driving a livery cab. Mind-boggling holdups ended in gunfights and cold-blooded executions. People killed for a hundred dollars, for twenty, for the joy of hearing their guns go "bang." Most of the victims were Hispanic, but there were Chinese, Koreans, Haitians and Middle Easterners, too, trying to make a living one pack of M&M's at a time in Washington Heights, the South Bronx, East Harlem, Bushwick Avenue.

I wanted to hear those stories from the mouths of the people who lived behind those counters day after day. But this time I would see the fear, feel it, as they did. It made for a newspaper story, a New York story, that is as honest as I have ever done.

Harlem, March 1994

"One man has already died behind the counter of the grocery where Omar Rosario works," I wrote, "murdered in a tiny business where customers pay in pennies and promises. Before he goes to work he slips on his bulletproof vest, slides a black 9-millimeter pistol into his waistband, and gives himself to God. It is early on a Wednesday night and the store's lights gleam like new money among the dead street lights at the corner of 139th Street and Edgecombe Avenue. The door opens and a young man with a puny mustache walks in, one arm hidden deep inside his baggy, half-open coat. Rosario thinks he has a machine gun or sawed-off shotgun. Rosario takes out his pistol and eases it halfway into the pocket of his pants, his finger on the trigger. He faces the man and lets him see the gun in his hand. He wants to make it clear that if the young man pulls a gun, he will kill him. The young man drifts around the front of the store as the last two customers walk out, but everywhere he goes Rosario is beside him, as if in a dance. They stare into each other's eyes for five minutes, silent, and the tension is sickening. Finally the young man turns and goes out. Rosario stares out the door, gun in hand. His face is pale."

I did not even know what was going on at first. The young man squeezed by me at one point in the cramped store and I felt, through his jacket, through mine, the hard shape that could only be a gun.

Only when Franco eased up beside me and said, softly, "We have stepped in it," did I really understand what was happening. There was no place to hide in a store like that, no place to run. They were between us and the door. We just had to stand and watch and hope that when it started, the shooting, it would be quick and clean. But I had little faith in that. When two country boys pull their pistols and start poppin', chances are that they will hit what they are shooting at. They practice, blowing beer cans off fence posts, or stalking deer through the pines. But city boys can't shoot for shit. It is why they kill so many children and innocent bystanders. They keep their guns in their waistbands because they like the way it feels against their skin, but they are amateurs at killing.

As they danced, I slipped the notebook into my back pocket. I figured it was unwise for a man about to hold up a store to see me recording it for the readers of the *New York Times*. Then I heard the soft click of Franco's camera. He was literally shooting from the hip, the camera hanging from its strap, down around his waist. He was trying to be as quiet, as discreet, as possible, but to me every frame he snapped off seemed like a tap shoe on a tile floor. I was worried about getting shot. He was doing his job. Franco is not an amateur. He hits what he aims at.

When it was over, Rosario walked out to stand in the cold rain with an employee, Pablo Mendoza. They scan the street, waiting for the man to come back. A half-hour later they are still there, watching. I am embarrassed. I feel like I'm in the way of something important. I guess survival is pretty important.

I ask him why he faced down the man, why he didn't just give him what he wanted. But Rosario, whose hands shake as he wipes his face, tells me he cannot trust the robbers anymore to take the money and go. "I do not resolve it, if I do not act first, he will take my money, make me lie down on the floor, and shoot me in back of the head," he says. There is no posturing here, only a young man who is tired of being scared every time the door opens.

"Not one bullet will I use to protect a piece of candy," Rosario says. "But I will kill ten before I let one pull a gun on me." The previous owner of the store, Henry A. Medina, was killed on November 16, 1992, by two men in ski masks. Medina was opening the register to give them the cash when one man shot him in the heart. His killers were never found.

"When I leave here, I am like a bird in the air, flying," Rosario said. "I am free."

"Rosario thinks he can sense the spirit of the previous owner wafting around the place late at night," I wrote. "He believes in God. He likes to think that maybe it is an angel. But there are no angels on Edgecombe after dark." I had no right to say that.

I did not even know what a bodega was when I came to New York City. It means, basically, "store," but I learned it can also mean freedom, respect, dignity.

For a week or so, Franco and I drove from tiny store to tiny store, interviewing people who had lost loved ones to bullets, talking to people who had narrowly escaped death. It would be wrong to say that we found that life is cheap there, behind the rows of breath mints. It is not cheap at all. People like to glamorize the high rollers on Wall Street, when they write of New York. They should come down here, to Leon Bodega at 289 Bushwick, to see what risk is all about.

"Domingo Leon, the 40-year-old owner, has a bullet hole in the arm of his leather jacket," I wrote. "The dry cleaner took the bloodstain out, mostly. Domingo Angeles wears the pants he wore when he was shot in the hip. He still has the bullet, lodged deep in his lower back. The difference between rich people and poor people is that poor people still wear the clothes they were wearing when they were shot. They save them from the emergency room floor. Along with a friend, Manuel Celado, who was shot twice in the chest, the men are survivors of a violent bodega robbery last year. But no one died. 'Milagroso,' Leon said. The men are all members of an extended family that draws much of its income from the bodega. It does not make anyone rich, but it is exactly what Leon was searching for when he left Moca, a village in the Dominican Republic, more than 20 years ago. He saved his money and opened in 1982. No one holds the keys to his livelihood, so no one can make him bow his head. People who have never been poor, who have never had to live on their knees, do not understand what it means to him.

"On Feb. 23, about 10 P.M., four young men burst into the bodega and one put a gun to Celado's head. Leon grabbed at it, in reflex, and the robbers started shooting. Angeles grabbed the gun of one young man and the hammer chewed a groove in his hand as the man jerked over and over on the trigger. Finally one of the bullets hit him in the hip. He lay on the floor, pretending to be dead, quietly praying the men would not shoot again. One robber dragged the bleeding Celado into a storeroom and started beating him in the head with a gun, trying to make him tell where the store kept its money. When Leon ran into the room the man shot him in the arm and ran. A few hours after being shot, while Celado and Angeles lay in the hospital, Leon was back at the cash register of his bodega. Blood still seeped from the bandage. 'I have nine children,' he said. Angeles was back at work a few days later. He is still in pain, the bullet grating against muscle tissue. He thinks of finding safer work, but refuses to leave his friends in danger."

Celado almost died from his bullet wounds. Now he just sits thin and frail in a dark car outside the bodega, serving as the lookout. It is his job to spot suspicious people, and warn his friends. He will shout "holope!" and run inside and lock the door.

We left him there, sitting in the dark car, left them with their dangerous lives, to have some oxtails and rice and drive on to the next tragedy. New York is a supermarket for tragedy. Its streets are just aisles, and the selection is first-rate.

We make one more stop, on Fulton Avenue in the South Bronx. Behind the cash register, an inch-thick, bulletproof plastic shield surrounds Antonio Mueses like a security blanket. He still feels cold inside it. Mueses and his brother, Rafael, used to run the bodega together. Afraid of the killings and shootings they read about in the newspaper, they hired a man last summer to put up a shield. The man took the money but did not build it, and on July 25 his brother was shot dead. His brother had two children. "If the man had built the shield," Mueses says, and shrugs. The shield looks like a good one, though, nice and thick.

The story on the bodegas ran at the bottom of the front page. People told me it was a "real New York story," and I was proud of it. A friend told me that I "lent dignity" to the people in it, but that was wrong. All I did was write what was there. I would have sent a copy of it to my momma, but I decided to wait, for a happy one.

It would be nice to believe that people back in Alabama were following my stories in the *New York Times,* but that would be a lie. You have to drive an hour to even find one, and then it costs a dollar. Who has a dollar for a paper?

But now and then other papers would run my stories, off the *New York Times* wire, and someone would cut them out and send them to my momma. She started a new scrapbook.

31
Coming home

You hear them more than you see them. People always say they sound like freight trains rumbling across the sky, and maybe that is it, exactly. We hunkered down in hallways or storm shelters three or four times a year, when I was a boy, waiting for the tornadoes to go away. Momma prayed. I saw only one, my whole life, a fat gray snake writhing in the sky over the Crystal Springs community, not far from home. I tried not to be afraid, but I was.

I lost my fear of them over time. In my adult life, the bad winds were just one more story, written about strangers. The names were strange names, the dead were benignly alien to me. I wish it had stayed that way.

It was Palm Sunday, 1994, in the *New York Times* newsroom. The Associated Press moved a story that a tornado had destroyed a church in northeastern Alabama, toppling a wall onto its congregation, killing twenty people, including six children. The dateline read "Piedmont," the town where I was born. The editors on the national desk asked me if I would be the rewrite man on the information coming in. First, I called my momma to make sure she and my kinfolks were fine. They were. Then, I wrote about death in my backyard. I knew the names, I knew the place, I knew the color of the ground and the smell of the grass and the height of the trees.

It was not a good story, just another story about dying in the paper of record. It didn't mention the small patent-leather children's shoes scattered in the ruin, brand-new Easter shoes, bought especially for church, that church, for that day. For some reason I thought not about the rubble and the dying but about mommas leading toddlers through the Dollar Store or the Wal-Mart, searching for the perfect shoes.

I wanted to do more than give a body count punctuated by a few quotes. It deserved more than that.

The next day I flew to Atlanta, rented a car, and went home to the little community that straddled the Calhoun-Cherokee county line. It was a brilliant, beautiful day, and if you didn't see the tin from old roofs wrapped like foil in the branches of trees, if you didn't notice blank spaces on the spring grass where houses were supposed to be, you would have thought everything was just fine. As I drove, too fast, toward the church, a man in a pickup waved at me, and I forgot to wave back. The city does change you.

People who believe I was just speeding to another compelling story are dead wrong. Any reporter who has had to write about his or her own people—like the reporters who covered the bombing in Oklahoma City—will tell you that they do so with great reluctance, but knowing they might do the story better than a stranger.

I found instead of a church a pile of sticks and crushed red brick, with a scrawny cross made from scrap stuck up in its center. People pulled their cars and pickups over to the side of the road and walked up, to look at it. I remember that men took their hats off.

I remember there were still some buttercups out, and that the rain had turned the red clay to slick mud. It was why no one I ever knew had white carpet. That mud, it was harder to get out than bloodstains.

I looked at it for a while, then did my job. I talked to the survivors. I jotted names I didn't have to ask to spell and ages I didn't really need. I had played softball against their nephews, gone to school with their sons and daughters, and, probably, waved at every one of them at one time or another as my car met their car on a strip of blacktop.

I found them troubled by more than grief. You do not die in church in northeastern Alabama. You do not die under the eye of God, under His hand, in His house. You cannot. Later, when I asked Momma what people were saying, how they made of sense of it, she just sat there, with not much to say. Others I asked wouldn't look me in the face. I guess what I sensed was not anger, but doubt.

As I stood just outside the crime scene tape—a crime of nature, I guess—that ringed the pitiful pile of rubble, I tried, like I always do, to re-create the thing in my mind, to see it. The survivors had filled my head with it.

The destruction of the little country church and the deaths, including the pastor's four-year-old daughter, had taken just a second, maybe two. The children had been putting on a play, and in the middle of praising His name, six of the little ones and fourteen grownups were crushed to death. Most of them died instantly. There had been screams, of pain and fear, and some merely shifted the direction of their prayers, like a car changing gears on a hill. There had been almost no warning—just those uneasy glances as the winds pounded the walls—but where better to be in a storm, than here.

They are country people, so instead of lying helpless they tried to help each other. The wounded were carried off on stretchers fashioned from the splintered pews. In a makeshift morgue in the National Guard Armory in Piedmont, volunteers wiped the faces of the dead children before zipping up the body bags. The bags were too long, and had to be rolled up from the bottom. Outside, grown, tough men sobbed into the arms of other men, who held them like babies.

The funerals lasted all week in the surrounding towns, and obituaries filled an entire page in the local newspaper. No one died. People merely said that God took them. He took Miz Ruth Peek, sixty-four, and Mr. Cicero Peek, seventy-two. He took Derek Watson, who died with his wife, Glenda Kay, and their daughter, Jessica. Everyone knew Derek; he worked at the Super Valu. He took four-year-old Hannah Clem, the pastor's daughter, and Earl Abbott, whose wife played the organ. Earl's brother was the one, Rudy, who coached baseball and told me that people like me and him couldn't fail.

I learned from my momma and kin that two other churches were destroyed during services, but those congregations somehow survived. The winds had snapped two-hundred-year-old trees and ruined houses and lives in five states that day, but Goshen was the centerpiece of the agony. The same winds had ravaged Spring Garden, Rock Run, Possum Trot, Bennefield's Gap, Knighten's Crossroad and Webster's Chapel. At Mount Gilead Church, about ten miles from Goshen, the wind had pulled tombstones from the earth and smashed them to pieces.

I knew that over two counties there would be pickle jars on the counters of stores, filled with quarters and wadded-up dollar bills, for the victims' families. The funerals would be a hardship for many of them, the children of farmers, mill workers, seamstresses, carpenters and steelworkers, some who had moved on to other work, some who stood in the places where their fathers and mothers had stood at sewing plants and cotton mills. The mill, I knew, had just had a new round of layoffs.

I went to the funeral home one night myself, half as a reporter, half as a man whose obligation it was to be there. The line in the door was fifty yards long, and as I walked by people would throw up an arm and say, "Hey, boy. Where you been?" I shook a dozen hands, and hugged a man whose name I could not really remember. Maybe he had gotten fat, or I had grown stupid.

Later, in the dark in the parking lot, I jotted down what they said, what they felt. The people said the same thing. How awful, how sad, and how hard to understand.

"We are trained from birth not to question God," one young woman, Robyn Tucker King, told me. I met her outside the funeral home, where the cars half filled the parking lot of the nearby football field. "But why?" she said. "Why a church? Why those little children? Why? Why? Why?"

"It was church," said Jerri Kernes, delivering flowers to the funeral home. "It isn't supposed to happen in church."

I ran into Sam Goss on my way to the car. Everyone knows Sam, too. He runs the filling station, and believes in heaven the same way he believes that walking in the Coosa River will get him wet. He smoked a cigarette, cried some, and talked about Glory.

"It's hard not to question God in this," he said. "But they say there ain't no tears in heaven. We're the ones left to hurt. You see, God took them because he knew they were ready to go. He's just giving all the rest of us a second chance." I don't know, for sure, if anyone in that little town of five thousand or so ever shook their fist at God. I don't know for sure how many felt their faith slip away from them, in the dark nights after that awful thing. But I doubt if it is many. Life can be hard here without some faith. I remember what Vera Stewart, Piedmont's seventy-year-old mayor, told me when I called her about the tragedy. Piedmont, she reminded me, has two doctors' offices, and twenty churches. "As long as we have our faith, we are as strong as our faith," Mrs. Stewart said. "Because no matter how dark it is, if I have faith, I have a song in the night."

The minister of the Goshen church, the Reverend Kelly Clem, took a few minutes to talk to me beside the ruins of her church. I remember feeling a great surprise that the minister of a little country church in my part of the world was a woman. I hadn't known we had gotten so progressive. When I saw her, her face was covered with bruises from the falling bricks, and her eyes had that weary look that would have been hopelessness, if something inside—or from On High—had not been propping her up. She had spent all her time since the disaster ministering to the grieving parishioners, to the heartsick.

You hate this part, as a reporter, you hate to look into the eyes of a woman who has seen her child taken away forever. But maybe even worse, I felt like I was insulting her, her beliefs, to ask for an explanation of this disaster in a sacred, holy place.

She just smiled at me, a little wearily. "This might shake people's faith for a long time," said Mrs. Clem. "I think that is normal. But having your faith shaken is not the same as losing it." She explained that God did not send the storm that killed their daughter. She explained to me the

distinction between God's laws and the laws of nature, something the-
ologians have debated for years. "My God is a God of hope," said her
husband, Dale Clem, also a minister. "It is never His will for anyone to
die."

I had been taught as a child that He controlled everything, even the
wind. At the funeral for the Clems' daughter, the presiding minister told
the congregation that it was okay to be confused. "People have asked,
why did it happen in a church," said the Reverend Bobby Green. "There
is no reason. Our faith is not determined by reason. Our faith is under-
girded by belief, when there is no reason."

In the Bible, Palm Sunday is a day of destruction, not hope, he said.
Hope comes later, on Easter Sunday. I stood with the mourners and said
the Lord's Prayer, the only one I know all the way through.

It was my first time home as the big shot newspaper reporter, the *New
York Times* guy, but few people there knew or cared. They had lost track
of me, a few papers ago. They asked me how I liked Birmingham, and if
I was still married. When I told them I was a *New York Times* reporter
now, they looked at me funny. I am sure that a few of them thought I was
lying, or crazy. I wrote my story at the *Gadsden Times,* just a short drive
away. The *New York Times* owned it now, like me, and the nice people
there let me write my story there.

The *Gadsden Times* had just gotten in a new chair, one of those very
fancy ergonomically correct jobs with more adjustments than a barber's
chair. They insisted that I take it, since I was visitin.' It was a fine chair.

I wrote the story over two days. It was important to me that it be
good, I guess because I wanted people there to think well of me, but also
because it was my responsibility. I was one of them. Nothing that had
ever happened, over all the years I had been away, had changed that. I
began it this way:

This is a place where grandmothers hold babies on their laps under the stars and whisper in their ears that the lights in the sky are

holes in the floor of heaven. This is a place where the song "Jesus Loves Me" has rocked generations to sleep, and heaven is not a concept, but a destination. Yet in this place where many things, even storms, are viewed as God's will, people strong in their faith and their children have died in, of all places, a church. The destruction of this little country church and the deaths—including the pastor's vivacious 4-year-old daughter—have shaken the faith of many people who live in this deeply religious corner of Alabama, about 80 miles northeast of Birmingham. It is not that it has turned them against God, only that it has hurt them in a place usually safe from hurt, like a bruise on the soul.

I flew back to Manhattan on Saturday, and met some reporter friends for a late dinner at a Cuban joint on Broadway, uptown. As we ate, talking about worthless stuff that reporters are expert at, I noticed a young man—he had to be a student—eating alone at a counter and reading an early copy of the Sunday *Times*.

The story was there, on the front page, with a picture of that raggedy cross, and a headline that said something about an anchor of faith holding. I asked him if I could see it, and he said something to the effect of, "Get your own." So I read over his shoulder, to the jump.

"I wrote that," I said.

He didn't bother to turn around.

But the fact is that I didn't give a damn what he thought of it. Over the next few weeks, I would learn that editors back home reran the story in the Alabama papers. For weeks, months, people wrote me letters, letters from strangers, letters from home. It wasn't that I had gotten it right—God knows I mess up a lot—but that I had gotten it true.

I was back there, less than a year later, in the false spring we always get during February. The congregation stood not in a church but, as I wrote, in the promise of one. They sang "Amazing Grace" in a green field specked with red anthills, and I noticed it was hard to tell when people were praying and when they were just checking their feet. I saw some grown men cry. I saw people I knew, and people who were alone who should not have been. I saw gaps in families. They had come to this old cornfield just a mile or so from the site of the old church to start over, and consecrate the ground. One by one, starting with the children, they poured cups of red dirt from the old site and mixed it into the clay of the new one.

Of the more than eighty parishioners who were injured, most have healed. A few, like fifty-five-year-old Joyce Woods, whose foot was crushed, still hobble. For her and the others, Sunday's service was a time of celebration and joy, said her husband, Franklin.

It was the first time I had ever seen the Reverend Clem when her face had not been swollen and purple. She spoke beside a rough-hewn cross held together by a rusty nail. It was the same cross that parishioners stuck into the church rubble the day after the tornado hit. Pictures of that cross, rising from the destruction, have appeared in newspapers and magazines around the world. When the service ended, she asked the children in the congregation to join her at the altar of grass for a surprise. She asked them if there were any children in heaven they wanted to send a message to. One little boy nodded his head. Together, they opened a plastic bag full of brightly colored helium-filled balloons and turned them loose. The balloons rose into the pale blue sky. The pastor's other daughter, three-year-old Sarah, watched them fly. It is nice to believe that balloons can rise so high.

Patricia Abbott, Earl's widow, played the church organ in the middle of a field of new grass.

I went to look at the new church the other day. It seemed like a fine church, a modern-looking sanctuary with a lot of angles, the way they build churches now. I couldn't help but think back to Hollis Crossroads, the last time I had been in a church that did not involve a wedding or funeral, or work. I bet it is still standing. A hurricane couldn't knock it down. I hope they still have Dinner on the Ground. I would like to see it, see all those people coming together like that, sometime when I drive by. Maybe I would even stop.

No, I reckon not.

32

Dining out with no money,
and living with no life

I come from a place where every town has one certified nut bag.
Every society needs one, I guess.

I know New York is a big place, but it seems to have a few more than
its share. It would be hard to shoot an arrow down any street in the five
boroughs—well, maybe not Staten Island—and not skewer a nut bag
sooner or later. I do not say this unkindly. I consider myself a nut bag, too.

But of all the unusual people I met in my brief time in that unusual
city, perhaps the most unusual was the man who would become known
as the Serial Diner.

I met him in May 1994. An old girlfriend, Rachel, told me that her
sister, a public defender in Manhattan, was representing a man who was
systematically eating his way into prison. "Sounds like a newspaper article to me," she said.

"Has to be," I said.

I have always been a one-dimensional reporter. I find rich people
dull, lulled by their own comfort. When you have nothing, it forces your
mind into gymnastics. Some days, your imagination has to do a double-
back-flip just to find a way to eat. That is why I feel such affection for
Gangaram Mahes.

He was between court hearings, in the holding cell downtown, just a roly-poly, bald-headed man, who talked to me through a cage. He told me his entire life story from behind that wire screen, but he had to rush the ending. They were serving chicken for lunch. "Tasty," he said.

"He is a thief who never runs," I wrote, "a criminal who picks his teeth as the police close in. To be arrested, to go home to a cell at Rikers Island, is his plan when he picks up the menu. Homeless off and on for several years, he steals dinner from the restaurants because he wants the courts to return him to a place in New York where he is guaranteed three meals a day. In a prison system filled with repeat offenders, he is the city's only serial diner. He has committed the same crime at least 31 times, always pleads guilty and never urges his lawyer to bargain for a reduced sentence. He is just tunneling inside again, with knife and fork."

He could snatch a purse or shoplift from a bodega, but he has settled on this, at least in part because he figures it doesn't really hurt anyone. The loss he forces on the restaurant owners will be recovered with the first overpriced meal. That is one reason why he prefers to dine in midtown, because—in a place where a chicken salad sandwich can cost fifteen dollars—he figures he is just one more thief.

But he knows the police will not see it that way. They will come and get him, and take him home.

"It's tough on the outside," said Mahes. This stay, for ninety days, he earned for stealing a swordfish steak.

To him, as violent and demeaning as jail sometimes is, it is better than drifting from shelter to shelter or living in cardboard boxes. "I like to live decent," he said. "I like to be clean."

Christina Swarns, Rachel's sister and the young Legal Aid lawyer defending him, made sure I saw the seriousness of his case, made sure I wouldn't write some wiseass piece about him.

"It's funny at first, 'The Serial Eater,'" she said. "But it's a very sad thing. How bad is it, his life, that he would prefer prison?"

"On one hand," I wrote, "is a man who goes to jail at will without hurting anyone, who steals only expensive New York restaurant food. Instead of throwing a rock through a window, he orders a T-bone. On the other hand is a man who seems to have abandoned hope of ever having anything better, who prefers society's idea of punishment to his place in the society, said Ms. Swarns. In the past two years, he has seldom been free more than a few days before enjoying an illegal entree. He patronized the American Festival Cafe and the Taj Mahal in Manhattan, and Tony Roma's in two boroughs. He chooses restaurants that are not too cheap, not too expensive. If a restaurant is too pretentious, it might not seat him. If it is too cheap, he might not be arrested for stealing its food. 'If they really wanted to punish him,' said Ms. Swarns, 'they would stand outside Rikers and say, "You go away."' Instead, Mahes does 90 days for stealing fish. It costs taxpayers $162 a day to feed, clothe and house him at Rikers Island. His 90-day sentence will cost them $14,580, to punish him for refusing to pay the $51.31 check. In five years he has cost them more than $250,000."

Your tax dollars at work.

It occurs to me, as I look around me in the visiting room, that I have seen the inside of a lot of prisons for a man who has committed relatively few crimes. All around us are inmates who just want to go home. Mahes is already there. He has no expectations, so there are no disappointments: he does not envy people who are free, because they are free to suffer.

Life is eating, eating is life. "Last night," he told me, "we had beef stew."

He is a talker, this Gangaram. He poured his life story out to me and I didn't even have to ask a question. Raised in poverty and fear as a child in Guyana, he left for the United States in 1976, when he was 18. His myth of New York shimmered in the distance. "I thought it was going to be milk and honey," he said. What he found was a country in a recession, with lines for gas, lines for work. Looking for refuge again, he joined the army. The army took care of its own; clothed them, fed them. He would have stayed, but five years and one drug addiction later he was on the street. He wandered to Florida and Virginia to pick collards and peaches in migrant camps where conditions were barely human. One camp fed its workers just once a day. He went home to Guyana, and returned to the South Bronx with a wife, who left him. For years he drifted, homeless, drinking himself happy. "I would drink to forget how the day passed." By the late 1980s, the one constant in his life was jail. He had done time for a string of misdemeanors. Jail took care of its own; clothed them, fed them. Getting inside was easy. All he had to do was pretend to be part of the mainstream, the middle class. Then, when the waiter brought the check, he told the truth.

"But in that golden space of time between being shown to his table and the second the check arrives," I wrote, "he is as good as anybody. He has the same rights, the same respect, the same choices. He can ask for a corner table. He can ask for one with a view. Because he looks like everyone else, he is, temporarily. He just happens to be an awful tipper, at the moment of truth. He likes a glass of Johnnie Walker and the chicken and rib platter at Tony Roma's. 'No dessert, but they did offer.' He was fond of the buffet at an Indian restaurant in midtown, but it closed."

A shadow passes over his face as he wonders aloud if he had anything to do with that. "The curried lamb," he said, wistfully.

He is in the Big House this time because of a night out at the American Festival Cafe at Rockefeller Center. "He had very good taste," the manager recalled. "I think he was drinking Chivas Regal."

I ask him if he is planning to continue this life forever, and he says that no, he thinks about doing right, getting a job, but the routine is so easy, so dependable. He has no family, no friends, just a plan for getting by, that works.

I think about him, too, from time to time. I wonder if he is in or out, and then I realize that it really doesn't matter. Wherever he is, he's eatin' good.

The *Times* had agreed to put me up free for my first six months, and as that deadline neared I began to search for an apartment of my own. I settled on the Upper West Side, near the corner of 110th and Broadway.

The homeless were five to a block, there had been a fatal stabbing two doors down. It was a real neighborhood.

I told my momma it was safe as a church.

I had two rooms, a galley kitchen and a view of nothing. It cost just $1,185.50 a month, and it was on the subway line to Times Square, a straight shot. Across the street there was a place that sold hot dogs for fifty cents.

I told my momma I was eating right.

My belongings arrived in early July. I walked around the opened boxes and thought to myself that a thirty-five-year-old man should have more stuff than this. There was a couch and chair, book shelves, a bed, a television and stereo, some pictures.

I told my momma my life was rich and full.

It took me a day or two to get the pictures nailed up and the books on the shelves, some of the same books my daddy had bought me so many years before. I tried to remember how many cities those books had been in, but I lost count. I wondered if he would have ever believed it, that his son would be sitting in New York, holding a copy of *Riders of the Purple Sage*.

I got everything in its place, perfectly. I do not think of myself as anal-retentive, but when you have lived by yourself as long as I have, it takes a while to get the couch and chair lined up just right, and to decide which books should be on the second shelf, and the third, or maybe the fourth. Or maybe the whole shelf needs to move. But finally, the pictures were straight, the books aligned, the kitchen . . . well, since I didn't own any dishes, there was not much to do there. Except for the forty-five-pound-pull Ben Pearson bow and arrows on the wall, a legacy from my childhood, it was a real New York apartment. I felt at home, more or less. I should have known better than to get comfortable.

The next day, the foreign desk asked me if I would like to go back to Haiti. A week later I was disembarking at what they used to call Duvalier Airport, searching the sky for smoke, and the ground for bodies, again.

I told my momma I was going to spend a few weeks in the Caribbean.

33

Buying bodies,
eating lobster

Not much had changed in three years. The cruelties were still off the scale of sanity. Government thugs chased away the Argentinian ambassador by setting two live roosters on fire and flinging them, smoking, squawking, kicking, over the consulate wall. Men with machetes made a game of disfiguring beautiful women. Political prisoners, how many we will never know, just disappeared into mass graves. Pigs rooted for the bodies after every hard rain. The gleaming Mercedes and Land Rovers of the ruling class still hurtled past babies with protruding empty bellies. Horribly deformed children walked on all fours through the streets like animals. The police still killed the poor at random, and stole the bodies. That way they could charge their families as much as a hundred dollars to get them back, for burial. I would not want to come to Haiti in the nighttime. I would not want to wake up here the morning after, after dreams of a more sane life, and have this place be the first thing my eyes would see.

Every morning, photographers made "the body run." They cruised the more isolated streets, roads and pig trails of Port-au-Prince just after dawn, and most days they found what they were looking for. Bodies with their hands and feet bound by wire, their faces peeled away, fingers hacked off, probably for fun. Politics, Haitian style. The military government headed by the aristocratic Raoul Cedras sanctioned the killings and left the bodies in the street for the same reason politicians in my native South tacked cardboard political signs on fence posts, only I guess the dead are cheaper. The message was simple: Follow Aristide, and follow him to your death. As the U.S. government's patience waned with the despotic military government, as ragged, half-starved Haitians continued to wash up on beaches in Fort Lauderdale, ruining the view from the condo canyons, the forced return of Haiti's Savior seemed to inch closer. Haiti's rulers, from the beginning, had known just one way to hold power: kill and kill and kill again.

My job was to write about those human rights abuses, and day after day after day I listened to the stories of frightened people, interviewing them behind the locked gates of safe houses and in dark rooms in the endless slums and, once, lying in the floorboard of my four-wheel-drive as I circled and circled the city, my eyes darting constantly to the rearview mirror. Once again, I knew I really had no business here, no real experience at this, but I tried hard. To cover that story dispassionately was beyond me. It may be that it made me a poor analyst of the sociopolitical situation. I just know that word of it had to get out, had to ring out, and for the first time I truly realized the impact of the newspaper for which I worked.

An ultra-conservative commentator for a brainless cable TV show said we exaggerated the killing. I would have liked to have tied that son of a bitch to me with a rope, and made him see what I saw, hear what I heard.

I looked into the eyes of twelve- and thirteen-year-old girls who had been gang-raped, and I will never forget the emptiness there, the blank, used-up, hopeless stares, as if someone had just snatched the life out of them and left the shell to wander. I shook the hands of men who had their fingers crushed with rifle butts, and sat under a tree with a man who had tried to hold a woman's insides in her body after she had been hacked again and again with machetes. I don't remember how many people I talked to who had seen their loved ones hauled away never to be seen again.

I know that some of them could have lied to me, some of them almost certainly did, and I tried to use in the newspaper only what I was most certain of. I remember one morning standing outside an old monastery, staring down at a bloodstain on a driveway. The night before, a beloved priest had been shot to death by thugs loyal to the military government, as he fumbled with the gate. The priest had been troublesome to the rich. He had once tried to organize the laborers who worked their fields. The government, of course, denied any involvement, and could not explain how the police arrived even before anyone called them, and took the body away.

As I looked down at that stain, I knew it would be hard to write too much or too strongly of the people who spread this misery. If they would kill a priest, why would they not kill a peasant without a second thought, or torture them for sport, or debase them. Common sense told me that much.

Sometimes it was unclear who was to blame. I walked through a nursery where the babies were doomed by a lack of medicine, medicine I would later learn was stolen by the military. But the military blamed the embargo, said it was killing the poor. One man stood over an emaciated baby, trying to get the child to grasp his finger with its tiny hand. The child—strange, I cannot remember if it was a boy or girl—lay as if dead. I took the man out in the hall and gave him some money, I cannot remember how much, and he grabbed both my hands and pressed his forehead to them.

I talked to a man who ran an orphanage who showed me the complaints he had filed with police, who had targeted the older children. I talked to a young prostitute who was forced to submit a dozen, two dozen, countless times a day, to soldiers who never paid. Her one possession was a tiny television. The soldiers destroyed it.

And around and around and around it goes. We are staying, me and most of the other reporters, in a nice hotel called the Montana, up the mountain in Pétionville. A man with a sawed-off shotgun guards the gate. But somehow the body merchants always sneak through. They lurk in the lobby, and sidle up to you with a polite "Monsieur? Excuse me, please.

But I have a body for you." They offer to take you to a place where a body has been dumped, for a price.

At the bar of the Montana Hotel, the foreign correspondents drink rum punches and discuss which restaurants are still open and which have been closed by the impending hostilities. A few of them befriend me, help me, and I will always appreciate that. One of the first people I see is Daniel Morel, but a different one. He has a wife and child now, and has a little more gray in his beard. He still looks like a man you do not want to mess with on a dark night. *"New York Times?"* he says, and laughs out loud. I am not sure if he is happy for me, or incredulous, but again he leads me to the good stories.

It would be a lie to say we had it rough there. On Fridays, as the people starved down the hill, there was shrimp curry. On Sundays, there was lobster on the grill. You couldn't even hear the gunshots, we were up so high.

The uprising I had predicted never came, of course. Only Clinton could force change now. The only question then was whether it would be a shooting war to bring Aristide back, or a negotiated return.

God help me, but as I watched the people suffer under the government's brutality, I wished for a war. I knew it could not last long. The commander in chief only came in from 2 P.M. to 4 P.M. They had only one functioning aircraft, and while none of the boats in the Haitian navy could run, one of them could float.

Their weapons were good only for terror of an unarmed civilian population. I knew that, with the first sight of a U.S. Marine, they would run.

I will never forget the night I heard a plane—it sounded like it was running too good to be Haitian—buzz by the hotel late one night. I thought the invasion was on. I thought the Americans were coming, and I jumped up and ran downstairs to find that the only thing that had dropped onto Haiti that night were transistor radios, which the U.S. government had parachuted down as instruments of propaganda. I later learned that the bad guys were confiscating them and selling them. As one of my uncles used to say, what a way to run a whorehouse.

The military tried to work its population into some kind of anger at the expected invasion, but the big despots had to bribe smaller despots with rum just to get them out in respectable numbers. I saw one man at both an anti-Aristide meeting and a pro-Aristide meeting a week apart. The government had voodoo priests block off the streets with hexes painted on the blacktop. A volunteer militia trained in the city square with rifles that had no bullets. The rifles were taken back up again after CNN had shot footage of the defiant Haitians. Cedras knew better than to let the people take weapons home. They might find a bullet somewhere. "So, what good is a militia if the attack comes at night?" I asked one officer. He shrugged.

But it never happened, of course. Jimmy Carter came and brokered an unusual three-legged dog of a peace that spared the despots and absurdly married the U.S. military with the same soldiers who had been the instruments of torture and terror. I always liked Jimmy, until then. Aristide would return, but there would be no sweeping justice, no mass executions by flaming necklace, no satisfaction.

For two days I stood outside the military headquarters and watched them hammer out that arrangement, listening to the bought-and-paid-for government supporters sing and chant that "if you come, we will eat you." Twice I got knocked down. It was bad theater.

The U.S. war machine landed and had to be careful not to shoot the cameramen who came to record it. U.S. officials paid Cedras money to rent a villa from him. Good Lord.

The killing didn't stop right away. For a full day and part of another, the soldiers hid behind walls, and did not intervene as the police and military clubbed dancing, cheering Haitians who came to greet them. The Haitian soldiers bashed one man's skull in with a stick of firewood and stole his body, to sell back to his wife.

I have seldom been so sick to my stomach in my life, but I guess diplomacy is complicated. All I know is that, in an effort to disperse the crowd, one Haitian soldier started firing tear gas into the masses. In most places in the world, you aim high and lob the grenade into the crowd. In Haiti, there is no such sensibility. The soldier fired it head-high, but it miraculously missed ripping anyone's head off at the neck—including mine—and landed against a government building a hundred yards away, which caught on fire, briefly.

I interviewed the American soldiers I saw and time and time again they said they wanted to stop the beating and the killings, that it made them sick, too. But they had their orders. They were young, they were from places like Niagara Falls and Fort Smith and Pensacola, and they were completely unprepared, morally, politically, for this place. I guess you could say their view was simplistic. We had that much in common.

A day or so later, pro-Aristide Haitians unwisely attacked a pro-government stronghold with rocks. The people inside put up with it for a while, then came out and started firing into the crowd. The packed bodies turned and ran, and I ran with them, watching a senior foreign correspondent closely, to see when it was right to run and when you were supposed to stand. Later I would learn that another journalist had been shot in the head, just yards away.

When the U.S. soldiers finally moved out from behind their wall and tried to set things right, I talked one platoon into letting me go with them. I wrote it for the *New York Times Sunday Magazine,* at a dollar a word, but I would have done it for nothing. Hell, I would have gone along for the ride. It was the only time in Haiti I felt any hope.

"The heroes of Third Platoon fumble toward history with canteens full of grape Kool-Aid," I wrote, "scanning the rooftops for snipers and trying hard not to run over their admirers. Their deep-green Humvees weave along streets packed with ragged but cheering people who believe these young men have delivered them from evil. 'We go where they tell us,' said Sgt. Paul Stevenson, a blond, blue-eyed 24-year-old from Midland, Mich., who enlisted in the Army to escape the inertia of his hometown. 'But this is a place we need to be. The people want us here. They dance for us and serenade us. I've been in this Army since I was 18 and I've seen countries get their freedom in the Eastern Bloc: the East Germans, the old Czechoslovakia. But this . . . you ride through these slums and see people starving on the streets. The next thing you know they're running beside you, cheering, making you feel like royalty.'

"How often in a black man's life, asks Pfc. Vondrain Smith, does he walk through a crowd of people of his own color and see them throw flowers at his feet? 'It's a good feeling being cheered,' he says. 'I've never been cheered before.' Smith, 19, has never been so far away from home and he did not expect to feel any love for Haiti. His kin in Hampton, S.C., said black people had enough to worry about at home. 'I like these people,' he says, looking out on a group of children who stare at him like he fell from the sky. 'They like me back.' The others echo him. 'We're doing good,' says Pfc. Paul Brady, from Billerica, Mass., who is 19 but looks 15. 'We know what they've done to people here. We're here to make sure that it doesn't happen anymore. It stops now.' Brady, a recruiter's poster boy, is well spoken and mannerly, from middle-class parents in a nice, peaceful middle-class town. When he goes home, he will probably go back to college. But he has the sense that, whatever happens after Haiti, this will be the most important thing he ever does.

"They patrol the city in Humvee caravans of two, three and four, guns loaded but not cocked and ready to fire, since this is a peacekeeping mission. The gunners in the turret, the most exposed and most at risk, wear two bulletproof vests. The drivers and navigators keep one eye on their windows, afraid someone will drop in a grenade. And always there are the Haitians pressing in on them, curious and friendly but so many and so close that the men know they would never see an attacker coming in time. Ask Richard Rice, the 38-year-old platoon sergeant, what he thinks of the morality of his mission and he barks: 'Sir, I don't think. I react. If my Government tells me I am here to do good, I'm here to do good.' He has enough trouble watching out for his 27 overgrown children in a military operation that has no precedent. In a year, Rice will retire. He plans to sit on his front porch in a rocking chair, in the center of 105 acres of rich bottom land in Maysville, Ky., and watch the chickens peck. Haiti will seem a distant memory, but he can only have that peace of mind if all the young soldiers in his command leave Haiti alive. 'I came here with 27,' he says, and the words seem riveted in the air. 'And I'm by God gonna leave with 27.'

"Rice—a lean, tall, hard-looking black man with arms like telephone poles—is worried. He was for most of his career a soldier of the cold war.

He worked a fence line in Korea, where razor wire divided friends and enemies, where soldiers were not expected to ride through towns drumming up good will. This post-cold-war mission seems to write new doctrine each day. Helicopters pound through the blue sky and blare a taped message in Creole on the humanitarian, democratic and peaceful intent of the 20,000 armed soldiers here. 'These guys are more at risk because it is a walk-in mission instead of a forced occupation,' he said. 'If it had been a forced occupation, we would have just taken all these weapons out there. My job is to make sure they are prepared,' but for what, no one is quite sure. More than anything, the men are afraid of a repeat of Somalia, where crowds first greeted American troops with smiles and later dragged their mutilated bodies through the streets, laughing as they did so. That image is burned into the mind of every soldier in the Third Platoon. They have heard stories about Père Lebrun. The poor of Haiti, the soldiers know, have their cruel dark side.

"But when the soldiers write home, they mention none of this. The thing Pfc. Jeff Harris hates worse than anything else is lying to his momma. In elegant script, he writes long, heartfelt letters home to Columbus, Miss., that describe Haiti as being safe, so his mother will not worry. 'You only write your momma the good stuff,' says Harris, who turned 21 in Haiti. He has the soft accent of the Delta. He also writes to a dark-haired beauty named Amanda Smith, whom he plans to marry if she will have him. He has two photos of her. He keeps them next to his *Playboy* magazine."

I liked Pfc. Harris the most. We talked about barbecue and deer hunting and hush puppies—the kind you eat, not the kind you wear to poetry readings—and about lying to our mommas. I rode with the soldiers for a few days, finding out who they were, where they were from, what they thought. I found them to be afraid, not of guns or grenades, but of the magic of the place. I saw it when we drove by a man sitting buck naked at the side of a winding road. His face was painted mustard yellow. His fingers tapped the ground in time to a song only he could hear. "Is that some kind of voodoo?" asked Private Matthew Gunn.

"No," said the squad's interpreter. "Just a crazy person."

My last day with them, we stopped to rest in the shade high up in one of the mountain neighborhoods. A thin, slight man with a camera around his neck walked timidly to the soldiers and asked if he could show them some photographs. He said that for three years he has documented atrocities in this neighborhood, hoping that someday the people who committed them will be punished. The stack of photos is two inches thick. They show gunshot wounds to the head, mutilations, bodies hacked and burned. One is a young, beautiful woman, her breasts and shoulders crisscrossed with slashes. "I wish you could have come sooner," the man said.

One by one the soldiers flip through them, then they go sit quiet. Some of them sit alone. I have never seen them do that before. No one looks at anyone else. "I knew they killed people," Harris finally says, "but I didn't know they done that." He looks disgusted, like he needs to hit someone. "I never seen nothing like that."

I remember that Brady did not say anything, not for a long time, that he just stared off into the trees. As we left the children ran alongside the Humvees, as they always did, but one little boy, as I wrote in my story, ran longer and farther than the rest, shouting, "Hooray." I wanted to go home.

I left before I finished the story. I did not wait for the triumphant return of Aristide. I flew to Miami, closed the curtains on a hotel room in Coconut Grove, near my old house. I slept a long time. I did not dream of Haiti, then, but sometimes I do.

The phone woke me up. It was the national editor of the *Times*. She told me they were promoting me, to national correspondent. I was going to cover the South, from the Atlanta Bureau. I was going home.

I called my momma. She asked me how my cruise had been, and I told her, "long." She told me, funny, she thought she had seen a picture of me on the news, in a crowd of terrified, running people. But she forgot all about it when I told her the news, that I was coming home. "Thank God," she said. I told her I would see her at Thanksgiving, I would see all of them. But I was only partly right.

Months later, I got a letter from Private Brady's momma. She thanked me for the story, for explaining her son's mission, how important it was. I meant to write her back, but I never did. I did not know what to say. Maybe I would just write:

Dear Mrs. Brady:

Your son seems like a fine boy. I hope he gets home to you, safe. And I hope he doesn't dream.

3
GETTING EVEN
WITH LIFE

34

Gone South

I t happens a lot, especially in places where the people live far apart,
separated by a few miles, a few fields, a few hundred fence posts. I
knock on their door, and tell them I am a reporter for the *New York
Times*. I see the doubt and sometimes even suspicion in their eyes.

"You don't sound like no *New York Times*," a state patrolman down in
south Georgia told me.

"You sound like me," a woman told me in a courtroom in South Carolina. She was paying me a compliment, I believe.

Sometimes, I have to show them my identification. It is not always
good to be home—my homecoming brought as much sadness as joy—
but it is an honor, by God.

To work in the Southern Bureau of the *New York Times* is to grab on
to the flapping coattails of newspaper history, and hope your hands are
clean. Legends did this job, in times of national crisis, in times when hatred and night riders ruled the region where I was born, and their stories
helped define it for the rest of the world. To be a Southerner in this job
is to live a dream, even if you never really dared to dream it. I am not going to poor-mouth too much—I wanted this job because I felt I could do
it with some insight, without asking some college professor what I should

feel—but it is as daunting as it is satisfying, to cover your home for strangers.

There have been many Southerners in the job before, of course, but it was a little odd, being the offspring of poor, white Southerners, working for the newspaper that had been so unpopular among my people for its often unflattering depictions of them. The *Times* was the ultimate pointy-head establishment, the ultimate outside agitator, the target of our hatred, and here I was, a modern-day extension of it.

But it feels right, doing this. I know how this part of the world is, how it works, and I know how it used to be, how it used to work. I thought, as I walked into work that first day, that I had an understanding of its meanness, its insecurities, its fragility, and its great good. I had lived much of it.

I had gaps in my knowledge, of course. I knew a good bit about poor whites and poor blacks and working people of all colors, but all I knew about the gentility was that I didn't like them much. Yankee reporters love to hobnob with the gentility, and the gentility love to have them around. They secretly despise each other, over the crab puffs, but not nearly as much as they disdain the nasal-voiced crackers who keep their cars running and their houses clean. I don't find the rich folks down here to be very interesting, and, they talk funny. If I have to hear one more penny loafer–wearing, pink-jowled, bow-tied geek who doesn't know how to pronounce his *r*'s talk about how his "mutha" grew up in the Big House in "Jaw-ja," I will bust. We may sound like trash, us up-country peckerwoods, but at least by God you can understand what we're saying.

Anyway, except in politics and business, rich people seldom make news. Their money, like wings, carries them above the hardships and dangers of normal folks, and keeps them out of the newspaper between cotillions. If I should ever own a newspaper I shall set the society page on fire. I shall chase the society matrons out of my newsroom with a cattle prod when they come in with pictures from the debut. I shall . . .

It is nice to dream.

My understanding of those beneath the gentry helped me, and no place did I use that knowledge, my own life, more than in the story of the old washerwoman in Hattiesburg, Mississippi, Miss Oseola McCarty. She became famous when, in anticipation of her own death, she gave her life savings to the local university as an endowment for scholarships earmarked for poor students. The wizened, gentle old woman had made her living washing and ironing for the rich folks, saving her dollar bills and pocket change over a long lifetime. In the end she had more than $150,000, and, at age eighty-seven, she just handed it to strangers in the belief that her money could do good.

As we talked, in her little house on Miller Street, I had a hard time keeping my mind in the here and now. Her house was filled with clothes, other people's clothes. They surrounded us, in bundles, in neat rows on hangers, as other people's clothes had surrounded me in our own little house, a long, long time ago. As she talked about making them look nice, for parties she was never invited to, weddings she never saw, I heard a voice in my head telling me not to play in the piles of laundry. I smelled the clean, strong scent of bleach and soap and starch, again.

When I sat down to write my story, I closed my eyes and saw not an old black woman but a young white one. Like Miss McCarty, my momma had worn old tennis shoes with holes cut out, or worn through. Like her, she had sweated for hours in hot, airless rooms for dimes and quarters. I let some of the admiration I had for her creep into this story of a stranger, but I don't think it hurt it much. It was, some people told me, the best story I ever wrote, in this job I was born to do.

The *Times* had never made me a hard promise that I would get to do it, but the editors had hired me specifically for it, I would learn some time later. First I had to prove myself in places where I was not part of the landscape, but after just a little over six months in that crowded, frenetic newsroom in New York, and a couple more in the dark, miserable twilight of Haiti, I was as close to home as I would perhaps ever be. It was a marriage so perfect, in my mind's eye, that I was almost surprised when I got a cold, or stubbed my toe, or got a parking ticket, because such things do not belong in dreams.

From the eleventh-story window of the bureau office on Peachtree Street in busy, sprawling Atlanta, you cannot see forever, but on a clear day you can almost see Alabama. Some nights, as the sun sets over the hills that border my state from this one, so close, I stand at that high-up window and lean my forehead to the cool glass. It is not a prayer, really, only something like it.

It was fall of 1994, when I finally got here. I rented an apartment in mid-town and became an urban Southerner, again, because Atlanta has Los Angeles–class traffic and I am not going to waste big chunks of my life trying to get home to a house I would rarely see. I had not been in the city of Atlanta for more than ten years—you don't have to get anywhere near the downtown to get to the airport, the first leg on my journeys home—and I found it to be as I remembered it: big, new, gleaming, at least on first glance, till you found its warts. I knew, from reading about it, that it was about as Southern as a snowmobile, a pretentious city striving for some kind of ridiculous national or international acclaim, or—as one native son once said—just a lot of really nice conventions. I have always been uncomfortable around people who are somehow ashamed of their heritage, who went to speech school to get rid of their accents. Atlanta is like that. It tears down its history with wrecking balls, and builds something bland and homogenized in its place.

But that is harsh. Atlanta is a good place. You won't get shot here nearly as quick as Miami or New Orleans, cities I love, and it is much warmer than Manhattan and Boston. It has green, that lovely green, and nice, safe neighborhoods, if you can afford them and don't mind the drive.

The place I settled into was an old four-unit apartment building where passersby were prone to steal the mail—the mail police told me so in a letter, which they mailed to me at home, risking it—and the washing machine danced back and forth in the closet like a mentally deranged great-aunt. But it had a fireplace and hardwood floors you could slide across in your socks and a good shower, and I spent a day just putting books on the shelves. I guess it is a form of mental illness, but I am careful about it. I put the good, old stuff—Robert Penn Warren,

Faulkner, Eudora Welty, Capote, Dickens, Wolfe, Tennessee Williams, Steinbeck—on the top shelf, in case of floods. It does not matter that I am on the second floor, the ritual continues. I did it in Los Angeles and I was on the eighteenth floor, with not a river in sight. They didn't even have time to get dusty, there.

From the stoop in my apartment in midtown Atlanta, I can hear the distant roar of high school football games on Friday nights. It is not a real football state, this Georgia, not like Alabama, but it beats nothing. For lunch, sometimes, we walk down to Thelma's on Luckie Street and get some collards with pepper sauce and sweet potato soufflé, or drive out toward the federal prison to Harold's, for barbecue and cracklin' corn-bread. Because it is Atlanta they charge you twice what it's worth, but it is mighty good barbecue.

I live precisely two blocks from the Krispy Kreme doughnut factory, and I can smell them from my front yard. Trying to explain how good they are to someone who has never had one is like telling a celibate priest about young love. Four blocks away is the Kentucky Fried Chicken. I have all I need to sustain life, well, almost. Love flies in for the weekends, sometimes, on Valujet.

My neighborhood is a potluck supper of a place: white, black, straight, gay, rich, poor, peaceful, violent, nuts, punks, homeless and some just a paycheck or two away from it. Over on Ponce de Leon, a dys-functional parade of crack dealers, emaciated prostitutes and transves-tite party boys remind you that you live in a big city, but there are crickets at night in the summertime. I like to go to sleep listening to them, unless it is Saturday night, when their fiddling is often interrupted by young men in leather chaps and no shirts engaged in a slap fight. Some nights you are serenaded by nature, some nights you are jolted awake by cries of "Bitch." But that's life in the big city, isn't it.

I am seldom here. I ride the whirlwind of my newspaper's travel budget, doing things and seeing places I could never afford on my own, living a life I could never afford. I live for sweet, long days—weeks, if I can swing it—in the elegant old Pontchartrain Hotel in New Orleans, where the sound of the rattling old streetcar rocks you to sleep and, if you are good, they put pralines on your pillow at night. I write late into the night at the Tutweiler in downtown Birmingham, and try hard to turn down that second cheeseburger at Milo's over by UAB, which has the best one in the whole wide world. In Baton Rouge, in Jackson, in Nashville, in Charlotte, in Columbia and Spartanburg and Macon and a hundred smaller places at the side of the road, I have learned how to feel at ease in a borrowed bed. On the Gulf Coast, I sit by myself on the beach until well after dark, until the sunset is just a memory over Mobile. You learn not to mind being by yourself, doing things by yourself, when you are on the road as much as I am. It is loneliness, maybe, but it is a warm and fuzzy kind. I used to not mind it at all. I mind it a little more, the older I get. But just a little.

There is a sense of urgency in me, a sense that time is running out, but it has to do with the life I left behind, not the one I would begin, if I was so inclined. I am running out of time to keep my promise, to buy her the house, to try and rewrite history so late in the volume of our lives. I have saved forty thousand dollars, which is enough to buy or build a small house in Alabama, but not nearly enough to buy her the nice house I want, a house she would be proud of. I am too ignorant to realize that she would be proud of anything. I decide to save some more, at least enough for a decent two-bedroom cottage, and in the meantime my momma just gets a little older. I kick myself, mentally, for not saving more, sooner, for realizing so late what I should do. I soothe myself the same way I always do, by telling myself I was just young and stupid. I still refuse to buy it on time, because I am so unsure that this dream will last. I am older now, and the conformist in me tells me I should start building a real life of some kind, any kind, but that cannot happen yet, if ever. It has to wait, until my debt to the old life, however ridiculous it might sound, is paid.

Meanwhile, the casualties grow. Another girlfriend, a beautiful young woman named Kelley who rides horses, wins journalism awards and has a rich daddy, is giving up on me. "Will you ever have time for me?" she asked, and I should have lied and said yes. I told her I didn't know.

So, another good, loving, decent woman slips away, and I don't even try to keep her. If it happens to you once or twice in your life, you are a tragic figure. If it happens to you thirty times, you are a womanizer. I don't know what I am. I just know I have never been lonely for too long, that I never spent as much time as I should have, grieving. I don't have time to worry about it, much. I have a plane to catch, always a plane to catch.

Lost in the stories, in the telling, I find my satisfaction, contentment, peace, even in the most tragic ones. Only one thing is missing, really, in that part of my life. Like most reporters, I want the big award, the one that forever alters your obituary. I have some trophies, but there is no Pulitzer Prize in my living room. So, no matter how good life gets, I stare at a blank space on the wall that only I can see. I know it is a sad state for a man to be in, but it would be a lie to say it didn't matter to me. I want it so bad I dream of it. I want it for me, selfishly, and for her, because of what it would bring her, at least what I hope it would bring. I am simple-minded, of course, to look for such magic elixirs, such cure-alls, but I search for them, anyway.

The move makes it easy for me to go home when I want, on any weekend, but the nice, warm feeling of being in close touch again in my family is short-lived. It is blown away by the ranting of a drunk man, by the sound of screeching tires, by the smell of old beer.

I am still helpless to do anything to protect my momma from the torture of worry that my little brother inflicts with his drinking and fighting and life on the teetering edge. Some mothers would have given up, banished him. Not mine. He is more than just a son to a woman who has already lost one. He is her baby. And he is still my little brother, who disarms me with a grin, who tells me, naw, he ain't in no trouble, but he could sure use a carton of cigarettes.

So I just keep moving, from hotel to hotel and plane to plane and story to story, getting lost in that never-ending journey. The job, this perfect job, has brought me back within the orbit of my family, but going home is such a mix of sweetness and sadness that I let weeks, sometimes even months go by between visits. My momma calls every week, and can't figure out why I make it home so seldom, being so close.

Once, I even tried to run away, again.

The *New York Times* job in east Africa came open, after I had been in the South less than a year, and I told the foreign editor I thought I could handle it. He seemed to agree. But Joe Lelyveld and Gene Roberts, the legendary Philadelphia editor, and now our managing editor, told me the story was here, in this country, as the whole nation seemed to grow meaner, less patient. Lelyveld, that supposedly frosty man who had always been warm to me, seemed troubled by my desire to chase something else. Why would I leave, when they gave me exactly what I wanted?

I told myself it was my own nervous feet. I have always been a little afraid of being left behind. To be a real foreign correspondent—Haiti had been only temporary—was one more thing to try, to prove I could do, even though I had not proven myself where I was, not really. In the end, it didn't matter. Roberts, especially, seemed to want me to stay, and arguing with him is like staring at a rock and waiting for it to hop up in the air and twirl. A rock is a rock.

They were right of course, anyway.

The story was here.

35

Abigail

Some days, sadness is all there is. In the fall of 1994 I went to New Orleans to write about the people held hostage by violence in a New Orleans housing project. I captured the stories of dead innocents and other great sadnesses in my notebook, like butterflies pressed between the pages of a science project. Then I went back to hide in the frayed opulence of the old Pontchartrain Hotel on St. Charles. But the sadness spilled out there, too, as if the notebook had fluttered open, letting it out. I knew a reporter once who stretched rubber bands around her notebooks, I thought, at the time, to mark her place. But maybe that wasn't it at all.

The phone rang and it was my sister-in-law, Teresa, calling on behalf of the family. Miss Ab was dead, she told me, of the pneumonia.

I packed my bag for home, rode the jet plane to Atlanta, and told my grandmother good-bye. It would be nice to believe that she knew it was me just one more time.

I took my place among the other young men in the parking lot of K. L. Brown's funeral home, not far from the football stadium. The older men eased on inside, their thin, bony fingers on the elbows of their wives. It is always that way: the old men and women and young women go inside, but the young men linger outside, not talking much, just smoking, standing, waiting as long as they can. We don't do death well, us young men.

I found Sam and Mark there, just standing, quiet. Sam's eyes were red-rimmed and bleak. It was just like him, to have done his crying in private. Most likely it was in his shop, the door closed, maybe even locked. "Hey, son," he said, and shook my hand. "We wondered if they would find you."

I had stopped in Atlanta to put on my one suit, a blue wool suit I wore in my interview to fool the *New York Times* into thinking I might be respectable. I knew, as I looked around the parking lot at the people who actually worked for a living, that I was overdressed.

Sam does not own a suit. There has seldom been any need for one. He borrowed our cousin-by-marriage Tony's leisure suit to get married in, the same suit I borrowed to go to the homecoming dance. One suit would do us all, when we were young. At the funeral he wore a dress-up pair of blue jeans and clean work boots, like about everybody else there. Grandma wouldn't have known us, if we had all had on ties.

Mark said, "Hey," quietly, and just stared at the ground. When he did look up, his face was nothing short of stricken. He was stone-cold sober. I knew he would be. A bad man, a man bad clean through, doesn't grieve, not really. Mark grieves. I reached out and squeezed his arm, hard, at the muscle.

I looked them over closely, as if, so close to death, it forces you to take careful inventory of the other lives that are close to you, important to you. Sam does everything except sleep in his hat, the one with Fruit of the Loom on it, so it always strikes me as odd when I see him with it off, and that is only at funerals. He was nearing forty, and as he had gotten older he had come to look more and more like my grandfather. He still looked solid, still seemed indestructible. His handshake was still like iron, and as I squeezed back he had looked me in the eye and smiled, briefly, to say: "Is that all you got?"

Mark was thin and pale, all long muscles and bone, and looked older than he should have. Indestructible, too, in his own way.

All my male cousins, close and distant, were there, people I had not seen in decades, but that is the way of it, with funerals. I shook hands, asked them how their mommas was, told them I was over in Atlanta now, to come and see me. They nodded politely. Atlanta is only a couple of hours away, but it is light-years from this. There is nothing in Atlanta these folks want.

The funeral director stuck his head out and said we might want to mosey inside. I said hello to the old women and shook hands with the men, and one after another they said they were proud of me.

I didn't know what to say, so I didn't say anything. You hear it all the time, how gracious and strong salt-of-the-earth people can be. I know it to be true, for dead certain.

I looked for Momma, but she wasn't there. She couldn't come, my aunts told me. She didn't think she could stand it. So she did as she has always done. She hunkered down in that little house, and waited for the sadness to pass.

My uncle John told me it would be okay, if I wanted, to go and sit with her, after I saw my grandma. I noticed for the first time that his hair was completely, purely white.

The funeral chapel is built on a sloping floor, toward the casket. You hear it said, too, how natural someone looks. Well, Grandma really did look like she was just asleep, like she was just taking one of those afternoon naps that old people take. And for reasons I cannot explain, that clawed at my guts.

I felt lonely then. This is the time when you need somebody. This is the time when it is good to have a wife, and children, to absorb your grief, to hold on to you. This is when you pay, and pay and pay, for pretending that you don't need anybody.

I didn't hear the words the preacher said over her, but I know exactly how it went. The preacher would assure those left behind that she was in a better place. There would be no doubt of that. Rejoice.

Well, she is. A woman who pretends to forget to eat so that her children will have more, like she had, like my own mother had, doesn't have to worry about getting in.

I left before the first song was sung. I went and sat with Momma. She asked me, her eyes miserable, if people would think badly of her, not going. I told her no.

We talked about her mother for an hour, until the kinfolks started to trickle in. The next day was Thanksgiving.

I don't think a lot about where or how I want to be buried. I think sometimes it would be nice to be laid to rest under an oak tree, but that probably won't happen. They've cut all the oak trees down in the Jacksonville cemetery. And that is where I belong, I guess.

I know I do not want to be buried during football season. In Jacksonville, during football season, the marching band practices not far from the cemetery, so that the dignity of the sermon is lost sometimes, with tubas in the background.

I had to come back to the same funeral home, the same cemetery, less than a year later. One of the best, most generous men I have ever known, Tony Estes, the one who married my cousin Jackie and loaned us his suit, died in a car wreck.

It was hot, so I guess it was still summer. I remember it rained but the sun still shone on us. It happens a lot, in the late afternoon here.

A lot of people came, because Tony had a lot of friends. I guess that's about the best thing you can say about a man.

As the minister said his words, I could hear the band tuning up, in the distance. It is almost always football season, down here.

36

Mrs. Smith, and family

It is one of the first things you learn about writing a story. Mrs. Edna Baggs taught it to me in the tenth grade at Jacksonville High School, and I paid attention, mostly. They call it "The Five W's and H" rule. Every news story has to have the Who, the What, the When, the Where, the Why, and the How. It is an old-fashioned concept, maybe, in the new media, like describing a hammer to someone who has only used a nail gun, but leave out one of those elements of story, and there is no satisfaction in the telling or the reading.

The murder of two little boys in the fall of 1994 in the rural textile mill country of northern South Carolina haunted this whole country, as we answered those questions, or tried to answer them, one by one. The Why of it, the only one left unanswered, haunts me still.

Why.

The satellite trucks stretched for two blocks on the little town's Main Street, and even more television crews filled a parking lot across from the stately old county courthouse. The circus is definitely in town, I thought, as I drove into Union, South Carolina, to cover what an editor had described as "that horrific abduction down in South Carolina." I headed over to a semicircle of television reporters, all scrambling for twelve perfect seconds of breaking news, until I could glimpse the object of their desire behind a battery of microphones.

I got there just in time to see the pale young woman blink into the eye of the electronic nation, Live, and beg the heartless kidnapper and carjacker to look into his own heart, and return her stolen babies.

"Whoever has my children . . . please, please bring them home where they belong. They are missed and loved more than any children in the world."

Then, apparently on the chance that her two young sons were watching, she sobbed: "I feel in my heart you're OK. And your momma and daddy will be waiting for you when you get home. I put my faith in the Lord that He will bring them home to us."

I believed her. I wrote a story about that awful abduction on October 25, 1994, when a black man in a stocking cap jumped into her car at a dark crossroads, ordered her out at gunpoint, and sped away with her sons, Michael, four, and Alex, fourteen months, as the young mother fell to her knees in the road and screamed in rage and terror at those fading taillights.

I wrote of the increasingly frantic search, of the grim determination of the stoic Southern law officers, of the united community, praying as only we down here can pray, for miracles. And, as the days slipped by, I was slow to believe in anything except the young mother's grief, which she reminded us continuously about, every time a television flickered on.

People in Union and surrounding towns started wearing yellow ribbons. They packed churches, believing that their condensed prayer might do more than individual ones. The young mother, her tears dry, went on TV again. "I can't imagine why anyone would want to do such a thing," she said. She guessed that it could only be the work of a "sick and unstable person."

The would-be rescuers turned to bloodhounds, horses and helicopters. On October 26, a film of a convenience store robbery in North Carolina showed a man matching her description of the kidnapper; witnesses described a car resembling her Mazda, and the search shifted there. Law officers and volunteers searched a North Carolina national forest after two hunters reported seeing a car matching the Mazda's description, and hope shifted there. On the 28th, officers searched a wooded area outside Union after a twelve-year-old girl reported seeing a man matching the suspect's description, and the satellite trucks rumbled back into Union.

The investigators, led by a plain-spoken, quietly intelligent sheriff named Howard Wells, admitted that they had no leads. It was as if the two little boys had just winked out of existence with those vanishing taillights.

Then, I think it was on the 29th, we all began to suspect—reporters, searchers, even the people on their knees—that we were fools.

I never, ever call my momma from assignments like this, but I was back home in Atlanta on a Sunday when she called me. She had long since caught on to the kind of stories I was drawn to, or ordered to, and asked me if I had been "to that bad thing in South Carolina." She asked me if I believed the momma had killed those babies, and I asked her why she asked me that. But before she could answer it, I suddenly knew.

"Momma," I said, "if it was us, when we were little, and a man had shoved a gun in your face and told you to get out of the car without us, what would you have done?"

"I would be dead," she said. "He would have had to have shot me."

It was the truth of it, of course. The tragedy we had been spoon-fed by a twenty-three-year-old textile mill secretary would turn out to be an unspeakable act, one that made people as far away as New York City hug their children an extra time at night.

The night they disappeared, she dressed her children in neat clothes, drove to the lake and then parked her car on the steep boat ramp. She stepped out, released the hand brake, and let that car carry her children to their deaths by slow suffocation under the water. They were still strapped in their seats.

After nine days of lies, she told her story, sobbing, to the quiet country sheriff. She did not volunteer it. The sheriff had tricked her with a lie

of his own, into confessing, and asked God to forgive him for it, because
he was a thoroughly decent man.

As a journalist, of course, I dropped the ball. I should have raised the
possibility of her involvement. I knew that in most cases like this, the
parents are involved. A simple line about that would have, at least, raised
the possibility of a hoax. I was dumb.

The horror of what she had done left us to wonder why. Maybe,
as her lawyers said, she had killed them because she was so deeply de-
pressed, because she had been sexually abused by her own stepfather,
a corpulent leading Republican and devoutly religious man named Bev
Russell, then used by every man she had ever gone to, searching for
love. Her lawyers painted her crime as a failed murder-suicide, saying that, after that lifetime of sexual abuse and emotional abuse at
the hands of her stepfather and other men, she wanted to die with
her children. It sounded too much like daytime TV to me, and even as I
tried to feel sorry for her—and I did feel disgust for the men who had
used her so—I kept envisioning those children at the cold bottom of
that lake.

The prosecution seemed to be dealing with a totally different woman.
The children were dead because Susan Smith wanted to rid herself of an
obstacle in her campaign for the affection of a rich man's son she had
dated, a man who did not want her ready-made family, the baggage that
came with her. Union exists because of the textile mills, where men and
women work for low wages in the deafening clatter and hum of the great
machines. Susan, a brown-haired, not unlovely woman who was getting
out of a bad marriage, worked for the mill's owner in an office where the
clatter of the machines could not reach, and went to hot tub parties with
the mill owner's son.

Nine days after the big lie, as the police cruisers and divers con-
verged on the lake, the water looked almost black. Visibility was only
about a foot when diver Steve Morrow floated up to the burgundy
Mazda that lay upside down in the cold water. "I had to put my light
against the window, and peered in," he said. "I was able to see a small
hand pressed against the glass."

Inside the car with the bodies of her sons was a letter from the man she loved telling her that their relationship would never work, in part because of her children, in part because their worlds were just too different.

Someone should have told her how hard it is to fight your way from one side of the tracks to the other. Someone should have told her that just because they invite you into a dark room, that doesn't mean they'll take you to the dance.

Every day at precisely 12:25 P.M., the local radio station in Union has its litany of the dead. It is not a complicated or dramatic process. The radio announcer just reads the obituaries from the local paper out loud. People here say the program is very popular. It tells the town who has passed from their midst in a respectful and very concise manner. Every death gets a few seconds, and sometimes the whole list is a single name. It is a short program. It is a small town.

The murder of two innocents took death to a proportion this town had never experienced, robbed it of its dignity, and shattered custom like a swinging baseball bat against an heirloom vase. It was suddenly terrifying and sickening and, ultimately, shameful.

It required more than a monotone sendoff, spiked with static. It ushered in the world.

I was part of the zoo, too, just a little less obvious. I fit in. I knew the dialects. I had cotton mills in my blood, and some days I felt guilty, for spreading this story so far and wide.

No matter which Susan Smith you believed in, the murder trial of that young woman was like running barefoot through Johnson grass. No matter how detached any reporter was—and I had learned to be pretty detached by now, at least detached enough to keep my sanity—the evidence shocked and sickened. Some news magazines called it the story of the year, as she went on trial for her life.

To me, it was pure American gothic, showing the small-town, milltown South in its worst possible light, and I hated that. I had met some nice people in Union, but their normal, decent voices would be drowned out by the awfulness, the selfishness, the horror of the testimony that unfolded over the next few months.

The worst day was the testimony of the lover who spurned her, Tom Findlay. Known in Union as "The Catch," I had expected a handsome man, but in Union, good looks don't feed the bulldog. He was a baldish, average-looking man from Mountain Brook, Alabama, an affluent Birmingham suburb where teenagers often get their driver's license and their first BMW at the same time, and lived in an apartment in his father's mansion, on an estate in the woods outside Union. He was the crown prince of a town of 10,000 people, most of them just one paycheck ahead of poverty.

Susan Smith's husband had worked in the grocery store. How compelling, to be invited to the Big House.

But her love was wasted on the rich man's son.

"Like I told you before, there are some things about you that aren't suited for me, and yes, I mean your children," he had written her in his letter, on October 17, just eight days before she drowned her sons. "With all the crazy, mixed-up things that take place in this world today, I just don't have the desire to bring another life into it. And I don't want to be responsible for anyone else's children, either."

It wasn't just the children that kept them apart, the county prosecutor said of the twenty-eight-year-old man, Tom Findlay, and Susan Smith. He had also written that their backgrounds—he was a child of privilege, she a child of a mill worker who committed suicide when his wife left him—would never mesh.

"We are just two totally different people," his letter said, "and eventually, those differences would cause us to break up."

It sounded like high school stuff to me, but then I have never been a romantic.

At one point in his letter to Mrs. Smith, he wrote that he was disappointed in her for an affair she had had with a married man and for kissing a man during a hot tub party at Findlay's home. "If you want to catch a nice guy like me," he wrote her, "you have to be a nice girl."

The prosecution introduced the letter and Mr. Findlay's testimony in an effort to portray Mrs. Smith as so maliciously selfish that she was prepared to trade the lives of her children for a chance to reclaim him. And all the way through that day's testimony, all I could think was, what a fool she was. I learned that even as her babies lay under the lake, she twice asked friends to tell Findlay to call her.

I could have told her about the dance.

Her estranged husband wanted her dead. His hand vibrated so badly as he held the pictures of his two sons up to the jury that they were a just a blur of two little boys on the sand at Myrtle Beach. One network correspondent cried out loud.

He had been a much better father than a husband, and had gone to her house long after they had split up, and demanded sex from her, according to the testimony. But his grief was real.

"Michael didn't like water on his face," he said, between his sobs. "He would try to climb out of the bathtub" when water splashed onto his face. He would have to shield Michael's face with his hand, when he rinsed his hair.

The defense, led by a smart man, David Bruck of Columbia, South Carolina, had a simple argument. She was not insane, only desperate for love. It drove her to a promiscuous love life, where men used her instead of loving her. I will never forget the day her stepfather came to court, the one who first molested her when she was fifteen, and how he joined hands with other family members in the courtroom, to pray for his stepdaughter. I guess he has asked God to forgive him.

The man who had caught her was Union County sheriff Howard Wells, a complicated man who collects guns but pops Supreme Court decisions off the top of his head. He did it with a simple lie. He told her he knew she was not telling the truth because his deputies were working drug surveillance at the crossroads where she said her children were stolen, the night of the alleged abduction.

"This could not have happened as you said," he told her, sitting face to face with her in a small room in a church gymnasium, where they had gone to get away from reporters. There had been, in truth, no such deputies at the intersection. "I told her I would release it to the media" because her lie about a black carjacker was causing deep pain among blacks, and he said he owed it to the town to end the racial divisiveness it had caused.

She broke then. She asked him to pray with her, he said, and face to face, holding hands, they did. "I'm so ashamed," she told him, and asked for his gun so that she could kill herself. But that might have just been Susan acting, too.

The jury couldn't kill her, of course.

"This young woman is in a lake of fire," said the lawyer, David Bruck. "That's her punishment."

It might have been different if it really had been a black carjacker. Then I'm pretty sure there would have been an execution. Carolina gives the condemned a choice. They choose the needle, or they can ride the lightning.

One of the four blacks among the jurors, John Dunn, said he did not resent Mrs. Smith for having chosen to blame a black man and in fact understood why she had done so. What better alibi to offer, Mr. Dunn said, then a lie that she knew people would believe?

Almost on cue, as the county court clerk read off the verdict that spared her life, a hard rain started to fall, washing away for a little while a summer heat wave that had lasted throughout this trial.

"Poetic justice," said Andy Wallace, a state investigator, as he watched the rain run down the street.

❖   ❖   ❖

One thing has always bothered me. If you believe her lawyers, if you believe the theory of a failed suicide, then it happened this way. She drove to the lake and parked her car on the boat ramp's steep incline, pausing as she steeled herself for what she was about to do. She let go of the hand brake, reconsidered and pulled it up again, then let it go and—in some instinct for survival—hurled herself from the car.

Yet her clothes were not torn or dirtied. Her clothes were neat and clean when she walked to a nearby house to tell her lie.

The only possible way it could have happened is if she stood outside the car, leaned in to let go the hand brake, and jumped back, letting the car roll into the lake.

People in Union said it didn't really matter. It was over, wasn't it?

But it wasn't really over. It never will be. The lake became a shrine, complete with monuments to the two boys. People came from all over the world to see it.

I had to go back to Union in September of 1996. The unthinkable had happened again, but this time an accident. This time the lake swallowed up a family of five and two other people who had come to see the monuments to Susan Smith's sons. The new victims—four of them children, one an infant—were shining the headlights of their truck on the memorials when the truck somehow rolled into the water. The five people inside drowned, including those four children. Two adults who had been standing outside the truck drowned when they swam out to try to save the others. When rescue workers arrived at the lake late Saturday night, the body of a child floated on the surface. The next day, some said it was God, punishing the town for its leniency. I don't think so. The tragedy was that anyone would want to see that place, that anyone would go.

I hated the Susan Smith story, for its hopelessness, and I guess maybe I hated it because a part of me understood her, the desire to be something else.

She will be eligible for parole in 2025. Her looks will be long gone then. She will have to live out the rest of her life as a mill worker's daughter who killed her babies.

Who knows. Maybe some nut bag will come and rescue her in her old age, because of her celebrity. Some nut bag with money. And she will get to put on her party dress, after all.

37

Monsters

I understood nothing of the bombers who killed the innocents in Oklahoma City, who reduced the federal building to rubble and turned the day-care center, where the babies had slumbered in the windows, to a jumble of concrete chunks and broken toys. I wrote of it because they told me to, because I wanted to, but I do not like to think much about it now. I will not, for more than few a minutes at a time. I tried to give a short talk about it once, to other reporters, and while my mouth kept moving, I stumbled in my mind over the bloody rubber gloves tossed in the rain, and the smell of, what? Dust. And the faces of men and women who had seen something we should never have to look at.

You pour it all into your stories, as your fingers hover above the computer keyboard, but when you get up, when it is done, you block much of it out. You have to feel for the people you write about or the words don't amount to much, but you learn to put it down.

I remember one night in Oklahoma City, a dinner with the other reporters, laughing a little, whistling past the graveyard as we coldheartedly discussed the stories we had written and still had to write. And all that time, at the neighboring table, sat a woman whose little girl had been killed in the blast. Later, her friends lashed out at us, and all I could say, sitting there, white-faced, was how sorry we were to be so insensitive. There was no way we could have known, of course, how close we were to someone who could never, ever block it out.

I walked away but something made me turn around and go back, to explain myself, to try to make her understand that every reporter at that table was sick at heart, too, of what they had seen. I guess she believed me. I hope she did.

I have never been ashamed of being a reporter. I have been afraid, and angry, and heartsick, but never ashamed. I lay awake a long, long time that night, sorry about what had happened, but not ashamed.

It goes way beyond the craft itself. That assignment, the story of the year, was in my eighteenth year as a reporter, in the role, the only one I have ever felt at peace with, of paid storyteller.

It had pulled me out of poverty, literally. It had shown me the world, and I did not mind that the world was so often on fire when I got there. It gave me an education, from books at Harvard, from a thousand stories where I was forced to understand something an hour before deadline. It gave me pride and money, but more pride. It saved me. It surely did. My mother gave me the boost up, and what I found, on the other side of that wall, was this.

Of course, she was still there, surrounded by those old sadnesses. Nothing seemed to change, on her side, except the calendar.

Houses burn in the country all the time. The wiring is often homemade, and over the years the boards dry out and wires short out, and then one night as you drive back from town you see a dull orange glow in the distance, and you wish, quite selfishly, that the flames have consumed someone else's lifetime of hard work and dreams. House insurance is not a given, not here. The only insurance some have—is luck.

My grandmother's little house had burned in the summer of 1993. That should have been enough bad luck. Two years later, my little brother's house burned to the ground. I was in the Piedmont region of Virginia, as the flames licked up into the oaks, writing about floods. The volunteer fire department came fast, but much too late. My momma came, in terror.

Was he inside? she asked the fireman.

He said he could not say for sure. He did not think so, but he could not say for sure.

She was in agony, for hours. His truck was gone from the driveway, but that meant nothing. He was always breaking down on deserted roads and walking out. My brother Sam drove his Ford Bronco through the northern part of the county, searching for Mark, but found nothing. No one had seen him.

Finally, several hours later, my kinfolks found him safe.

My momma took days to stop shaking.

I finally made it home five days later. I told him I would help pay for his lumber, if he wanted to build it back. He started laying block for the foundation less than a month after the blaze, planning a smaller house this time.

Sometimes, things like that will shake people up enough to make them change. I have seen it happen with fires, with deaths, even surgery. My momma hoped it would be so with him. We do have some luck in this life, but not that much. Momma just stepped back on the treadmill of worry and hopelessness, and kept walking.

I had been selfish long enough. It was time, past time, to begin paying her back, in the only ways I knew how.

38

Validation

On the eleventh floor of the building at West 43rd Street in New York, there is a long hallway lined with the faces of winners of the Pulitzer Prize. The black-and-white photographs peer down from the walls, framed beside prizewinning stories of wars and upheavals and great tragedies, datelined Berlin, Bejing, Johannesburg, Moscow, any place news has been committed. I remember one day in winter or early spring, 1994, I drummed up the courage to walk between the pictures of the educated, dignified ladies and gentlemen. As I browsed, dreaming, I heard people approaching around the dogleg in the hall. For a silly moment, I wondered if I had the right to be there. For a moment, I was that little boy in the dime store again, just before the old woman behind the counter told me I didn't have enough money to buy what I was looking for.

It was Arthur Sulzberger Jr., the publisher, and Max Frankel, the retiring executive editor. Of all people, to catch me dreaming. But Frankel smiled, warm, not mocking. He knew why I'd come there. I wonder how many others he had seen there just like me. Hundreds?

"Next year," he said, "it will be you." He was being nice, to the new boy.

It was a good moment, the kind you would like to press between the pages of a book, or hide in your sock drawer, so you could touch it again.

❋   ❋   ❋

I will never forget the first journalism award I ever won. It was for sports writing, in the category of stock car racing, and when they announced my name in that banquet hall in Pell City—the same city where they make the discount dentures—I was proud, so proud. That, as near as I can figure, was about sixteen years ago. I hung it on a bedroom wall, so I could see it when I woke up in the mornings. It was a simple certificate mounted under Plexiglas on fake wood, but it was pure gold to me. I won some more, as the years went by, better ones, until finally that first one just didn't matter to me anymore, and I grew tired of lugging it and others like it around. But throwing it away was unthinkable. I put it in a box with my baseball glove—my knees were shot by now—and some other pieces of my pleasant, obsolete past, and gave them to my momma for safekeeping. I expected it to collect dust and spiders in one of her closets.

I went home one weekend to find it on the wall in my bedroom, along with a few other plaques, a few other distant milestones. I didn't ask her why she put it on the wall, because I believe I understood. It was proof that outsiders believed that her boy had done good. It did not matter that it was the Alabama Sportswriters Association or the Alabama Associated Press. They had my name on them, and the words, "First Place."

The house fire ruined them in 1993, along with her GED diploma and my high school graduation picture. The fire, which started in the little room that had been my bedroom, blackened the certificates and warped the Plexiglas frames. The scrapbook of yellowed newspaper clippings—a lifetime of them—vanished in ashes, but it was the awards that she hated losing most, because they represented praise, validation.

"I don't tell you a lot," she told me one day, sitting in the living room that still smelled of smoke, "but I am very proud of you. I look at you and know I didn't do no bad job, not altogether."

No, not altogether.

When I was a baby, it was common for men in my part of Alabama to leave home for jobs in the automobile assembly plants in Detroit, a lonely crusade away from their kin and sweethearts. They cooked on hot plates and dreamed of their momma's kitchen, and lived in rented rooms that looked out on smokestacks and black snow. They could stand it only because it was temporary. They saved their greenbacks in the company's credit union, not for retirement but for that sweet day when they went back home for good.

It was expected of them, after they made enough money to buy a few acres of land and build a two-bedroom house. Sometimes, of course, they came home as changed men. They learned to drink and they learned to take the Lord's name in vain, some of them. I cannot tell you how many times I have heard some old woman say: "He never did cuss none, before he went to Michigan." But it didn't matter, just so long as you came on home. Only the most selfish young men made their fortune and stayed away, leaving their daddies and—worse—their mommas, to grow old alone.

I used to believe my momma sat in sadness, waiting for me to come home for good. I used to believe that if my mother had had her way, I would live in a little house next to her, with children chasing lightning bugs through the dark, with a wife at my side, to chase the loneliness away.

I was wrong. "I'm glad you got out," she has told me, a dozen times.

She worries that I will die old and alone, and she disapproves of my running around and acting a fool, a man my age. She wishes I was closer to Jesus, and I see the clouds collect in her mind when I say I can take care of myself, that I am living life as I want to live it, free and loose, that I have no regrets. But she never nags. I sat down with her once, a long time ago, and told her that this job is who I am, what I have instead of a wife and children, in place of a garden and a house with a porch swing. She understood that.

When kinfolks and others tell her, "Rick don't come home much, does he," she always defends me. She tells them how busy I am, and relays my latest promise to get home as soon as I can. "The only way Ricky can eat at your house," she told one aunt, "is if it's cooked and ready when he pulls up in the driveway. That, or you throw it in his mouth as he drives by." She tells them I have an important job, that I fly in airplanes near every week, that I have a special card that lets me rent a different-colored Pontiac in every city I go to. And sometimes, a Cadillac.

"One day," she told me, "maybe you can come home." Maybe someday, she said, when I have what I want, when the car I am chasing like some mutt just stops, and I have to decide: "Fine. I've caught it. Now what?"

I was in Washington, D.C., the day before the Pulitzers were announced, to interview the new president of the National Rifle Association, an ornery woman who was a champion black powder shooter and cheerleader sponsor. I had known I was a finalist for the prize, but I had come close before. The thought of sitting by the phone in our bureau office in Atlanta was abhorrent to me, so I planned a day-trip to Washington to fill my mind until the awards had been announced and my disappointment had faded. I didn't even pack a bag; I just needed to be in motion.

Later, when I called in to check my messages, Susan Taylor, the office manager and one of the best people I know, told me that my big boss, Joe Lelyveld, was looking for me. I knew right then that I had either won the thing, or I was fired. I called him from the bathroom phone of a strip mall restaurant called Ruby Tuesday's.

"Can you be in New York tomorrow, and have lunch with me?" he asked, and I told him yes, sir. "I can't tell you why," he said, "but I will demystify you, tomorrow."

I called Susan back and told her, "We might have won."

I didn't have a toothbrush or a change of clothes. I got to New York too late to buy anything except the toothbrush. The night before the second-greatest day of my life, I washed my underwear in the sink with fruit-scented shampoo, and hung them on a lamp to dry. I was careful not to let the cloth droop down and actually touch the bulb. I had started a small fire in the Medallion Hotel in Oklahoma City doing that, once.

I was supposed to meet him at the Café des Artists—I truly didn't know that this was a pretty swank place—and I got there much too early, my suit wrinkled, my shirt a day old, my underwear smelling of peaches. I had not brought a coat, and, of course, it started to snow. But I needed to walk. I walked up to Broadway, the snow and sleet stinging my cheeks and sticking in my hair, but if I was cold I can't remember it. I was numb, but it had nothing to do with the temperature, just that odd feeling of walking outside yourself, of distance.

I had plenty of time to think. I knew that I had had a good career, that editors had trusted me with important stories, that I had survived the people who tried to block my way, that I had made the people who had helped me proud of me. But I barely thought of them, as the yellow taxis flowed and honked and the lunchtime crowds poured down the sidewalks through the last snow of the year. I thought instead of a woman in Alabama, who was probably soaking beans and flipping through the King James Bible, a woman who didn't even know what the Pulitzer was.

This glorious thing, this prize, was validation of my mother's sacrifice. It was payment—not in full, but a payment nonetheless—for her sweat, and her blood. "Now, people will speak to her when they see her on the street," explained one editor, a Southern man who knows something of snobbery, of class.

I will not lie and say that I was not thrilled to get it. Maybe I didn't even deserve it, but by some miracle it had happened, and several times since that day I have felt like pumping my fist in the air and letting out a howl. Even though she was oblivious to all this—I had not called her because I was afraid it might not come true—she was with me then, on that sidewalk, in that big city, just as sure as if she had been walking beside me. I wasn't even sure, though, how I would tell her. I would have to explain it first, give shape to it, before it would matter to her what we now held, both of us.

What I felt mostly was relief. I knew that this would bring her attention, respect. It would be a chance for me to spread the word of what she had done for me, and the words would have real weight, because of the prize itself.

Later, at the table, over honest-to-God champagne that did not come from the Piggly Wiggly, Lelyveld told me that I had won the prize for feature writing, along with Robert D. McFadden, for spot news reporting, and Robert B. Semple Jr., for editorials. (Now that I have a Pulitzer, I may also get a middle initial.) The glasses clinked and people smiled but I don't remember smiling, just that relief, that sweet relief.

One of the men had the beginnings of tears in his eyes, and he got up from the table to call his wife. Lelyveld looked at me and asked me, "What now?" and I truthfully didn't know. It was like the fights in the playground when I was a boy, when you take one last blind swing, wipe the dirt out of your eyes, and realize that the other boys you were fighting, biting and gouging have left the field of honor to you, and run for the teacher.

But instead there was Lelyveld, and Gene Roberts, and Howell Raines, the legends, raising glasses to me. I don't give a damn how corny it sounds, it was nice.

Later that afternoon, we walked into the newsroom of the *New York Times* to applause.

People who have lived a long time have called this day the best day of their lives. Lelyveld stood on a desk and said nice things about us, about me, and I tried to say something that made sense. For the first time in my life, I really had nothing to say. I felt stupid, as if, by whittling down the chip on my shoulder, I had nicked away part of my brain.

Then I went looking for a phone, to call my momma. It had been more than an hour since the announcement, plenty of time to discover a miscount in votes or a mistake in the order of finish. It was safe now, I figured.

I know how silly and paranoid that sounds, especially coming from a man who gets a perverse thrill from taking chances. But it is a common condition of being poor white trash: you are always afraid that the good things in your life are temporary, that someone can take them away, because you have no power beyond your own brute strength to stop them.

But this thing was ours now. No one could take it away from us.

The phone was busy. It was probably my aunt Jo, I figured. It usually was, when the phone was busy. I finally got her, on the fifth try.

"Momma, you remember that big award I told you about, the one I said I probably wouldn't win? Well, I won it."

"Well," she said.

"It's the Pulitzer Prize, Momma. It's the highest honor you can win in our business.

"Well," she said, "thank God." One reporter had already called her, and she truly had not known what he was talking about.

She truthfully had never heard of the Pulitzer. But as soon as she hung up her phone, it started to ring. It seemed like every newspaper in Alabama called her, over the next twenty-four hours. The *Anniston Star* took a picture of her and ran it on the front page, in color. The *Jacksonville News* interviewed her, and the *Birmingham News*, and the *Mobile Press Register*. Story after story ran, saying nice things about her son, about her. Instead of talking about the prize—she could not pronounce it, she was so afraid of saying it wrong—she just said she was proud of me, that she always had been, and that she sure hoped I had brought a coat to New York, because I wasn't good at remembering things like that, and it was supposed to get cold.

She had not been to a beauty shop in twenty years, and she was ashamed of her hair, and her mouth, because it still didn't have any teeth in it. When the *Star* photographer called, she called me, in a panic. "They want to take my picture," she said. "They want to come in the house." I told her she didn't have to let them, not if she didn't want to, but she thought somehow she would be letting me down if she refused.

I have the paper folded in my desk. The photographer had her hold a framed picture of me, one of those that had survived the fire, more or less.

At first glance, the newspaper photo looks like one of those pictures you see in the paper when a teenager is killed in a car wreck, just a grim-faced momma staring down at the likeness of a fresh-faced boy. She told me she would have liked to have smiled, to appear happy, but she was afraid that if she grinned people could see her gums.

I did not really notice, not for a long time, that in the photograph she is sitting in the yard.

I told her that day that we would have to travel to New York to accept the prize, but she just said, no, she couldn't do that, she could never do anything like that. It was not the plane ride that frightened her: she had never been on a plane or even near one, unless you count the one they stuck up on a big pedestal near a rest stop down between Montgomery and Troy. It was the people she couldn't face, all those fancy people.

I told her how silly she was acting, that she had to go, that we were as good as anybody, that we could dress up and hold our heads high and pass ourselves off as the gentry, and if they caught on, we wouldn't give a damn. I told her it was easy, but no matter how much I coaxed her and reassured her she just said no in a tiny voice. The program called for a short cocktail party-reception, which she equated with people dripping in diamonds, and a lunch, where she would not know which fork to use, and would not be able to chew the food because she didn't have any teeth. I told her we would get her some damn teeth, I told her we would get her some nice clothes, I promised that I would not leave her side for even a second. She just apologized, over and over, for letting me down, for not being there with me.

I gave up after a while. I had to make myself understand, had to tell myself that all my momma's experiences with people in suits had been bad. She had always been on her knees to them, cleaning their floors. She did not think she belonged, even for just a little while. I think she was afraid just as I have always been afraid, that they would spot the imposter in their midst, that they would ask her to clear the table.

I could have called one of the ex-girlfriends, but somehow that seemed wrong. This was not a date, it was something precious, and I called my momma one last time to beg her to go.

"I been thinking about it," she said, "and I reckon I can do it." I almost dropped the phone.

The phone had rung steady for days and days. Kinfolks we had not heard from in years suddenly called her, to say how proud they were. Teachers from elementary school called to tell her that they always knew I was something special. Perfect strangers had called, to say how proud they were that someone in our town had won something so grand. They stopped their cars when they saw her in the yard. People did speak to her on the street, people who had never spoken to her before.

Finally, she had just swallowed down her fear and hitched up her man's britches, and decided that if this thing was so important to them, then it must be ever so important to me.

We only had a week or two to get ready, and the kinfolks, God bless them, mobilized. My momma didn't own a suitcase because there was no place she had ever really wanted to go—we used to pack our clothes in paper sacks when we went to Pensacola to play in the water—and didn't have any dress-up clothes. Within a week, she had five suitcases and three hanging bags and more dresses than she needed. My cousin gave her a permanent and she practiced smiling in front of the mirror, so that she could seem friendly and still not reveal that she didn't have a tooth in her head. She still refused to get new dentures. There wasn't time, she said, to get them made at Pell City, and all my arguments to have someone else make them were ignored. "Costs too much," she said, and went back to practicing.

The kinfolks had little faith that I could care for her in the big city— I think they were afraid I would lose her or let her get hit by a taxi—and they recruited my cousin Jackie, who was the only one who had flown before, to accompany her.

The *Times* offered to fly us up for free, but I told my momma we could take a car or a bus or drive, if she would feel better that way. She just said no, that wasn't what she was afraid of, and on an unseasonably hot day in May, we worked our way through Hartsfield International Airport in Atlanta, on our great adventure.

She made it fine through the X-ray machine, but when it came time to get on the plane, we had a little confusion. My momma had never been to an airport, and she believed that you had to walk out on the tarmac to get on the plane, like Elvis in *Blue Hawaii*. When I took her in tow and led her down the ramp at the loading gate, she said she didn't think she'd go into that confining place, she'd just wait and get on the plane, thank you very much. I told her, Ma, this is how you get on the plane, and she didn't like that one damn bit, because she couldn't see the thing she was getting on.

We sat in first class, in the front row. That was when my momma asked me the first of what I estimate to be one million questions.

How big was it? How many people rode on it? Where did they sit? How many pilots did it take to fly it? Did I reckon they was any good at what they did? Were we moving yet? Could we feel it move? Did we get to sit in the front row because we won the Pulitzer? Had I ever flown this plane before and did I reckon it was a pretty good one, because she had seen on the TV that some of them wasn't? Would we see a movie—she had heard they had movies sometimes—and would it have cussing in it? Would we be flying over water, which she certainly hoped we would not be, and was there a raft?

That was before the plane had moved. When we finally pushed back from the gate and the plane gave that little, reassuring lurch that tells you that, indeed, you might actually be flying somewhere today, Momma's eyes got big.

Then the questions poured. Was it supposed to make so much racket just rolling on the ground? If they brought you food, did you have to eat it? How did the man flying the plane know where to go? How did he keep from getting lost above the clouds? How high would we fly? How fast would we go? Did the flight attendants (she called them "them ladies") ever get to sit down or did they fly the whole time standing up? Did I think anyone would mind if she prayed?

Finally, the plane taxied down the runway and, with a shudder that was less than reassuring, slipped into the sky. My momma watched it for a second or two out the window, until we got about as high as a barn loft, then refused to look out the window the rest of the trip.

She did not whimper, even though she was scared to death, and I pat-
ted her like an idiot and told her everything was fine. She nodded her
head, swallowed, and fixed me with one of those hard looks that she
hadn't used on me since I was a little boy.

"Ricky," she said, "what keeps us in the air?"

I truly did not know. But considering the situation, I thought it best
to lie. I told her that the plane was held aloft by the air being forced
through the whirling turbine engines, which did something, which did
something else, which resulted in "thrust." Yeah, thrust. That's it.
"Thrust," I said gravely, knowingly, "keeps it aloft."

They served us a meal on a white tablecloth, which she marveled at,
and she admired the tiny little salt and pepper shakers, saying, "Why, I
never have seen such a purty thing." She didn't think much of the food,
the stringy chicken. But the meal took her mind off the fact we were
soaring so high above the ground, so it was a blessing.

We talked the whole time, saying nothing, and she made it just fine
until we started to come down, and she prayed again.

I thought we were home free when we landed with just a mild bump
and walked safely off the plane, and I had forgotten about the escalator.
Momma had never seen one, and I had to keep an arm around her, to
guide her down. She would come to refer to it as "that thang that eats
your toes."

But it was the taxi ride that damn near killed us. I had warned her
that the taxi drivers blistered through bumper-to-bumper traffic like
they had stole something and were trying to get away, but it was still the
wildest ride of her life. Ma, Cousin Jackie and I were wedged tight in the
backseat—Momma, the precious cargo, in the middle—and my greatest
fear was that one of the doors would pop open from the strain of three
bodies slammed against it at every twist and turn. Momma seemed to be
out of questions, or maybe she was just too terrified to speak. By the time
the taxi made it to the hotel in Times Square, she was pale and rubber-
legged.

But there was still one man-made hurdle left to leap. Momma had
never been in an elevator either, and this was a glass-enclosed one that

shot you heavenward like a crystal bullet. This was a woman who had never, until that day, been higher than a rooftop, when she used to help her daddy nail down shingles. I was treating her like a human yo-yo.

Over the next three days, she had her first room service, had someone make her bed the first time in her adult life, and watched a television with more than three channels, 6, 13, and 40.

I loved that time, seeing her experience those big city things. But what I will always treasure are the walks we took in midtown Manhattan, through the sea of people. It is true, the cliché, about people being in such a hurry. Not her. The sea parted around her, and she took her time down Broadway, across 45th Street, down to the Empire State Building. She did not want me to hold her hand because she said it made her look helpless, so I just tried to stay close to her, with Jackie's help. If I lost my momma in midtown Manhattan I could not have returned home. They would have killed me.

We did lose her, once. I was lost in thought about something, musing along, staring at the ground, for a whole block. I noticed I was missing someone. I panicked. I hurried back, searching the mass of faces, and found her standing in the center of the sidewalk, her head tilted back, just looking at the skyscrapers, wondrous.

"I never would have believed it," she said, and I nodded my head. It wasn't that she couldn't believe how tall the buildings are, only that she was here to see them.

For dinner, because she was tired, we went to the buffet at the hotel. She liked the roasted peppers, although they were hard to gum. But I noticed she had her eye on the dessert buffet, this dazzling array of sweets that was unlike anything she had ever seen. I walked her to the cakes, pies and puddings and she said, "Okay, I can do it from here." When she came back to the table my timid momma had a fruit torte, a wedge of chocolate mousse cake, a plate of strawberries, a slice of what looked like mango cheesecake and a parfait tucked under her arm.

My momma is not a heavy woman—she eats desserts on Thanksgiving, Christmas and Halloween, if there is candy the trick-or-treaters don't eat—but she had never seen temptation like this. If I had done it, she would have told me I would be sick as a dog. But how do you scold your momma for digging deep into the first dessert buffet she ever saw.

After dark I led her out into Times Square again, into the colors that actually seemed to throb through the canyons of buildings, and we just stood and looked and looked and looked.

"Well," she said, "I wouldn't want to pay their light bill."

That night I made sure she and Jackie were locked safe in their room, and I took a walk alone through Times Square. It was warm, too warm for the season—seems that all my time in New York is spent either sweating or freezing—and I wound up back at the *Times*, back in the gloom of the Pulitzer walk.

I couldn't help but wonder again how I would ever fit in here, among these people. I told myself that I had reached the same place, I had only started from a different direction, and, truthfully, had to travel a good part of the way by pickup. I told myself I belonged on that wall, after all, with the pipe-smoking foreign correspondents and elegant writers and crusading reporters. Among so many holy men and women, I guess there is room for one Elmer Gantry.

She was already dressed pretty as a picture when I knocked on her door that next morning, for the Pulitzer lunch. I had not seen her dressed up like that since my wedding, a million years ago.

She was scared again, so very scared. I told she looked good, that there was no reason to be afraid of these people. She didn't say anything. She just looked stricken. I chattered on the way to Columbia, showing her my Upper West Side apartment building, where I had lived for almost a week before Haiti, but she just sat quiet.

The reception was full when we got there, so we stood just inside the door. When I touched her shoulder, it was shaking.

Then, one by one, the editors of the *New York Times* came by to pay my mother homage, to tell her what a fine son she had raised, and how proud they were of me, and for her. Joe Lelyveld just said, "I know who this is," and smiled. Gene Roberts came up and talked Southern to her, and others came up to say kind things, welcoming things.

For the first time in her life, the people she knew only as "the rich folks"—wealth is a relative thing—were being nice to her, by the dozen.

We sat a table with the president of the university, the publisher of the *New York Times* and other dignified folks. Arthur Sulzberger Jr. switched the nametags so that she could sit between him and me, and he treated her like a queen. All the way through the lunch, he chatted with her, kept her at ease when other people dragged my attention away from her.

I had seen my mother cry from pain and grief and misery, when I was a child. I had never seen her cry from happiness until they called out my name and I walked up to get that prize, then handed it to her. She did not sob, she would never do that, but there were tears there.

We shared a taxi with Lelyveld back to the *New York Times*, where a photographer, Chester Higgins, flung his arms around my mother's neck and gave her a big hug, just for being my momma. Roberts invited her into his office to sit a spell and catch her breath, and gave her a copy of the full-page ad the *Times* had run after the awards were announced, and a *New York Times* carry bag with a tape of the interview I had done with Charlie Rose.

That night, I heard her talking to one of my aunts on the phone. "We had codfish, I think it was, and dessert but I didn't get to eat it because that was when Ricky was going up to get his prize, and I met all the people and they was real nice and seemed to think a lot of Ricky, and a man named Chester hugged my neck."

I went to a dinner party in my honor that night. Momma was passed out in the bed, dead tired. People at the party said they were sorry she didn't come. My momma, I thought: The toast of the Apple. When I got home I found her awake again. She and cousin Jackie had ordered room service, and got a cheeseburger big as God, one apiece. They couldn't eat it all, and my momma was ashamed to put it out in the hall for the waiters to pick up. "I don't want nobody to think I'm wasteful," she said. I told her not to worry.

I asked her what she thought of her day, and she said she never would have believed it, the place, the people.

"I'm glad I come," she said.

It was late and I left them then to go to bed, left the Prize tucked in my momma's purse.

Friends of mine had said that she would really only enjoy the trip after it was done, after she was home and could replay it in her mind.

They were right. She enthralled the kinfolks with tales of the city, of flight, of the ceremony in the library rotunda that looked like a castle. But mostly she talked of the people she met. "It's the nicest I've been treated in a long time."

A week or two later, she came to Atlanta with Sam, his wife, Teresa, and their daughter Meredith to have fried chicken and potato salad with me, her second big trip in less than a month. "Your momma's become a world traveler," Teresa said.

We took a walk down Peachtree Street. At one point Momma stared up at the skyscrapers and made a dismissive grunt.

"Ain't nothin' like New York," she said. "Now, them's some buildin's."

It wouldn't have been the same, that award, if she had not been there to share it, to share the honor, the pure joy of it.

I have not always been a nice man in my life. In a selfish way that had nothing to do with my momma's sacrifice, I wanted that prize and even dreamed of winning it. I wanted it to shove down the throats of the people who questioned my sophistication, my very existence among them. The honor it brings to others, hell, to anyone, came to me and I embraced it.

Maybe there is nothing special at all about us. Maybe there is validation in it for every mother and father.

Maybe the only thing that makes it seem so special to me, where my mother is concerned, is a simple matter of distance, of space between two points.

On one end is the tall woman dragging that cotton sack with a tow-headed little boy on back. On the other end is Times Square at night, and a room service cheeseburger, and the Pulitzer Prize.

We had to get on a jet plane, Momma, to fly so far.

39

1.3 acres

The squirrels have been raiding the old hickory nut tree in the neat, green front yard, leaving a carpet of dark hulls on the lawn. It is a way to tell the character of a person. Show them a squirrel with a jaw full of hickory nuts, and if they don't smile, there is something bad wrong with them. I thought it was a good sign, that tree. It is hard to be lonely with a yard full of gray squirrels. The old, ugly dog, Gizzard, can chase them if he's able.

I believe my momma will be happy here.

The four-bedroom house, made of beige brick with dark green shutters, sits on top of a hill—she had always wanted to live on a hill—but it is not so steep that she will have a hard time walking down to the mail box every afternoon. It has a porch on the front, and in the summertime she can sit there in the cool of the evening and snap beans, or peel taters, or just wave at the cars. In the back, behind the backyard, are more hills, and in the fall the hardwoods and pines form a backdrop of red and gold and green. In the summer, the honeysuckle runs from tree to tree, smelling so good. "I would spend all my time here," she told me when we first walked the little piece of land behind the house.

I kept my promise to my mother on November 2, 1996. I took every dollar I had and bought her a house, a good house, the first thing of any real value she has ever owned. She never had a wedding ring, or a decent car, or even a set of furniture that matched. Or teeth that fit. But she had a home now, a home of her own. I was happy and sad at the same time as I handed the realtor the money, happy that it had finally come true, sad that it had taken so long to accomplish.

Like I said earlier, I could have bought her one on credit, a long time ago, and I guess I should have. But if I had bought her a house on the installment plan, and something had happened to me, if I had lost my job and the dream had died and my world had turned to shit the way I have always feared it might, she would have lost it. The only thing worse than doing without is to be given something and then have it snatched away, and I could not take that chance. It is a sad thing, maybe, to go through life with an outlook like that, but that's the way it is. Maybe someday that will change. I hope it does.

But this way, no one can take it away from her no matter what happens to me. The thing is done: 1.3 acres, with room for squirrels and ugly dogs and family. If it had been up to me, I would have bought her a white Victorian house in town, one of those homes where she used to scrub floors, where the people wore the clothes she ironed. I would have done it for the pure poetic justice of it, to strike back at the past. But she wanted nothing to do with those houses, nothing to do with town. She wanted to walk in the pines and smell the wood smoke and plant rose of Sharon on the chert-rock banks. She wanted her dog, the remarkably unattractive Gizzard, to live out his last, limping days in the country, not in some pen, the neighbors complaining every time he felt like baying at the moon. She wanted to live as she had always lived, in the pines, with room for a small garden and space to pace away your troubles, only on her own ground.

She was afraid to want it, really, afraid because it cost so much, afraid because she thought it was a hardship on me, afraid because it seemed all wrong, a son buying her a house when he should have been buying one for himself, and beginning a family. "It ought to be the other way," she told me once. "It ought to be me, doing for you, not you doing for me."

I don't think I have ever quite made it clear to her that I would never, ever be able to start building that part of my life as long as this part, this promise, was unfinished. It would be like building on sand.

She picked the house out herself, after months of riding the back-roads in Calhoun County, because she thought it was pretty, because it was close to my brother Sam's house and my other kinfolks, because the hill always seemed to have a good breeze on it, other reasons, some silly, some not. We must have looked at a hundred houses before this one caught her eye and her heart. We went to look at it on a hot day in the early fall, scuffed along the wall-to-wall carpet, opened the oven in the nice, roomy kitchen where she will can her jellies and peppers and green tomatoes. We flushed the toilets in all three bathrooms, walked down into the full basement and the downstairs "family room," twisted the dial on the thermostat to hear the heat pump click on like a Trojan. I saw her reach up to feel the cool air rush in, like magic, and saw her smile.

"I won't run it, 'cept on the real hot days," she told me, and I told her she should run it any damn time she wanted. In the basement–family room, there is a fancy new wood heater with a rock fireplace, which she said she will use sometimes. I made it plain to her that the reason for buying it was so she could grow old in some comfort, that she doesn't have to tote in wood anymore—or trip over the extension cords to the dangerous electric space heaters—to stay warm. She pretended not to hear me—I know she heard me but there is no arguing with my momma's back—and went on talking about how the wood heater would heat that whole house, if she blocked off the space she didn't need.

She gave the living room, dining room, den and upstairs bedrooms just a passing glance, but kept wandering back to the kitchen, with so many cabinets, so much space, such nice, clean space. I knew she was deciding where the flour tins would go. I knew she was placing, in her mind's eye, green tomatoes on the windowsills, so they could ripen. I knew she was searching for a place to plug in her coffee pot—she had never had anything to drink in her whole life except coffee and water and buttermilk—and I knew the house would not be complete until that warm, rich smell of strong coffee filled the rooms.

"It's a lot of house for one woman," the realtor said, but I told him no, it was just right.

Then he told me what he was asking for it, and saw my momma's eyes drop and her dream snap closed, because to a woman who had lived with next to nothing, that very reasonable price seemed impossible. She walked outside then and stood in the yard, and wouldn't talk about it much, after that. Now and then she would slip in conversation with my brothers and other kinfolks, and call it "my house." She drew pictures of it. But she never asked for it again.

It took a few months to close, until that November day when I showed up at her door unannounced, and told her she owned a house now, her house. She smiled, as wide as I have ever seen her smile, and the tears pooled in her eyes. She asked me if we could afford the mortgage payments, and I told her there were none, that she could run around and around in it banging on pots and pans with a hairbrush, and no one could do a thing about it. It was hers.

I will never, ever forget that day. She and my aunts were having a yard sale, selling canned pickles and quilts and homemade doodads, and though the wind blew strong and just a little cold the sky was electric blue, cloudless. It was a fine day, in every way.

We went for a drive to look at it. The previous residents had not moved out yet, so all we could do was sit in the car at the side of the road and look at it, which was all she wanted to do anyway. The hill behind it was on fire with color from the changing season—fall comes late down here—and we sat, not saying anything, until the light started to fail and we began to worry that the people in the house would call the law on us, for lurking down there at the foot of our own hill. Somehow it didn't matter that we could only sit at the side of the road and look up at it.

"It's a dream, ain't it. It's just a dream," she said, and I told her no. It was just us getting even with life, one more time.

❁   ❁   ❁

My brother Sam went to work on it as soon as it was hers, fixing all the little things it needed, making a pretty house much prettier. "I ain't got money," he said, "but I got labor." He sawed down unwanted, spindly trees, painted every inch of the thing that wasn't covered in brick, and crawled over it and under it, with a hammer in his hand and nails in his teeth, to make it perfect. He worked on it every day after his shift at the cotton mill, dragging brush out of the wooded area behind the house by flashlight. At night, from my apartment in Atlanta or whatever hotel room I was in that night, we schemed by telephone on what to do next, what colors to use, talking about any and everything we could do to it, until we finally just ran out of projects. I know he was as proud of it as she was, as I was, that he had watched her, helpless as I was, just existing in that borrowed home. One night we sat in his living room trying to decide between tan and off-white paint for the trim, and it struck us, how odd that was. "Did you ever think we'd be doing this?" I asked him, and he shook his head. There was no celebrating. You celebrate winning, not just catching up.

We tried hard to make it perfect. The house sits on Nisbet Lake Road, but that is kind of misleading because Nisbet Lake dried up a long time ago (and calling it Nisbet Hole in the Ground Road was not attractive). If we could have done it without going to prison, Sam and me would have broken the dam and filled that lake up again, so she could have ridden past water on her way to town. It would have been closer to perfect, as a family, if Mark had been with us, beside us, as we did these things for her and for us, as we built this nice, new life for her, safely away from the ruins of the old one. But he was off somewhere, grappling with his own ghosts.

"You can't fix everything," one of my old girlfriends told me, when I complained about those missing pieces of this life I was trying to reshape, re-create. "You think you can. But some things you can't buy and some things you can't just wish true."

❖   ❖   ❖

"Did you know it had a doorbell?" my momma asked me, right after we bought it. "I never had a doorbell." I asked her if the sound of it bothered her, and she shook her head. "I kind of like it."

Some weeks later I was talking to Sam on the telephone, asking if she had settled in. She has, he told me, but he was a little worried about one thing. "She rings her own doorbell," he said.

I told him to let her ring it till she wore it out.

I guess it was hard for her, even as much as she loved that new house, to leave the tiny house on Roy Webb Road, the one we had shared for so long with our grandma, the one that had been a refuge for us, from our daddy.

She lived there forty years, almost all her adult life, most of that time without hot water in the kitchen, with pipes that froze every winter, without room for even a decent-sized Christmas tree in the tiny front room, at least one bigger than a shrub.

Some of our kinfolks did not like the idea of me moving her out. I can't understand that.

"Margaret won't never be happy nowhere but in that little house," one of our kinfolks warned us, but it had never been hers, that little house. The fire a few years earlier that had started in my bedroom had turned most of my momma's keepsakes and memories to ashes. Almost all her pictures, my daddy's letters, our baby books—back then the hospital doctors gave you a book to fill in with the baby's first words, first song, other things—were gone. There were just the walls, and the memories they contained.

Life inside those walls had been bittersweet, certainly not always happy, but somehow better than the life we had so often run from, to escape. This was the house where we healed.

I do not know if my aunt Nita and uncle Ed, who own it, will ever rent it out, or if they will keep it as a shrine to my grandma. People, my people, do things like that.

My momma did not walk it one last time, trying to remember. You never know what you will prick yourself on when you feel back into the past. She packed her last bag and made sure the stove was off by patting the eyes, turned off the lights and left.

She did not cry, she did not show any emotion at all, as we drove her to her own house on the hill, at least not until we pulled into the driveway. "I'm gonna put a Christmas tree in every window," she announced. "In the living room, a big one, one you can walk around."

I did go back to the little house, to look and remember. I have seen movies where people walked through their empty houses, their footsteps echoing with memories. It wasn't that way. I couldn't take more than a few steps in any direction before having to turn around again. But in every cramped step there was a flash, like an old projector running backward. There was my momma in her bed, sick, after the death of my brother, and my brother Mark, a toddler with fat cheeks, sitting on the floor, laughing, showing his new teeth. There was my uncle John in the living room, before his hair turned white, fishing in his pocket for a silver dollar, and my uncle Ed at the door, his face unlined, telling us it was time to go to work, boys.

There was my grandma with a rag around her head, high on her medicine, shaking me awake at 3 A.M. instead of 7 A.M., shouting that it was time to go to school, and my poor momma taking her by the elbow and leading her back to bed. There was Sam, about ten years old and wearing a cowboy hat, staggering in from doing work no boy should have been asked to do, his boots tracking in mud, my momma cleaning it up without saying a word. There was me, about twelve, reading a book by the light of a naked 40-watt bulb dangling from a drop cord looped over a bent nail in the ceiling, the orange cord disappearing past the quilt nailed over the doorway to the living room, for privacy. There was my young-looking aunt Jo, balancing a plate of turkey and cornbread dressing on her knee, and my aunt Nita, her hair still a rich, dark brown, asking my momma if she needed anything from town.

Even though it was winter and dead quiet, I could hear the drone and rattle of the electric fan that made it bearable to sleep in the August heat, even though the fan sucked in the bugs that, sooner or later, found their way into at least one ear. I could hear the radio in my grandma's room, hear Bill Monroe in his high lonesome tenor singing about a boy going off to sea, his true love begging him to stay at home with her. I could hear Hank, and Merle, and Johnny Cash and June Carter Cash singing about Jackson, her calling him "you long-legged, guitar-picking man." I could hear The Word on that dusty TV.

They say you can't remember a smell, but I could smell the wood smoke and the Rose Hair Oil and the chicken shit that invariably crept into the house on the bottoms of feet, and the musty quilts our momma pulled up to our nose, and, stronger than anything, the smell of fatback, fried crisp, that smell that lasted all day and rode to school with you on your hands, so that you could put your hands to your face during history class and get hungry all over again.

I don't know. Maybe I did wrong. Maybe I should have let things alone and left her there. A friend, a good, well-meaning one, told me once that I was buying the house for me, for my own satisfaction, to meet my own sense of duty, and not really for her. But that friend had grown up middle class and comfortable, protected by her daddy's steady pay-checks, never forced to tote wood a hundred yards just to stay warm. If she wanted to be cold, she went camping. That friend had never seen the silverfish scurry by the hundreds across the floor because there were so many cracks and holes in the walls and floors, or felt a rat crawl across their legs at night. I doubt if her momma had ever stuffed cotton in her ears, to keep the bugs out. I doubt if she had ever flushed the toilet with buckets, not for a day, but for a winter. I doubt it.

Yet it planted some doubt in my mind. Was this house just my own selfish act. Had I taken her out of the only place on earth she could feel at home, even with all its hardships? I asked her, sometime later, if I had tried to fix something that wasn't broke.

My momma seldom gets mad at me now, at least that I can see, but she was mad at me then. "I wish everybody would quit telling me how I feel," she said. "They don't know nothin'." Then she stomped off—as

much as a sixty-year-old woman can stomp—over her wall-to-wall carpeting, to her big, clean kitchen, in the house where every time you have
company, it goes ding-dong.

It may sit empty a hundred years, that tiny house we grew up in, until
the pine trees out front—the ones Sam and my grandma planted when I
was just a boy—reach into the clouds. Funny, I cannot imagine anyone
in it except us. I guess everyone feels that way, when they leave a house
behind. But when I think about it now, for some reason my thoughts
carry me not through the yard or even into the house itself, but beneath
it. It takes me into that cool darkness where I used to play for hours in
the dirt, burying the cat-eye marbles, fake-gold buttons and bits of tin-
foil, only to go digging for them again in a week, a month, a year. In a stupid, silly way I search my grown-up memory for the things I reclaimed
there, and for the treasures that just disappeared in the soft ground. Like
it matters now.

40

The same

S o here we are, Daddy.
    I did what you didn't do. It took me a long time, all of your life, most of hers, perhaps even most of mine. But it is done. She wakes up in a house of her own, a real home, and she is as good as anybody on that road. She lives warm when it is cold and cool when it is hot and even has a bright light on a pole in the yard, to chase away the dark. She has cable, and garbage pickup, and county water. She still prefers to walk in the backyard instead of the front, out of sight. Some habits really do die hard, I reckon.

    I couldn't fix everything. I couldn't take any of the pain out of her mind. I couldn't give Sam back his childhood. I couldn't save my little brother from the same demons that consumed you, and maybe I didn't even try very hard. But there is time left for him. For reasons I cannot really explain, I believe that Mark will one day escape whatever it is that hunts him so mercilessly. I believe he has enough of Momma in him to just outlast it. I believe it.

    I have had a lot of luck in my life, Daddy. Some of it, maybe, I earned, but most of it was blind, dumb, stumbling luck. Maybe, when it is all said and done, that is the only difference between you and me. I got the luck.

I hear it said a lot, especially lately, what a good man I turned out to be, considering. I always feel like a poser when I hear that, because I know it's not true. I wrote once that I was "my momma's son," but that was a mistake, to claim that.

The truth is that, in so many ways, I am just like you. The meanness you had in you, I used to get where I am. But instead of spraying it out, like you did, I channeled it. I used it every time I told some loving soul that I had to say good-bye because my work was more important to me than them, or just because it was time to move on.

I used your coldness, the same way I used my momma's kindness, in my work. Because of her, I could understand the pain and sadness of the people I wrote about, and could make others feel it. But because of you I could turn my back on them when I was done and just walk away, free and clean. Think about it. What kind of man can do that, as much as I have, and live with himself?

Your hatred of responsibility, of ties, is in me just as strong as it was in you. I have no home, no children, no desire for them. I picked one responsibility, just one, and I met it. But, any fool can meet just one responsibility. Any lame idiot can set the bar so low, and clear it.

There have been a thousand nights when I would rather have been you, nights when I wanted nothing more in this world than to give up and drink myself into a good night's sleep. But that would have surely killed her, to see it. It would have put her in her grave. I do not know what will happen to me when she is gone, when the responsibility I picked up after you threw it down is fully met. I might be very, very tired then. The truth is that I can see myself wrapped around a bottle of bad likker for good company, that there are times when the very thought of that oblivion is so, so appealing. Luck or not, it has not always been easy being the raggedy-ass boy made good, the one the smart people like to have around, sometimes, to hear my rustic witticisms.

I am you, in better ways. I love the music as you did, and the women as long as they would someday go away, and sometimes a good fistfight just to let the rage out, and to see if my nerve is still there. Only it takes so much longer to get up now than it used to. I wonder, is that what finally happened to you?

I have never fought in a war, never experienced the hell you did. I have seen it, the killing and dying, but not on the scale of horror that consumed you. I wonder sometimes what might have happened if you had come home from that war crippled in body instead of spirit, if she had had to care for you, parking you in the sun, helping you to bed. Would you have lived? Would you have lasted?

There is no hate in me for you. I know that now. There is no profit in hating a dead man. I glimpsed the good in you when I was a little boy, and I saw it shine through you the day you gave me those books, the day you told me the story. I believe you told me the truth, mostly, about your war, and I believe that it took you from us, from me, allowing me only those glimmers of the man before. Like I said, I have to believe it. I have to, because without it there is only a clenched fist where your face would be, in my mind.

Some people tell me I should thank you, that by being the man you were, it forced me to be a different one. But I don't buy that "Boy Named Sue" bullshit. If I could talk to you again, I would want to know one thing. Did you ever think of us, those years we didn't hear from you. Did you ever think of us at all?

I am about the age you were, now, when you left us for that one, final time, when the telephone finally fell silent. Men in our family don't last long, anyway, do they? We only look indestructible. We come to pieces in time, in such short time.

I will always remember that last time we talked, after you had given up on living but so feared death. Even with your life so tenuous, you unscrewed that cap and hastened your death with that amber liquid. And I understood. I would have done the same.

Some people say I am more like her, of course. They say I look like her. But I'm not much like her. I wish I was, but I'm not.

She has proved she can outlast anything. As hard as life has been for her, she hates death, she despises it. She even hates funerals because she does not like to feel its breath.

She is good and patient, and devout, so that she is never alone, like you and me.

I don't really know why I think this, but I believe you would have liked to see Momma in her house. I think you would have liked it, since you always seemed to appreciate nice things. It is a pretty big house, not scary like the last one we lived in with you, but warm and big and friendly. It has no ghosts in it, not that I can feel. Still, ghosts have a way of finding your new address. You can't fool them by changing zip codes. I know. As much as I would like to be a dam, some barrier to the sadness that rolls through her life and her mind, I'm helpless. In the same way, there is no guarantee that the memories we make in her new house will be good ones. We can only try.

She jokes, sometimes, that she gets lost in it.

There would have been room for you.

41

Who we are

Mid-November 1996

There wasn't much to move, and memories don't weigh nothin' really. She took a chrome-and-vinyl couch and chair, leftovers from some doctor's office, and took her washing machine, which she had nicknamed "Old Smokey," because the house fire had blackened the white paint. Smokey didn't look like much, and, like my own machine in Atlanta, was prone to dance across the floor, as if possessed by demons on the spin cycle. But you couldn't kill him with a gun. "Still runs. Don't leak," Momma said, refusing to let us get her a new washer. That was by God that.

I was in Louisiana, I think, on the day she finished moving in. I would have liked to have been there. As it turns out, it was good that I was far away.

The night after my momma's first full day in her new house, my little brother came to see her. He was drinking, a little bit. We had all asked him not to come there, when he was. I don't know what right we had to say that, or to expect him to comply.

My big brother, Sam, drove up at about the same time, just to check on her. They faced off in the yard.

321

I guess they had to fight. They had to, because of who we are.

Sam fought because he believed he was protecting her, because he believed he was fighting in my place, because I had begged Mark to stay away from there when he was drinking. Mark fought because he felt he was being pushed away, unwanted, which I guess is about the worst feeling in the world.

So, on my momma's second night in her new house, a forty-year-old man and his thirty-three-year-old brother are fighting mean and earnest in the front yard of the very symbol of our new beginning. It was not two blowhards swinging at air and curses between the newsstands on Broadway. I wasn't there but I can tell you that it was dirty, chilling. Mark choked him until his eyes began to dim, and all Sam could think, as he fought to get loose, was that if Mark hurt him bad he would lose a day's work at the mill, and if you lose two, you're fired.

My momma introduced herself to her new neighbors not by taking them a jar of homemade jelly or some pickled banana pepper, but by running to them for help.

And somewhere, my daddy was laughing.

Finally, Sam broke free and they broke apart, and it was just over. No one wanted to fight any more. Sometimes, the anger just dies on you that way. There is no reason, no sense to it.

I heard about it two days later. I don't know if saying that it broke my heart is strong enough. It made me sick. I hung up the telephone and got in my car and just drove, not to home but away from it, going east on Interstate 20 until I crossed over the South Carolina border. I played the radio and drove. I turned around somewhere this side of Anderson, or maybe it was Greenville, and drove back home again.

Sam only did what he believed I would have done, or would have tried to do, if I was man enough. He did it to keep something good in her life from being tarnished.

But of course Momma didn't see it that way. She has tolerated drunks all her life; she is good at it. She expects it, like she expects the sun to rise in the morning. Instead of being angry at my little brother, her baby, she was mostly mad at Sam. I had never really seen him beat before, not even bowed, but he was hurt by that.

So, instead of fixing anything, I only built a stage, a prop, for another sadness. I felt an anger at Mark that almost scorched me, raw, but it faded over the days, as the resignation set in. As long as he is alive, as she is alive, she will care for him, nurture him, tolerate him, and that is exactly as it ought to be. How do you tell a mother not to love her baby.

Even though I couldn't make everything right with the simple purchase of a house, I wanted to believe it would at least be someplace fresh, free, for a while, of that lingering aroma of dusty pain. But what killed me, was when I heard my mother had left her new home, for a little while. She went back to the old little house, as she always had, even though it was empty, and sat in silence. There was no television, no phone, just my momma and an empty little house.

The house on Nisbet Lake Road sat empty for almost a week. My brother Sam would not go near it. My little brother Mark vowed he would never set foot in it again.

I begged her to go back, not to give up, and she told me that she never intended to stay away for long, that she just needed to let that bad beginning fade away, a little bit. But to me it was like all the things I had worked for were wasted.

And then I knew that maybe I had bought this house more to redo the past than to make her dreams come true. I felt sorry for Sam, for Mark, for her, but especially for me.

It got better, of course.

By Thanksgiving, Sam and Momma were working side by side again, again trying to make the house perfect, cosmetically. She held the ladder for him, passed him nails, cooked him biscuits as he did the little things that needed doing. I came home the day before Thanksgiving and hung pictures and fixed a broken lock and carried some broken limbs up into the woods. I felt like part of it.

My momma had fixed me a room. It had a spare bed with a box spring and two mattresses on it, so that it was a good four feet off the floor. When I dangled my legs over the side they didn't touch the floor, and for a minute I felt like a little boy again. I thought again what I had thought as a child, morbidly comforting: If I should die before I wake, at least God won't have to stoop over much to jerk me up into heaven. If He is inclined.

We had Thanksgiving dinner that next day, Sam and his family, Momma and me, my aunt Jo and uncle John. They have no children of their own, and have always eaten this meal with us. I guess it was the best food I have ever had. Momma used every rack in the oven and every eye on the stove in her new kitchen, and there were biscuits and dressing and mashed potatoes and pinto beans with a ham bone as big as my fist, and a turkey that fell off the bone . . . I was full as a tick. For the first time, ever, we all sat in the same room and ate, because it was the first time we, Momma, Sam and me, had ever had a room big enough to gather in. After a while my momma went and sat in a chair in the adjoining den, and Sam looked at me over the table and, without smiling, said: "Look how far away she is. And we're in the same room."

We tried hard not to notice the empty chair.

Momma said she slept good in her new house, mostly, but couldn't sleep on the cold nights. She thought about Mark then, and she has never been able to close her eyes when she is worried. Since his house burned down, he had been sleeping in his truck beside the ruins of his house, and on the cold nights he dressed in some thermal coveralls someone had given him, and shivered in the dark.

How could she sleep, knowing that?

But since his fight with Sam, something has happened to him. He has been cold-sober, working night and day to rebuild his house, this time out of concrete block. I guess it is anger that drives him, I don't know. But day after day he slaps those blocks together, and at night he crawls into the cab of a truck and goes to sleep.

We started painting the wood trim and concrete-block portions of my momma's house right after Thanksgiving. My momma paints as high as she can reach, and Sam paints the rest. There is still hurt in their faces, when they see each other, Momma and Sam, but that will fade, too.

She won't let me hire a painter. It doesn't bother her that it might take all winter—you can only paint on the warm, pretty days—and it doesn't bother her at all that the wooden part of the house is forest green in some places and "ivory" in others. She isn't like me, like I said.

The other night, in a light drizzle, we drove to Gadsden in the Bronco and got her a new couch. It was the first new piece of sitdown furniture she had ever owned.

The end of the couch stuck out into the rain, and my job was to ride in back of the Bronco and cover that end with a rain slicker. My momma held my ankle, to keep me from falling out the back.

For some reason I can't explain, about halfway home with the rain blowing in my face, I started to laugh, and pretty soon my momma started to laugh, and although I couldn't see him, in the darkened cab, I am sure Sam was grinning.

"You know, if you scoot on back there and sit on the very end of that thing, it won't get wet," he told me.

"I'll fall out," I said.

"Maybe not," he said.

When we got home I went into the guest bathroom—imagine that, a guest bathroom—to dry my face and hands. I noticed that the towel said "Emory University Hospital" on it. Stolen, no doubt, and given to my momma in one of those boxes of throwaway clothes. Just on a hunch I went into the next bathroom, and the towel there said "Peninsula Medical Center," and I started to laugh all over again. I walked back into the living room laughing, and saw my momma and Sam exchange one of those looks that they used to swap when I was little and did something odd.

Of course you can't buy respectability with a house. My momma has always been the most respectable person in my life, no matter what kind of shell surrounded her.

I really, truly had wanted her to have a place where she could be more comfortable, where she could more enjoy the good times in her life, and tolerate the bad. And she has that. She has exactly that. But I had to set my hopes on something higher. I wanted to redo the past, wanted to feel like we had won, after all.

Well, we have.

She has a split-level castle with stolen towels.

She has a four-bedroom, brick-façade mansion with vinyl den furniture scavenged from a closed-down doctor's office.

She has a home, which is more important than any of that other unadulterated pyscho-garbage.

She wanted it to be perfect, too. She even said, tearfully, that when my brothers rolled in the dirt, that "the splendor was lost." I don't know where she learned to talk like that. I guess she has been reading the *New York Times*.

But no, the goddamn splendor ain't lost. It ain't no ways lost.

"The thing we got to remember," I told her, sitting face to face, "is that we ain't gonna be any different here. We're just us. We just got a little bit better place to be us, in."

She smiled at that.

One day Mark will come back here, and while I am sure he and Sam will avoid each other for a while—it has never been unusual in my family for people to drive right on by your house if they don't like the looks of a car in the driveway—I know it can't last forever. It is a small county. Our corner of it is even smaller. All our young lives, we lived somewhere near the bottom of our society. We cannot afford, in the middle of our lives, to peck at each other now. Soon, too soon, we will be old men, and how silly we will be, gouging at each other with our arthritic hands, snapping at each other with our dentures. We may have to gum each other, since we ain't never had no luck at dentures, either.

It's not a dream. It's just a damn house, but the roof is first-rate, the heat pump is under warranty and the woods are covered in wildflowers. Some days, when the light is good, she searches the hill behind her house for the dormant plants she will transplant in the spring. She knows exactly where the property lines are, knows which trees and shrubs and weeds are hers.

This spring she can cover it up with flowers, but, it being us, it may just blossom with junk cars.

"No, it ain't gonna be that way," she told me. "It's gonna be purty. It's gonna be real purty."

It may be somewhere in between. We will live with that. For now, it is enough to see her walking her acre and a third, a little stooped over, with that ugly, ancient dog.

And I am grateful I could give her this much, before more time tumbled by, lost.

There ain't no way to make it perfect.

You do the best you can for the people left, a yard-fighting, teeth-gnashing, biscuit-eating, ugly-dog-raising, towel-stealing, television-praying, never-forgiving, hard-headed people that you love with all the strength in your body, once you finally figure out that they are who you are, and, in many ways, all there is.

I met a woman the other day. She told me she had heard me talk at a writing seminar, that I had "inspired" her. I nodded, politely. It seemed that she had grown up like me, kind of. She had been born in Charity Hospital in New Orleans, and wasn't dead sure who her daddy was. She and her momma had grown up in the welfare projects in Morgan City. She had bought candy with food stamps, waiting for all the other children to leave before paying at the counter, because she was ashamed of who she was. All her adult life, she said, she had pretended that part of her life had never happened, but when she heard me talk about who I was and where I came from, she thought that maybe it was okay not to be ashamed anymore.

"You use it," she said. "I don't mean anything bad by it. But you use it . . ."

Like a weapon, yes.

She said she had trouble with men. She said she was prone to just move on, when people got close to her. I nodded politely, again. She said she couldn't imagine children. There was just so much to do, wasn't there? So much to do, so very far to run, away from what? But it is the running that is important, after a while.

She is good. She is driven. She will make it, because what drives her is meaner than what drives most people. She will make it because, as someone told me once, people like you and me, we can't fail. I strongly suspect there are a lot of us. I never figured I was all that unique.

Several times I have found myself about to call and tell her not to put the nice things in her life on hold, not to wait for a time when she feels she has proven herself enough, has put enough distance between then and now, because that time might never come. I've been meaning to tell her not to look for some well-defined finish line, to tell her that sometimes you run right past it and don't even know it's there, like fence posts in the dark. I've been meaning to warn her, of all of that.

I will.

I like her. I would have liked to have spent some more time with her, but looking at me was too much like looking in the mirror, for her. She could see the strain of it, in my face maybe, maybe my eyes, could hear that old anger and lingering resentment on my lips. I guess it wasn't pretty, with that well-worn chip on my shoulder still sticking up, like a hump on my back.

But I swear, it seems lighter now. It seems a little bit lighter now.

42

Safe in the dark

I was bad to sleepwalk when I was a child. I would get out of bed and slip through the house, then out into the night. I would awaken to the crunch and sting of frost on the soles of my feet, or, in the summer, to the sound of crickets and night birds. Once I walked all the way to my aunt Nita's house, fifty yards away, knocked three, slow times on the door, and turned around and shuffled back home again, a pint-sized zombie in pajama bottoms with horses on them. I was never afraid when I would awaken, because the path, the trees, the dark outlines of the cars and pickups and small houses were all so familiar to me, and I have never been afraid of the dark. And I knew I would never be alone. The house we shared with my grandma wasn't big enough to afford my momma a bedroom, so she slept in the front room, on the couch. The banging of the screen door would wake her and she would follow me, not waking me because she had heard it was dangerous, that it was safer to just steer me back to my bed. But sometimes I would come to my senses outside and see her just standing there, beside me. I never cried. I just looked up, wondering. "You're okay, little man," she would tell me. "You just been travelin'."

About the Author

RICK BRAGG was awarded the Pulitzer Prize for feature writing in 1996. A national correspondent for the *New York Times,* he lives in Atlanta, Georgia.